# or
# Common Trauma
# Responses

# CBT for Common Trauma Responses

Michael J. Scott

SAGE

Los Angeles | London | New Delhi
Singapore | Washington DC

Los Angeles | London | New Delhi
Singapore | Washington DC

SAGE Publications Ltd
1 Oliver's Yard
55 City Road
London EC1Y 1SP

SAGE Publications Inc.
2455 Teller Road
Thousand Oaks, California 91320

SAGE Publications India Pvt Ltd
B 1/I 1 Mohan Cooperative Industrial Area
Mathura Road
New Delhi 110 044

SAGE Publications Asia-Pacific Pte Ltd
3 Church Street
#10-04 Samsung Hub
Singapore 049483

Editor: Alice Oven
Assistant editor: Kate Wharton
Production editor: Imogen Roome
Copyeditor: Sarah Bury
Proofreader: Audrey Scriven
Indexer: Bill Farrington
Marketing manager: Tamara Navaratnam
Typeset by: C&M Digitals (P) Ltd, Chennai, India
Printed by MPG Books Group, Bodmin, Cornwall

FSC
www.fsc.org
MIX
Paper from
responsible sources
FSC® C018575



First published 2013



**Library of Congress Control Number: 2012938456**

**British Library Cataloguing in Publication data**

A catalogue record for this book is available from the British Library

ISBN 978-1-4462-0864-9
ISBN 978-1-4462-0865-6 (pbk)

# CONTENTS

# Chapter One

## POST-TRAUMA RESPONSES AND CBT – AN OVERVIEW

*Cognitive behaviour therapy has its roots in the ideas of Epictetus, a Stoic philosopher in the first century AD, who said that 'people are disturbed not so much by things, as by the views which they take of them' (2011). It is as if people take a 'photograph' of the same situation from a different angle, for example people's differing reactions at a bus stop to the bus being late. But this also applies to extreme situations. Should this 'late bus' mount the pavement injuring those standing at the bus stop, in the long term there will be varying responses, including: phobia about travelling by bus, post-traumatic stress disorder, depression, etc. In this chapter the typical responses to trauma are described, together with the basics of a cognitive-behavioural approach to clients' problems.*

Adverse reactions to extreme trauma have been noted from antiquity. Samuel Pepys wrote in his diary on 2 September 1666 of the beginning of the Great Fire of London and five months later, on 28 February 1667, he wrote 'it is strange to think how to this very day I cannot sleep a night without great terrors of fire; and this very night I could not sleep until almost 2 in the morning through thoughts of fire' (Pepys 2003) – he was suffering from.... How did you complete the last sentence? Most commentators make reference to post-traumatic stress disorder (PTSD) in connection with Mr Pepys, and indeed this is a possibility. In Mr Pepys' case, the nightmares may have been taken by yourself and others as representative of PTSD, but in fact the diagnostic criteria for PTSD in *DSM IV TR* (American Psychiatric Association 2000) give equal weighting to other symptoms, such as concentration and connection with others. The diarist was assiduously completing his diaries and socialising, making a PTSD diagnosis unlikely. Mr Pepys probably suffered from a sub-syndromal level of PTSD, but

**Table 1.1** Common Trauma Responses

| **PTSD**<br>**Sub-syndromal PTSD** | | **Depression** | **Panic Disorder** |
|---|---|---|---|
| Severe Mental Illness | Borderline Personality Disorder | Phobia | Substance abuse/dependence |
| Pain/disfigurment/head injury | | | |
| **<u>Any</u> combination of the above difficulties** | | | |
| Adjustment Disorder | | *Prolonged duress stress disorder* | |

unfortunately he is not around to undergo a thorough diagnostic interview to decide the matter unequivocally and he may in any case have anticipated cognitive behaviour therapy (CBT) by writing about his trauma!

Trauma is ubiquitous. Half the adult population (61% of men and 51% of women) experience at least one traumatic event in their lifetime, with 10% of men and 6% of women reporting four or more types of trauma (Kessler et al. 1995). Despite this, only a significant minority suffer from the disorders shown in Table 1.1 (Kessler et al. 1995). Cognitive behavioural interventions post trauma are based on the tenet that the way in which the trauma and its consequences are appraised plays a pivotal role in whether the person suffers long-term debility (Ehlers and Clark 2000).

The common trauma responses are shown in Table 1.1.

Although PTSD is thought of as the prototypical trauma response, sub-syndromal PTSD is almost as common. In a study of 158 survivors of road traffic accidents (Blanchard and Hickling 1997), 39% developed PTSD and a further 29% developed sub-syndromal PTSD. The disorders in the first two rows of Table 1.1 can develop following a trauma either singly or, more usually, in some combination, for example in the Blanchard and Hickling study (1997), 53% of PTSD sufferers also suffered from depression and 21% with a phobia. A study by Zimmerman et al. (2008) found that 24% of PTSD sufferers were suffering from panic disorder. Many PTSD clients resort to substance abuse as a way of self-medicating (Hien et al. 2010) and this can make it more difficult to treat the underlying PTSD. Fezner et al. (2011) found that childhood trauma, assaultive violence and learning of trauma positively predicted the presence of alcohol use disorders. For those with PTSD, childhood trauma and assaultive violence both predicted alcohol use disorders (Fezner et al. 2011). In *DSM IV TR* (American Psychiatric Association 2000), a diagnosis of acute stress disorder (ASD) was included and it was thought that the development of this would be predictive of PTSD. However, it has subsequently been found (Bryant et al. 2011) that ASD does not adequately identify most people who develop PTSD and it is therefore not a focus in this volume.

Table 1.1 indicates that the development of severe mental illness (SMI), borderline personality disorder and substance dependence are often linked to trauma. PTSD is common among those with a severe mental illness, such as schizophrenia, bipolar disorder and treatment refractory major depression. A study by Mueser et al. (1998) found that using structured interviews, 42% met criteria for PTSD but a review of the clinical records found that only 2% of the sample carried an assigned diagnosis of PTSD. As such, a significant number of clients with SMI are not recognised and appropriately treated for their trauma-related difficulties. Leaving PTSD unaddressed among individuals with SMI almost certainly exacerbates their illness severity and hinders their care (Resnick et al. 2003). One in four of patients diagnosed with PTSD were also diagnosed with borderline personality disorder and 30% of individuals diagnosed with BPD were also diagnosed with PTSD (Pagura et al. 2010).

Trauma may cause impairment not only directly (primary traumatisation) but also indirectly via pain/disfigurement/head injury (secondary traumatisation), and the latter may then serve to complicate the former. For example, the pain that a person suffers following an accident may serve as a reminder of their accident and exacerbate, say, their PTSD. Thus the pain/disfigurement/head injury of row four in Table 1.1 can make the difficulties cited in the rows above (Table 1.1) more difficult to treat psychologically.

In *DSM IV TR* (American Psychiatric Association 2000), an adjustment disorder is a diagnosis of last resort and it stipulates that this label should not be used if the client meets diagnostic criteria for any other disorder. It is thus positioned in the bottom row of Table 1.1. Prolonged duress stress disorder (PDSD) is a term coined by Scott and Stradling (1994) to describe clients exhibiting PTSD symptoms but from chronic stressors such as bullying at work or caring for a relative with a progressive neurological disorder. PDSD is not a disorder included in *DSM IV TR* (it is thus in italics in Table 1.1), and there is a dearth of research on it. It is included by the author in Table 1.1 for its possible clinical value and descriptions of its usage are necessarily somewhat anecdotal.

The focus in this volume is on the CBT treatment of the disorders and combination of disorders in Table 1.1. Some of the responses to trauma in Table 1.1 are a direct consequence of the trauma/s (primary traumatisation), such as post-traumatic stress disorder (PTSD), depression, phobia, panic disorder, borderline personality disorder, and psychosis, while others are a response to a consequence of the trauma (secondary traumatisation), e.g. physical injury leading to problems with the management of pain, head injury leading to postconcussive syndrome or cognitive impairment, disfigurement leading to social anxiety. In this volume the treatment of primary traumatisation is dealt with in Parts One and Two, while the focus in Part Four is on secondary traumatisation. In Part Three the focus is on adaptations to treatment for children and those with a severe mental illness.

## CBT THEORY AND PRACTICE

One of the core theoretical concepts in CBT is that responses to stimuli are cognitively mediated (see Alford and Beck 1997, and Figure 1.1).

In Figure 1.1 the stimuli might be a hassle, such as the late arrival of a bus. Cognitive mediation theory suggests that it is not this *per se* that results in an

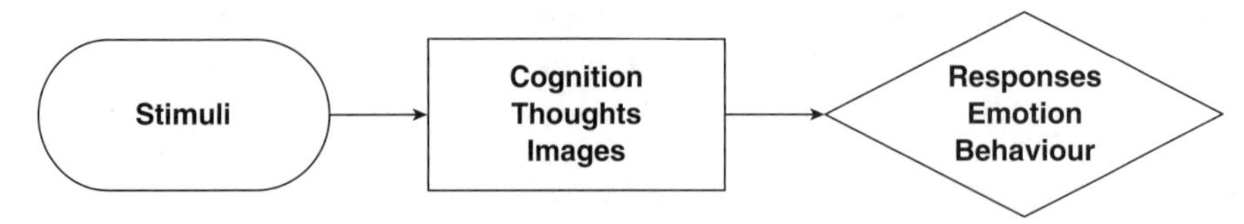


**Figure 1.1** Cognitive Mediation

emotional response, say of anger, but cognitions such as 'this is the second time this week that this has happened' and perhaps accompanying images of a withering look of disapproval from the boss when I arrive late for work. Because of the perceived injustice, I might push myself vigorously forward (behaviour) as people crowd on to the bus. In turn this might create a further negative stimuli in terms of anger from another would-be passenger as I step on their foot. Thus the chain in Figure 1.1 is actually part of a cycle, which can become a vicious circle if I in turn become angry with my fellow passenger. Cognitive behaviour therapy targets the thoughts, images, emotions and behaviours in Figure 1.1. Whereas cognitive mediation is held to be a necessary part of responding to a stimulus, CBT theory does not claim that cognition is the sole mediator. The stimuli–organism–response model (see Lazarus 2006) was a precursor to the cognitive model and emphasised that the physiology of the individual played a key role in determining an individual's response to any event. This has been incorporated in CBT conceptualisations of the interactions of physiology, emotions, behaviours and thoughts (see Figure 1.2) (Scott 2009).

The 'climate' in Figure 1.2 may consist of events such as hassles or extreme trauma, or the atmosphere in which an individual is 'breathing', for example excessive criticism or over-involvement from others, which has been found to be predictive of a relapse in clients with both depression and schizophrenia (see Hooley et al. 1986). For ease of illustration, climate is shown in Figure 1.2 as operating via cognition but it can exert its effects by any of the four 'ports' – cognitions, behaviour, emotion or physiology. Each of the four 'ports' reciprocally interact with each other. Thus, using the 'late bus' example mentioned earlier, if I managed to get on the bus, I might put my ipod on ('behaviour' in Figure 1.2), the music might lift my mood ('emotion' in Figure 1.2), leading me to feel less tense ('physiology' in Figure 1.2), which in turn might lead me to reconsider whether I should bother formally complaining to the bus company ('cognitions' in Figure 1.2). However, I may become so engrossed in my music that I miss my bus stop (back to 'behaviour' in Figure 1.2) and my new found tranquillity is lost (back to 'emotion' Figure 1.2).

In CBT the focus can be on the explicit content of the negative thought to derive more adaptive second thoughts, e.g. 'True, the bus is late today, but only by five minutes. It is not the end of the world'. However, if information is collected on my response to a wide variety of similar situations, it may be possible to infer an underlying dysfunctional attitude, e.g. 'If people just did what they are supposed to do, there would be no problems', and this silent assumption could also be a

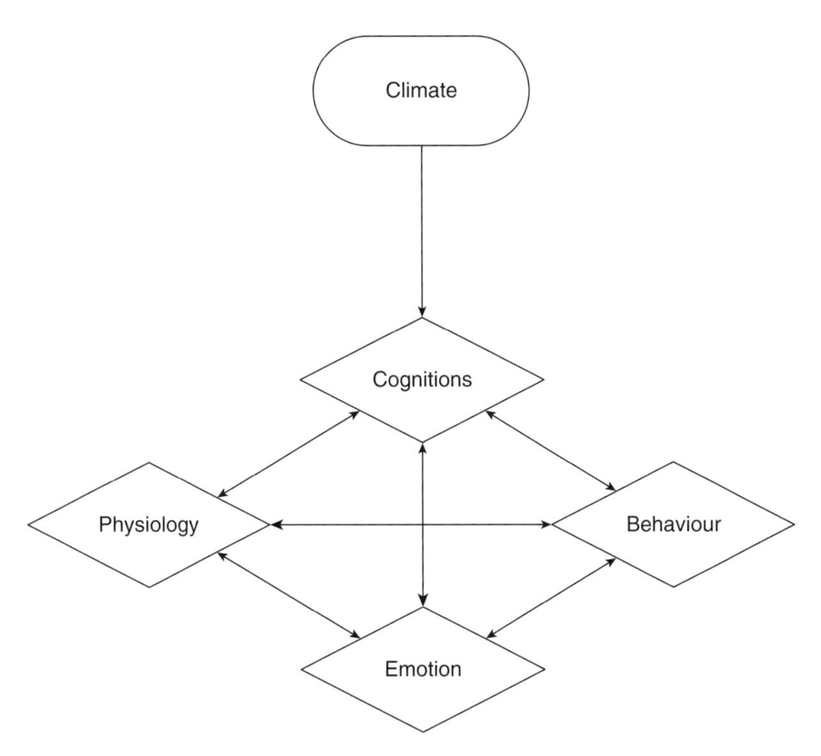


**Figure 1.2** Cognitions in Context (from Scott 2009)

target for CBT. Thus CBT can take place at the level of automatic thoughts or dysfunctional attitudes (the latter have also been termed 'schemas' – templates for processing information). CBT can take place not only at the level of content but also at the level of process. For example, in my focusing on the bus arriving late twice this week, a CBT therapist might conclude that this is yet another example of my using a mental filter, zooming in on the negative, amplifying its significance, neglecting that this was the first week in the last four weeks when the bus was late twice. Examples of such cognitive biases post trauma are shown in Table 1.2 (Scott and Stradling 2006).

The cognitive mediation model applies even when the stimulus is an extreme trauma. In these instances clients sometimes have images of a worse scenario, e.g. the death of their child in the trauma, although the child was not present. The CBT response might be to switch attention to an image of what the child was actually doing at that time.

One of the postulates of Beck's cognitive theory of emotional disorder (Alford and Beck 1997) is the cognitive content specificity hypothesis, i.e. the different disorders are distinguished by their differing cognitive content. This has led to different cognitive models for different disorders. For example, in panic disorder it is the catastrophic misinterpretation of bodily sensations that is hypothesised to play a pivotal role in the disorder and CBT treatment targets these both

**Table 1.2** Examples of Cognitive Biases among Traumatised Clients (Scott and Stradling 2006)

| | |
|---|---|
| 1. | Dichotomous thinking. Everything is seen in black and white terms, for example 'I am either in control of what's happening to me or I am not'. |
| 2. | Over-generalisation. Expecting a uniform response from a category of people because of the misdeeds of a member, for example 'All men are potential rapists'. |
| 3. | Mental filter. Seizing on a negative fragment of the situation and dwelling on it, for example 'I could have been killed in that encounter'. |
| 4. | Automatic discounting. Brushing aside the positive aspects of what was achieved in a trauma, for example for 'I was only doing my duty in saving the child'. |
| 5. | Jumping to conclusions. Assuming that it is known what others think, for example 'They all think I should be better by now, it was six weeks ago after all'. |
| 6. | Magnification and minimisation. Magnification of shortcomings and minimisation of strengths, for example 'Since the trauma, I'm so irritable with the family and just about manage to keep going to work'. |
| 7. | Emotional reasoning. Focusing on one's emotional state to draw conclusions about oneself, for example 'Since it happened, I'm frightened of my own shadow, I guess I'm just a wimp'. |
| 8. | 'Should' statements. Inappropriate use of moral imperatives – 'Shoulds', 'Musts', 'Haves', and 'Oughts' – for example 'It's ridiculous that since the attack I now have to take my daughter with me shopping. I should be able to go by myself'. |
| 9. | Labelling and mislabelling. For example 'I used to think of myself as a strong person. I could handle anything, but since it happened I'm just weak'. |
| 10. | Personalisation. Assuming that because something went wrong it must be one's own fault, for example 'I keep going over my handling of the situation. I must have made a mistake somewhere for the child to have died'. |

behaviourally and cognitively. Thus the evidence-based CBT protocols are largely diagnosis-specific (Butler et al. 2006).

## THE STRUCTURE OF CBT

CBT interventions are time-limited, typically involving 10–20 treatment sessions conducted either individually (Scott 2009) or in a group format (Scott 2011). They are psychoeducational in that they teach clients skills to better manage their difficulties and facilitate this by making use of self-help materials. (Traumatised clients and their friends and/or family may benefit from reading the book *Moving on after Trauma* (Scott 2008), and self-help manuals for depression and each of the anxiety disorders are freely available from www.routledgementalhealth.com/simply-effective-group-cognitive-behaviour-therapy and are published in Scott (2011).)

The skills focus in CBT means that great emphasis is placed on the client practising skills between sessions. A review of the client's homework is always placed on the negotiated agenda for a session. The emphasis on between-session practice and within-session refinement of that practice conveys a message that it is the learning of specific skills rather than the therapist that is important, thereby guarding against the client becoming dependent.

## CASE FORMULATION

A case formulation is a specific example of the cognitive model of a disorder. For example, a client might be diagnosed as suffering, say, from panic disorder. The cognitive model of the disorder (Clark 1986) highlights the pivotal role of the catastrophic misinterpretation of bodily sensations. For this particular client, the salient misinterpretation during a panic attack might be 'I'm having a heart attack' but for another client the catastrophising might focus on their shame of seeming 'mad' in public. Thus the case formulation is an individualised version of a specific (diagnosis-based) cognitive model. The distillation of a case formulation is an integral part of the assessment of a client and it guides the CBT treatment interventions. Case formulations (Weerasekera 1996) of disorders may be based on a 'key-lock' conceptualisation, i.e. an individual may have a particular predisposition/vulnerability (lock), but this, of itself, does not usher in debility until there is a precipitant (key that fits the lock). Thus in the development of depression, Beck (1983) has identified sociotropes that are addicted to approval. This predisposition does not cause problems until precipitated by a matching event, e.g. the break-up of a relationship. Other negative events, such as the failure to gain a promotion, would not 'open the door' to depression in this case. The nature of the vulnerability varies from disorder to disorder and different stressors may be pertinent to different disorders. Stressors exist on a continuum from no stress to extreme stress and distinguishing stress from extreme trauma is necessarily somewhat arbitrary. Case formulation (Weerasekera 1996) involves consideration of four factors (4Ps) – predisposing, precipitants, perpetuating factors (e.g. avoidance) and protective factors (e.g. social support).

## SUMMARY

1. Flashbacks/nightmares are not necessarily evidence of post-traumatic stress disorder.
2. PTSD usually occurs in conjunction with other disorders.
3. Trauma is involved in the development of many disorders.
4. The treatment of a post-trauma disorder can be complicated by pain/disfigurement/head injury.
5. An adjustment disorder is a response to an identifiable stressor but it is a diagnosis of last resort and should not be used if other disorders are present.

6. Prolonged duress stress disorder (PDSD) is not an official diagnosis but may be useful in understanding the symptoms of clients suffering the consequences of prolonged moderate stressors. Treatment reflects that of PTSD.
7. CBT is based on the notion that cognitive appraisal plays a pivotal role in a client's response to a situation.
8. Different disorders have different cognitive content: the cognitive content specificity hypothesis.
9. CBT targets the content of thoughts at the level of negative automatic thoughts and underlying dysfunctional attitudes (schemas).
10. CBT targets information-processing biases, e.g. a mental filter.
11. CBT targets the thoughts, images, behaviours and emotions involved in the maintenance of disorder. Thoughts, behaviours, emotion and physiology all affect each other.
12. CBT treatment is psychoeducational, emphasising a client practising skills outside the treatment session and an in-session review of such practice.

# Part One

## POST-TRAUMATIC STRESS DISORDER

# Chapter Two

## A *DSM V*-BASED CBT MODEL OF PTSD

*The proposed new criteria for PTSD in DSM V include exaggerated negative expectations about oneself, others or the world and the distorted blaming of self or others. The new model of PTSD described in this chapter includes these additional features and, arguably, makes it as relevant to helping clients who have suffered chronic physical and/or sexual abuse as to those suffering from a single, acute extreme trauma. It is suggested that the hallmark of PTSD is a state of 'terrified surprise'. The model can be used to explain to the client their particular expression of PTSD.*

Sufferers from PTSD are haunted by memories of a trauma (or traumas) and are almost constantly scared. In *DSM IV TR* (American Psychiatric Association 2000) and the proposed *DSM V* (American Psychiatric Association, in press: see Appendix I), criteria A defines the type of trauma that can lead to PTSD as involving either a threat to one's own or another's life, serious injury or sexual violation to oneself or others. Such trauma/s are the starting point of the CBT Model of PTSD presented in Figure 2.1.

The trauma is, to begin with at least, a surprise, and 'surprises' – whether for good or ill – are subject to reprocessing. In PTSD this occurs in the form of flashbacks and/or nightmares of the incident(s). These intrusions (criteria B) have a sensory quality – sights, sounds, smells – as well as occurring in imagery. Further, the trauma may lead to hyperarousal (criteria E), involving sleep disturbance, impaired concentration and irritability. However, in terms of the Model (Figure 2.1), the intrusions and hyperarousal are short-lived in the absence of persistent maladaptive appraisals. Maladaptive appraisals involve criteria D2 exaggerated negative expectations about one's self, others or the world, e.g. 'I am bad', 'No one can be trusted', 'I've lost my soul forever', 'My whole nervous system is

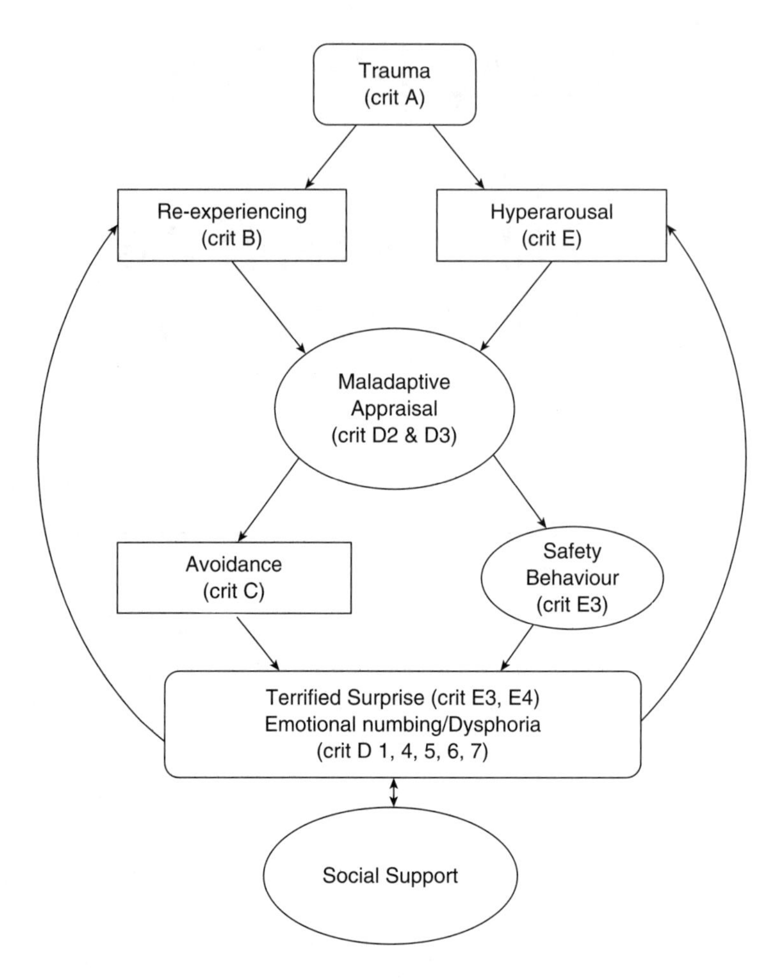


**Figure 2.1** A *DSM V*-based CBT Model of PTSD

permanently ruined', 'The world is completely dangerous', and Criteria D3 (the distorted blaming of self or others about the cause or consequences of the traumatic event(s)).

Earlier theories of PTSD (e.g. Ehlers and Clark 2000) suggested that in PTSD sufferers the traumatic memory is fragmented and poorly integrated, but more recent work (e.g. Lancaster et al. 2011) suggests that the opposite is the case, that the traumatic memory is overly integrated and the trauma becomes central to the person's identity. The centrality of the trauma to the individual sufferer's identity is reflected in the inclusion of criteria D2 and D3 in the proposed *DSM V* criteria for PTSD. Traumatised individuals with and without PTSD are distinguished by items on the Posttraumatic Cognitions Inventory (Foa, Ehlers et al. 1999) such as 'I have to be on guard all the time' and 'I can't deal with even the slightest upset'. Maladaptive appraisals are not so much of the trauma itself but of the meaning and significance attributed to the intrusions and hyperaousal symptoms. The intrusions may over time not be a replication of what happened, for example the victim of a serious road traffic accident may have 'flashbacks' of their children having been in the car at the time even though they were not present. Thus, in a sense, a person's memory is only as good as their last memory and it is to this that they are reacting.

Flashbacks and nightmares have a timeless quality. Unlike a memory they are not hooked to a particular time and place in the past but rather to varying degrees contain a sense of re-experiencing. They are the 'ghost' of what happened, leading to a feeling of being 'haunted'. The belief that the flashbacks and nightmares signal a real and present danger results in avoidance criteria C (e.g. a victim of a road traffic accident (RTA) avoiding driving and engaging in safety behaviours such as getting up in the night and checking the children are still breathing). The avoidance and safety behaviours prevent the sufferer learning that nothing bad would have happened in the absence of these behaviours and in turn this leads to the state of 'terrified surprise', typified by an exaggerated startle response (criteria E4) and hypervigilance (criteria E3), which are the hallmarks of the PTSD sufferer.

Avoidance of thoughts/images associated with the trauma (suppression) produces a rebound effect, increasing these intrusions (Wenzlaff and Wegner 2000). Fear is a feature of a phobia (albeit in a circumscribed way), thus fear or threat is not unique to PTSD, but a state of 'terrified surprise' is. While it subsumes a fear response, it is not confined to it. This state of terror can be mitigated by the support of others, but equally the PTSD sufferer loses the ability to elicit social support because of their emotional numbness, irritability, low mood and disengagement. (Social support has been found to be the biggest single predictor of recovery from PTSD; Brewin and Holmes 2003). The state of terror is reminiscent of their immediate response at the time of the trauma, increasing intrusions related to the trauma, probably through a process of mood-dependent recall (i.e. recalling preferentially that which was associated with a previous occurrence of the same emotional state). Further, the state of terrified surprise maintains hyperaousal, fuelling sleep, concentration and irritability problems, and may result in self-destructive or reckless behaviour.

A client's experience of PTSD can be individualised using the headings in Figure 2.2, putting into the boxes the specific symptoms that client has. For convenience, a blank version of Figure 2.2 is presented as Appendix F, for use in the construction of case formulation. The maladaptive appraisals may be distilled by asking the client: What they take the flashbacks/nightmares (intrusions – the vertical arrow) as meaning about today? What they make of their retreat into a 'bubble' (avoidance – right horizontal arrow)? Is it justified/useful? What do they take their retreat as meaning about themselves? What do they make of their irritability/jumpiness (hyperarousal – downward arrow)? What behaviours they feel they must perform 'on sentry duty' (hyperarousal – downward arrow)? What they believe to be the current threat level (negative mood – left horizontal arrow)?

The Posttraumatic Cognitions Inventory (Foa, Ehlers et al. 1999) can also be used to identify maladaptive appraisals. When Figure 2.2 is individualised in this

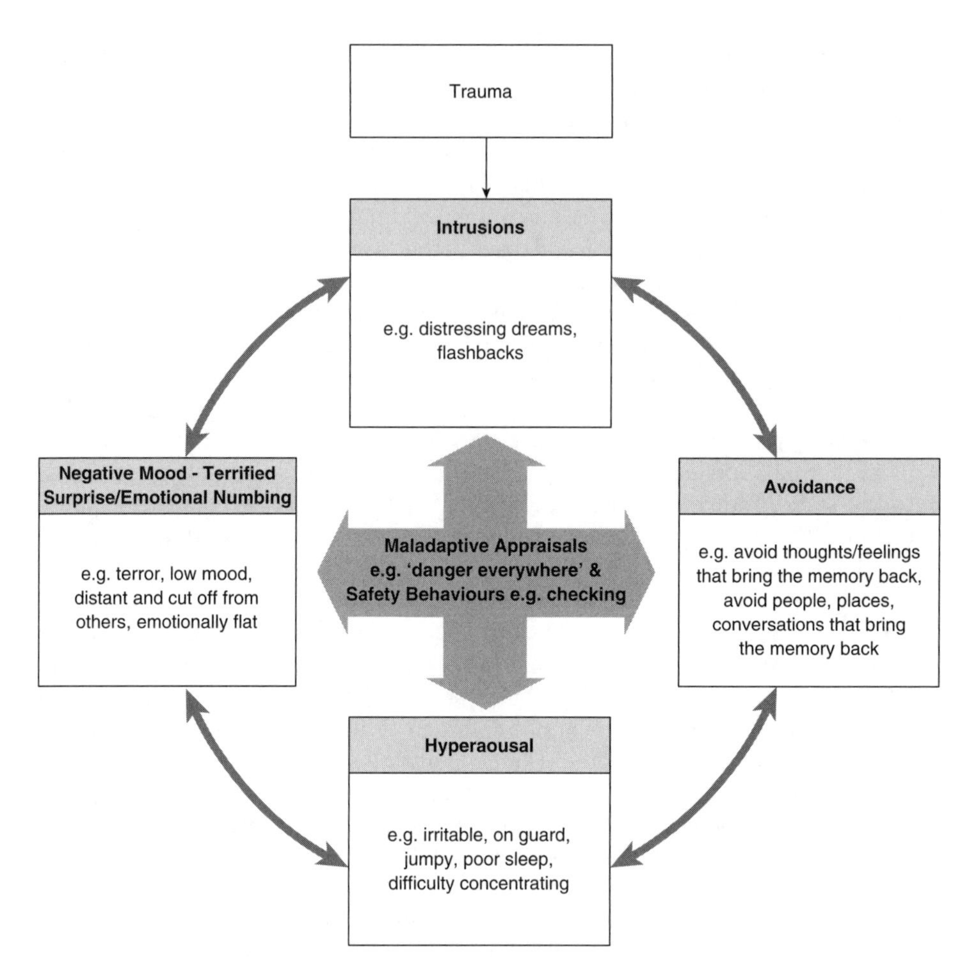


**Figure 2.2** The Persistence of Intrusions (adapted from Kaplan and Norton 1996)

*Source*: Adapted from the Balanced Scorecard by Roberts S. Kaplan and Dave P. Norton. Harvard Business School Press, 1996.

way it becomes the case formulation, i.e. a specific example of the cognitive model of the disorder. However, it should be noted that for ease of illustration the client version of Figure 2.2 leaves out social support and this is an essential ingredient of Figure 2.1 (A *DSM V*-based CBT Model of PTSD). It is suggested, therefore, that the intrapsychic focus of Figure 2.2 is supplemented with the interpersonal focus of Figure 2.3.

Figure 2.3 illustrates that the PTSD sufferer's tendency not to seek support (the 2 o'clock position and reflected in symptom D6 in the *DSM V* criteria) will likely result in no support being forthcoming (the 5 o'clock position), and this in turn may be subject to a maladaptive appraisal as to the futility of seeking

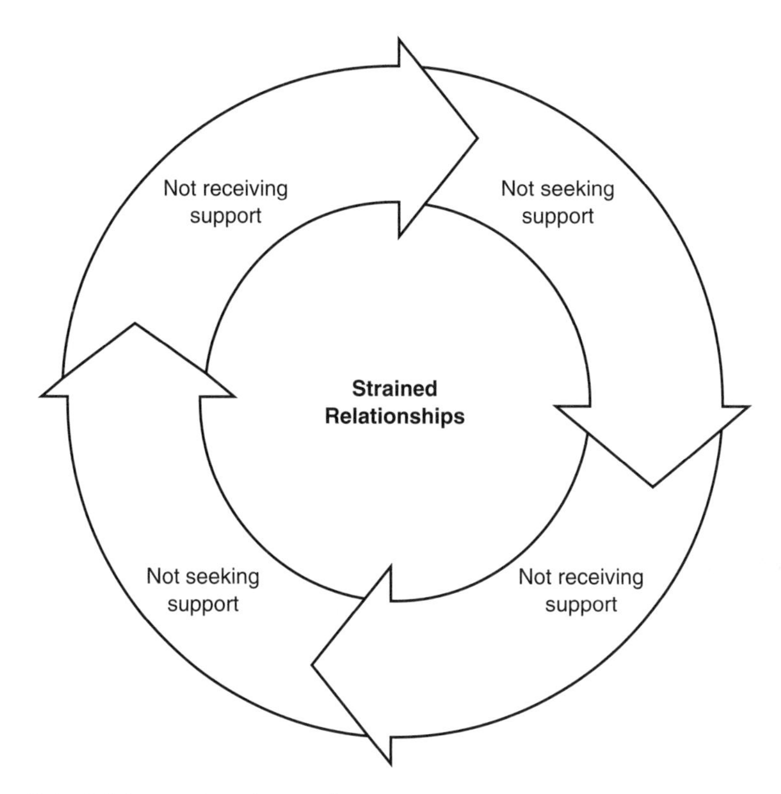


**Figure 2.3** Missing out on Support

support, confirming the 'wisdom' of not trying to elicit support (the 7 o'clock position) and setting up a vicious circle of no support being forthcoming (the 10 o'clock position) and strained relationships.

Flashbacks and nightmares (intrusions) are presented as a normal reaction to an extreme trauma. The intrusions in post-traumatic stress disorder are different from the unhappy memories that a person solely with depression might ruminate upon, in that they have a more immediate quality, involving some degree of re-experiencing. At its most extreme a person experiencing a dissociative flashback may experience a loss of awareness of their surroundings. Further the flashbacks/dreams are not experienced as being located at a particular time and place but have a 'now' quality. The persistence of the flashbacks/dreams can be explained using Figure 2.2. This figure also locates the role of each of the *DSM V* symptoms in maintaining PTSD (intrusions B1–5, avoidance C1–2, hyperarousal E1–5, negative mood D1, 4–7, maladaptive appraisals D2–3).

Using Figure 2.2, if flashbacks/nightmares are appraised as signalling a real and present danger, this generates a sense of threat/distress which will lead to actions designed to mitigate the supposed threat. However, these actions/coping responses are themselves so unusual (avoidance/safety behaviours) that they serve as a reminder of the intrusions, fuelling the intrusions. This in turn may be taken as signalling the need to be on high alert and the distress is transmuted into a state of terrified surprise. Thus a vicious circle is set up.

The proposed *DSM V* citeria for PTSD include two subtypes: 'Posttraumatic Stress Disorder – With Prominent Dissociative (Depersonalization/Derealization) Symptoms' and 'Posttraumatic Stress Disorder in Preschool Children'. The 'Dissociative' subtype requires that the person experiences ongoing symptoms of either depersonalisation ('feeling detached from , and as if one is an outside observer of, one's mental processes or body [e.g. feeling as though one is in a dream, sense of unreality of self or body, or time moving slowly]') and/or derealisation ('experiences of unreality of one's surroundings [e.g. world around the person is experienced as unreal, dreamlike, distant, or distorted]'). Preschool refers to less than six years of age.

## SUMMARY

1. Previous criteria for PTSD were criticised as being insufficiently relevant to the concerns of clients who had suffered chronic physical or sexual abuse or torture. The proposed *DSM V* criteria for PTSD take account of these shortcomings.
2. A new model of PTSD is described which suggests that a state of 'terrified surprise' is the signature of PTSD. This model includes exaggeratedly negative expectations and excessive self-blame.
3. The new model can be used to distil a comprehensive case formulation of a client's difficulties.

# Chapter Three

# ASSESSMENT AND ENGAGEMENT

*Clients have two pressing questions: 'What is wrong with me?' and 'Will I get better?' Answering the first question requires a reliable assessment. Vagueness about the answer is likely to increase a client's anxiety. There is no published evidence that PTSD can be reliably diagnosed without directly asking questions about each of the symptoms that comprise the diagnostic set. Evidence-based treatments for PTSD are diagnosis-specific. If the wrong disorder has been identified there is no evidence that this mistake can be compensated for by skilled therapy. This chapter begins by detailing the specifics of a reliable assessment. In order to answer the second question, 'Will I get better?', a client needs not only a credible and comprehensive story of their difficulties but also one which signposts the skills needed to move forward. The second half of this chapter explains how clients can be socialised into treatment by a translation of the neurobiology of PTSD into clinically useful analogies using simple illustrations.*

The process of characterising a client's distress and navigating through CBT treatment is shown in Figure 3.1.

The first step in defining a client's difficulties is a differential diagnosis – i.e. listing the range of possible diagnoses. A differential diagnosis is generated by both an open-ended interview and a comprehensive screening questionnaire/interview. The open-ended interview gives clients the opportunity to tell the story of their trauma, how they have been since, and how this compares with before the trauma.

The open-ended interview is followed by administering the 7-Minute Interview (see Appendix B)/First Step Questionnaire (see Appendix C), a screening device for the common psychiatric disorders. The screening questions for depression

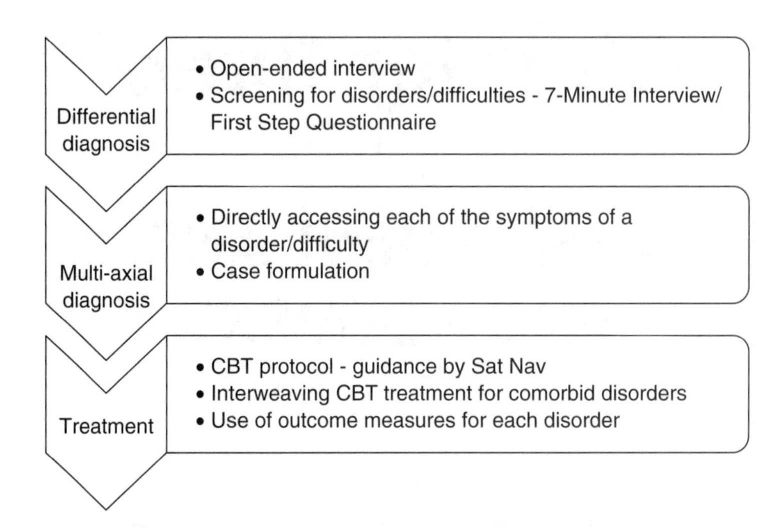


**Figure 3.1** Characterising Distress and Navigating through Treatment

in the 7-Minute Interview/First Step Questionnaire have been found to correctly identify 79% of those who are depressed (i.e. the sensitivity is 0.79) and correctly identify 94% of those who are not depressed (i.e. the specificity is 0.94). Importantly, including the question 'Is this something with which you would like help?' greatly reduced the number of false positives (Arroll et al. 2005). This question has therefore been added to the screening for other disorders.

The screening symptom questions for post-traumatic stress disorder (Prins et al. 2004), obsessive compulsive disorder (Fineberg et al. 2003) and substance abuse (Ewing 1984) have also been subjected to empirical investigation and found to be reliable. Further, the screening questions for generalised anxiety disorder (GAD) symptoms cover the same content area as the 2-item GAD scale that has been demonstrated to have a high sensitivity and specificity in detecting GAD (Kroenke et al. 2007). However, at this time the screening questions for other disorders have only a face validity. The self-report version of the screen 'The First Step Questionnaire – Revised' similarly awaits validation. Its strength is that it takes a client two to three minutes to complete and it takes the therapist only a minute to interpret using the guidance given for the correspondingly numbered items in the 7-Minute Health Screen. If a screen/questionnaire response for a disorder is positive, then a more detailed enquiry is made.

The second step in defining clients' difficulties is multi-axial diagnosis. This involves determining not only which disorder(s) a client is suffering from but also the contexts of those disorders, for example whether the disorder is complicated by pain and/or a head injury. The questions in Appendix H can be used to explore psychosocial stressors and gauge their severity. Diagnostic questions for depression and the anxiety disorders can be found in Scott (2011) (which is freely available as a CBT Pocketbook online at www.routledgementalhealth.com/

simply-effective-group-cognitive-behaviour-therapy). In Appendix A of this volume the questions with regard to PTSD have been updated to take into account the proposed *DSM V* criteria (American Psychiatric Association, in press). Having determined which disorder(s) the client is suffering from (i.e. what they are a 'case' of), the scene is set for an explanatory model of their problems. However, this is incomplete without taking into account any secondary traumatisation such as pain or cognitive impairment that the client might be suffering from as a consequence of their trauma. For example, if they are is suffering chronic pain following a trauma this may act as a reminder of the incident, leading to depressive rumination about it and therefore exacerbating any depression.

## RELIABLE ASSESSMENT

CBT's evidence base rests largely on the use of specific protocols for specific disorders, thus if a disorder is incorrectly identified the intervention will be inappropriate. Unless a diagnosis is made reliably a therapist may mistakenly conclude that a client's non-response to an intervention is because of their lack of therapeutic skill as opposed to diagnostic inaccuracy. Examinations of early CBT interventions post trauma (Roberts et al. 2009) suggest that the presence of a specific diagnosis may be the most important predictor of who benefits from trauma-focused CBT.

Therapists watching an open-ended interview being conducted have poor levels of agreement about diagnosis. This is often because different therapists place different emphasis on different symptoms and operate with different thresholds about whether a particular symptom is present at a clinically significant level. Not only do they disagree about the main disorder, they also stop at the first disorder they identify (Zimmerman and Mattia 2000) and miss additional disorders. This is a particular concern with PTSD clients as 75% of them suffer additional disorders (Kessler et al. 2005). Further, Kessler et al. (2005) found that a client's level of impairment will be strongly related to how many additional disorders they have.

Therapists can protect themselves from unreliable assessments by making a systematic enquiry about each of the symptoms that comprise likely disorders using the CBT Pocketbook (Scott 2011), or the SCID (First et al. 1997a and 1997b) for disorders not covered by the Pocketbook, such as borderline personality disorder. This broader sweep helps ensure that all the pertinent disorder(s) are identified as a prelude to intervention.

## PSYCHOMETRIC TESTS

The severity of a disorder should be gauged, if possible, using a psychometric test and a client's progress in treatment charted on the chosen test. Appropriate tests should also be administered for any additional disorders. IAPT (IAPT 2011) have usefully provided, as a free download at www.IAPT.com, outcome measures for depression and each of the anxiety disorders. For PTSD they recommend use of the Impact of Events Scale – Revised (IES-R) (Creamer et al. 2003) and suggest a cut-off of 33 or more to indicate 'caseness' of PTSD. However, Beck et al. (2008) found that when the IES-R was set against the 'gold standard' of a standardised diagnostic interview, as opposed to another psychometric test (as in the Creamer et al. (2003) study), the sensitivity of the IES-R was only 74.5% (i.e. it identified three out of four of those who had PTSD) and the specificity was 63.1% (i.e. of those who have not got PTSD about one in three would have been falsely identified as having PTSD and treated inappropriately). This illustrates that psychometric tests should not be used as a substitute for a diagnostic interview. Their proper place is as a measure of change once a disorder has been identified. In some instances, such as phobias, there are no standardised outcome measures, and IAPT (2011) have included in their package three suggested phobia scales.

## AN ENGAGING STORY

The cognitive mediation model described in Chapter One is not meant to indicate that cognitions are the sole determinant of responses to stimuli. Although it is useful to view human beings as information processors, and use the language of computers to account for distress (e.g. viewing PTSD as an example of arrested information processing), the analogy can be pushed too far. Humans do not have silicon chips, they are a biological organism. Indeed, the cognitive mediation model is a special case of the more general stimuli–organism–response model (Lazarus 2006). An appreciation of the neurobiology of PTSD can lead to clinically useful analogies that point the way forward for the client while simultaneously utilising the CBT perspective. This synthesis of cognition and neurobiology presents a more rounded view of human functioning.

The appraisals, coping behaviours and social interactions of an individual trauma victim do not occur in a vacuum but within a biological context. It is well established (LeDoux 1998) that fear reactions are mediated by the brain's amygdala, which operates as an alarm gauging whether a stimulus is a threat or not. In addition, it is a repository of emotional memory, remembering the sensory aspects sights, sounds, smell, etc., of an experience. The amygdala (LeDoux 1998) works on a perceptual matching, triggered whenever there is a stimulus that in some way matches the sensory experience that was recorded. In PTSD, the amygdala is hyperactive, operating with a low threshold for threat and often operating non-consciously, so that the person may react without knowing what they are reacting to. The PTSD sufferer may suffer an amygdala hijack in that their sensory experience undergoes little or no reining in by areas such as the medial prefrontal cortex which have become underactive (Brewin 2008). Further, under extreme stress verbal memories can be impaired by damage to the hippocampus (which is responsible for putting events into context and for the anticipation of forthcoming events).

It seems likely that memory retrieval is a dynamic process in that when a memory is retrieved it becomes available in a plastic state and is open to modification (Lee 2009; Diekelmann et al. 2011). For example, a juror may have a certain opinion about a defendant's performance in a trial, but if they have read something about the case in the newspaper after a day in court their memory of what they 'saw' in court can be altered – memory is thus only as good as the last memory. The reconsolidation of memory can result in the alteration of either the content of a traumatic memory (e.g. in a flashback seeing one's own children dismayed at the scene of a trauma even though they were not actually present) and/or the strength of the memory (e.g. increasing the strength by concluding that the memory is relevant to current day-to-day life). Thus memories are updated, and the therapeutic task is to ensure that traumatic memories are adaptively updated.

The same brain regions that are involved in remembering the past are also used in imagining the future (Schacter et al. 2007) and imagined events are constructed from episodic memory (remembered personal experience). This has led to the idea that individuals are involved in 'mental time travel' into both the past and future. The constructive episodic simulation hypothesis suggests that a crucial function of memory is to make information available for the simulation of future events. This hypothesis was advanced to explain why memory involves a constructive process of piecing together bits and pieces of information. For traumatised clients the event that is most salient is the trauma and, applying the constructive episodic simulation hypothesis, it seems likely that various aspects of the trauma may be put together to anticipate a forthcoming event. Thus, for example, a client traumatised by a fire engine crashing into her home, while she was at home, might subsequently suffer from PTSD, recover in the sense that she no longer meets the diagnostic criteria for the condition yet, since the incident, may still be troubled as she drives through traffic lights on green. Although she may no longer suffer thoughts/images of the trauma, nevertheless the bodily reactions are still those felt at the sound of the fire engine hitting her home, and despite nothing happening when she drives through the green traffic light, she may still be distressed by her imaginings. Aspects of the trauma become building blocks for the anticipation of events. Clinically, the goal is then to progressively marginalise the spontaneous trauma-based imagining by the deliberate graphic recall of instances when, in this context, there has been no harm.

The above biological considerations are consistent with Brewin's Dual Representation Theory of PTSD (Brewin and Holmes 2003). He suggests that there are two memory systems: one that encodes an experience at a sensory level and another that encodes the experience at a verbal level. In PTSD it is the sensory aspects that are preferentially retrieved. Such sensory memories may not be retrievable by verbal enquiry but can be triggered by reminders that are perceived, at a primarily non-conscious level, to match the trauma. These are termed SAMs (situationally accessible memories). In contrast, VAMs (verbally accessible memories) can be retrieved by verbal enquiry. Therapeutically, different types of treatment strategy are likely to be required depending on which aspect of the memory is being focused upon (e.g. exposure may be more pertinent to a SAMs, whereas cognitive restructuring may be more appropriate to VAMs).

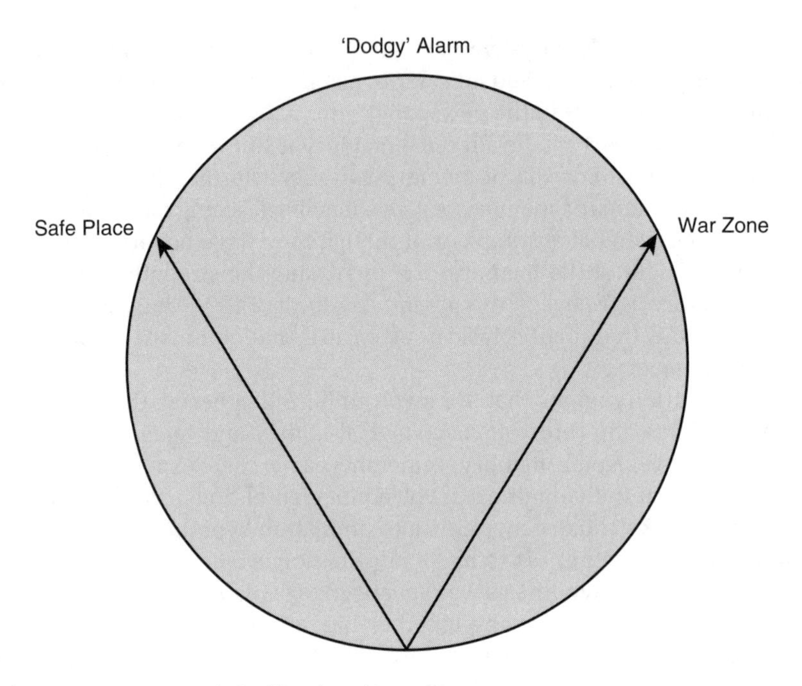


**Figure 3.2** The Amygdala 'Dodgy Alarm'

PTSD clients can be helped to conceptualise their difficulties by referring to their hypersensitive amygdala as an over-sensitive ('dodgy') alarm which is tripped by minor stressors that in any way resemble the original trauma. Figure 3.2 can be used to illustrate that it is as if, before the trauma, their alarm was set in a 'safe place' (10 o'clock position) but as a result of the incident(s) it has 'flipped' and now occupies the 'war zone' (the 2 o'clock position).

Figure 3.2 can be used to help the client normalise their symptoms. Avoidance can be presented as an intuitive recognition by the sufferer that they have an over-sensitive alarm. If it is tripped they are upset, so their coping strategy is to avoid tripping it by avoiding reminders. Similarly, safety behaviours are presented as an understandable coping strategy to being in a war zone. Likewise, sleep disturbance, poor concentration, irritability and an exaggerated startle response are probably the consequence of being in what is perceived as a 'war zone'. Figure 3.2 can also be used to explain the sense of detachment that PTSD sufferers experience. Relatives and friends perceive and operate as if they are in a 'safe place' but not so the trauma victim, resulting in the disconnection depicted in Figure 3.3.

The sense of disconnection that the PTSD sufferer experiences may lead to the emotional flatness depicted in Figure 3.4 as a lemonade bottle without the top on, possibly resulting in the depression which is often associated with PTSD.

Treatment can then be conceptualised as involving the resetting of the alarm. In order to achieve this, the client is encouraged to very gradually dare

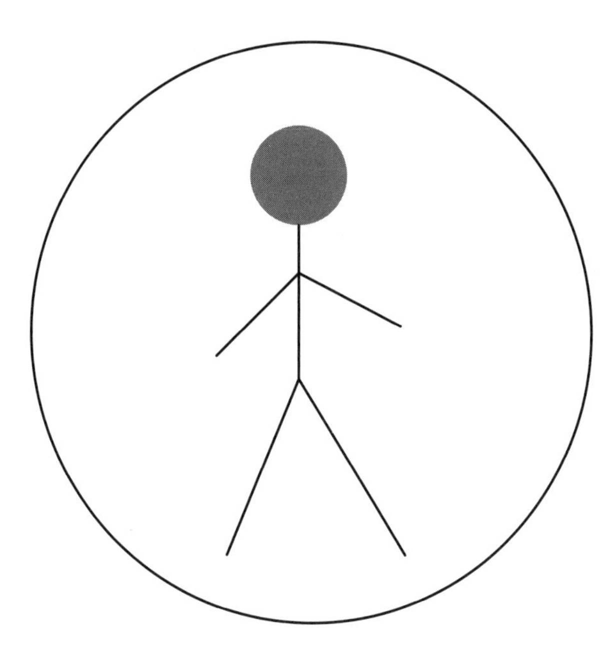

**Figure 3.3** The Bubble

themselves to do what has been avoided. Each 'dare' trips the alarm. While this experience is uncomfortable, information is collected that there is no threat and the alarm moves slightly anti-clockwise. There is also an emphasis on stretching the bubble (Figure 3.3) by gradually connecting with others – eliciting and maintaining social support. The treatment also focuses on the management of low mood/emotional flatness, depicted in Figure 3.4.

However, a client's imaginings can prevent them from attempting any 'dare'. In order to help circumvent this difficulty it can usefully be explained to the client that they carry with them a trauma-based 'construction kit' of the trauma. This 'kit' has a number of parts – bodily reactions to the trauma, emotions, thoughts/images and behaviours – and that in anticipating any event they may 'glue together' some parts of the trauma, suffer distress, and either avoid or endure the anticipated event with distress. Despite the fact their 'constructed model' is not borne out in practice, they may be debilitated by their imagining and may compound this by getting cross with themselves for the imaginings. It is suggested that they practise switching attention from what they have 'made' from the trauma-based construction kit to another 'kit' which contains all the experiences of a similar event to construct an alternative model. But it is important that this alternative model is constructed from detailed instances of past events. Thus, if a client has become fearful of going shopping since the trauma, they would recall very detailed pre-trauma instances of going into department stores, e.g. remembering the embarrassment when they walked out of a shop without

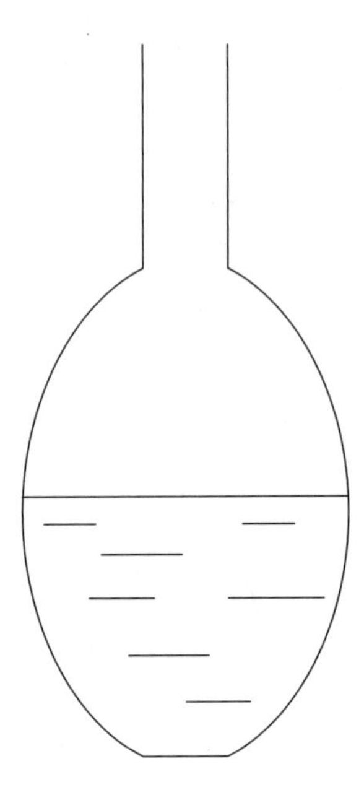

**Figure 3.4** Emotional Flatness

paying and were accosted by security guards, unexpectedly finding just the right gift for a loved one, etc. (Clients with both depression and schizophrenia have been found to use over-general memories to anticipate future events; see Schacter et al. 2007.) The PTSD Survival Manual – Revised (see Appendix G) provides clients with a description of PTSD symptoms and includes Figures 3.2–3.4 as well as figures illustrating the consequences of utilising a trauma-based construction kit as opposed to using a kit based on recalling similar events pre-trauma. The therapist should talk the client through the figures of the 'dodgy alarm', 'bubble' and 'lemonade bottle' in the Manual and gauge that client's expressions of the felt relevance of the diagrams before giving it to them to read for homework.

## SUMMARY

1. Routine open-ended interviews are unreliable and there is evidence that therapists stop their enquiry prematurely at the first disorder they believe they have identified.
2. A reliable assessment involves directly accessing each of the symptoms that comprise a diagnostic set. Because comorbidity is the norm, an enquiry should be made about multiple disorders. In this regard, a useful first step is to use a diagnostic screen.

3. Psychometric tests are not a substitute for diagnosis; they tend to yield false positives leading to inappropriate treatment. However, a psychometric test is a useful measure of change if it assesses a disorder already identified via a diagnostic interview.
4. An information processing model of a client's difficulties is incomplete without a biological model. When the biological model is translated into a clinically useful analogy it enhances further the client's sense of being understood. The analogies elaborated are such that they carry clear action implications.
5. A hypersensitive amygdala (the brain's alarm) likely plays a key role in the development of PTSD.
6. The interpersonal consequences of PTSD have been ignored in previous cognitive formulations. The alienation of the PTSD client is explained in terms of the marked difference in the sensitivity of their alarm from that of those around them. Further, this alienation often leads to a low mood/depression.
7. The client's alarm may be triggered externally and automatically by a perceptual matching and/or internally by unusual but not abnormal sensations, producing panic attacks.
8. Clients can be taught the cognitive and biological models using the PTSD Survival Manual – Revised.
9. It is suggested that PTSD is maintained by the automatic retrieval of aspects of the trauma to construct a model of any situation that may be objectively, even remotely, threatening. Although the model does not predict what actually happens, the client may nevertheless continue to be disturbed by the 'fright' that they have given themselves. The implication is that clients should be taught to travel back in time again but only in order to retrieve specific examples of what happened when they engaged in this activity pre-trauma.

# Chapter Four

## NON-TRAUMA-FOCUSED CBT

*Avoiding reminders of trauma and having conversations about it are symptoms of PTSD, therefore clients are likely to be reticent about therapy. Traditionally, the CBT treatment for PTSD is trauma-focused, although potentially this can drive a wedge between client and therapist. However, there is some evidence that a non-trauma-focused coping skills approach can be effective. A non-trauma-focused intervention increases the range of options available to the therapist. In some instances it may be the only option acceptable to the client and in other instances it can be a necessary stepping stone towards a trauma-focused intervention. The non-trauma-focused intervention described in this chapter has Self-Instruction Training (SIT) at its core. In SIT clients are taught coping self-statements for use in advance of PTSD stressors, statements to be used on encountering these stressors, and self-talk to be used when feeling overwhelmed, followed by a review and refinement of the coping skills. In the non-trauma-ocused CBT (NTFCBT) programme the focus is on the management of each of the domains of PTSD: intrusions, avoidance, maladaptive appraisals, hyperarousal and negative mood. The number of sessions required is typically 5–10, but the determinant of the number of sessions should be whether there has been adequate coverage of each domain. At the end of NTFCBT the client should be re-assessed and if still suffering from PTSD stepped up to TFCBT.*

Trauma-focused CBT (TFCBT) is an effective treatment for PTSD (Ehlers et al. 2010) as well as a NICE recommended treatment (NICE 2005a), and in the next chapter a TFCBT protocol is described. However, while TFCBT is effective, a significant minority fail to benefit – a review of outcome studies for PTSD, by Bradley et al. (2005) revealed that only 40–70% of patients recover with TFCBT. One of the diagnostic symptoms of PTSD is the avoidance of thinking and talking about the trauma, thus in trying to implement a trauma-focused intervention the therapist may face an uphill struggle. For example, Scott and Stradling (1997) found that, in routine practice, only 57% complied with an audiotape exposure treatment, while Zayfert et al. (2005) found that only 28% of those undergoing exposure therapy, in routine practice, completed treatment. This raises the question of whether there is a place for a non-trauma-focused intervention (NTFCBT).

An NTFCBT approach can operate as a first step in a stepped care approach and clients can, if necessary, then be stepped up to a TFCBT intervention. A possible advantage of an NTFCBT intervention at the front end of treatment is that it may better enhance a therapeutic alliance, creating a bond between therapist and client and making for a more collaborative focus on tasks and goals. An NTFCBT approach is particularly amenable to delivery in a group format, in that it circumnavigates the possibility of a re-traumatisation arising from exposure to fellow group members' traumas. In Chapter Six such an intervention is detailed.

## THE EVIDENCE BASE FOR A COPING SKILLS APPROACH

Stress Inoculation Training (Meichenbaum 1985) is a coping skills NTFCBT package consisting of Self-Instruction Training, problem solving and cognitive restructuring. In two studies, Foa et al. (1991, 1999a) compared TFCBT (in the form of prolonged exposure) with a version of Meichenbaum's (1985) NTFCBT package. At the end of treatment the latter was superior to the former, but at follow-up the TFCBT intervention appeared slightly superior to the NTFCBT package. However, Foa et al. used a truncated form of Meichenbaum's (1985) package, omitting the application and follow through phase. This final phase involves opportunities for clients to apply coping skills to a gradient of stressors and uses techniques such as imagery, modelling, role playing and graded in vivo exposure in order to prevent relapse. Thus despite Stress Inoculation Training not being properly implemented it was little different in outcome from TFCBT. The focus in the Foa et al. studies (1991, 1999a) was on adult female victims of assault and it is therefore unclear whether the results can be generalised to other populations.

A study by Cloitre et al. (2010) provides some encouragement that a skills-based approach extends the armamentarium of treatments for PTSD. These authors treated female adult survivors of child abuse. One component of their intervention focused on skills training for emotion regulation and interpersonal difficulties and this produced an additive gain in the subsequent TFCBT. Further support for the possible efficacy of an NTFCBT intervention comes from the work of Resick et al. (2008), who compared the efficacy of individual components of cognitive processing therapy: a trauma-focused intervention (written accounts), cognitive therapy only, and the full package. The non-trauma-focused intervention reported greater improvements in PTSD than the trauma-focused condition. Although TFCBT has the most evidence to support it at present, there is limited evidence that stress management is effective (Bisson and Andrew 2009). The

European Network for Traumatic Stress Guidelines (Bisson et al. 2010) notes that not all sufferers from PTSD benefit or can engage in TFCBT and recommend stress management as a second-line treatment.

## MECHANISM OF ACTION OF A COPING SKILLS APPROACH

It may be that the active ingredient in an NTFCBT programme is cognitive control, i.e. the ability to complete goal-directed behaviour by actively maintaining information while inhibiting irrelevant information. For example, a client might be fearful of enclosed spaces (e.g. having an MRI scan), and this fear might relate, say, to being trapped in a room following an explosion. In order to cope with the proposed MRI scan the client might engage in self-talk to the effect that they have never heard of anyone suffocating in a scanner, while at the same time recognising that thoughts/feelings might be generated that are relics of their trauma. Cognitive control would involve concentrating on the positive coping self statement and marginalising though accepting the 'relics'. It appears that cognitive control is associated with re-experiencing symptoms (Bomyea et al. 2012) – the more cognitive control, the less re-experiencing.

## FLEXIBILITY IN THE USE OF NTFCBT AND TFCBT

The CBT programmes described in this chapter and the next reflect different phases of intervention, an NTFCBT Phase and a TFCBT Phase, but there is not intended to be a rigid distinction between the phases time-wise. For example, a particular client may appear at the outset perfectly open to a TFCBT intervention (e.g. daily writing about the trauma may be an agreed homework task) but at the next session it may be discovered that the client only wrote about it once and they were extremely distressed by it, becoming very angry with their partner. In such a situation, Self-Instruction Training (SIT) can be applied to writing about the trauma, with coping self-statements distilled to be used prior to beginning writing, self-talk to be used when beginning to write, and coping self-statements to be used when feeling overwhelmed. Thus a component of the NTFCBT package may be adopted to facilitate the TFCBT, but if the latter still proves unacceptable to the client, the NTFCBT approach is continued. While in general it seems sensible, in terms of establishing a therapeutic alliance, to begin with an NTFCBT approach, there can be many occasions where TFCBT is acceptable from the outset.

## ORIENTATING THE CLIENT TOWARDS TREATMENT

It is very useful for clients to have to hand pertinent reading material to reinforce what is taught in the programme, and for this the PTSD Survival Manual (Scott

2011) has been revised and reproduced in Appendix G. As described in the previous chapter, the therapist should talk the client through Figures G.2–G.4 in this Appendix. For many sufferers the sense of isolation can be profound and this may be only partly mitigated by seeing a therapist. Reading about how other PTSD sufferers have coped and the steps they have taken to recover (*Moving on after Trauma:* Scott 2008) can greatly help them normalise their difficulties. Social support is a key predictor of recovery from PTSD and involving a significant other in the treatment programme helps them understand the effects of traumatisation and what needs to be done, ensuring generalisation beyond the treatment room. If a partner or relative attends some of the treatment sessions, the interpersonal difficulties that PTSD clients often present can be better addressed.

## BEYOND THE FIRST INTERVIEW

The first session is devoted primarily to assessment and this was covered in the previous chapter. However, such an assessment should not be regarded as a once and for all event. At all sessions the therapist has to be alert to information that comes to light that causes a revision of the initial opinion and an altering of direction. Therapists need to be aware of the operation of a confirmatory bias (Kahneman 2011, that is the tendency to look for information that confirms our initial conclusions. For example, a therapist may have initially concluded that a client was suffering from panic disorder but as treatment progresses there may be hints that these 'attacks' occur whenever the client is in the 'spotlight'. There is then a need to move around the confirmatory bias and ask clarifying questions: it may then become apparent that the client's social/evaluative concerns (social phobia) need to be the target rather than, say, catastrophic misinterpretations of bodily sensations (panic disorder).

The NTFCBT/TFCBT programme beyond the first interview may be conducted over 10–20 sessions. The structure of sessions from the second session onwards is shown in Table 4.1.

Each session begins with an enquiry into the client's functioning since the previous session and their response to the last session (see Table 4.1). These are both crucial to establishing a therapeutic alliance. The therapist has to strike a delicate balance with the client in enquiring about their welfare since the last session. On the one hand it is important for rapport building, but on the other hand it can squeeze key items off the agenda. Indeed, setting an the agenda for the session (item 2 in Table 4.1) should usually occur within a few minutes of its starting, though clearly in some instances (e.g. a sudden bereavement) this may be significantly later.

The third item in Table 4.1 relates to homework: if homework is not systematically reviewed in a session then the client will likely see it as having little importance. In reviewing homework the therapist should determine the client's self-efficacy with regard to the assignment, by asking whether the client believed they had the capacity to do the assignment and whether they

**Table 4.1** Structure of Sessions – Second Session Onwards

1. Enquiry about client's functioning since the previous session and response to last session
2. Setting of Agenda
3. Review of homework and reading – troubleshooting difficulties
4. Introduction to new material – use of SIT to target:
   - i Intrusions
   - ii Avoidance
   - iii Maladaptive appraisals
   - iv Hyperarousal
   - v Negative mood
5. Cognitive restructuring – Socratic dialogue, MOOD Thought Record
6. Problem Solving
7. Setting of homework

believed performing the homework would make a worthwhile difference. If the client felt that they lacked the capacity, then the size of the task may need to be temporarily reduced. If they believed that the homework was not relevant, namely that it would not make a worthwhile difference, the therapist should ponder whether in the setting of this assignment they had fully involved the client. Reading material should be regularly referred to and discussed throughout the programme, so that the client can become so familiar with it that it can constitute an important resource post treatment.

In some instances the therapist may need to engage in motivational interviewing with the client, presenting the non-compliance with the homework as a credible response and simply asking the client what a typical day in six weeks or six months would be like if they continued along this path. This is then juxtaposed with the terrain the therapist maps out over the next six months if there is completion of homework assignments but without minimising difficulties. In so doing the therapist creates in the client a state of cognitive dissonance, which is likely to be resolved by the client making a greater commitment to one path or the other.

The material to be introduced in the sessions (item 4 in Table 4.1) covers the application of SIT to the five domains of PTSD (see Figure 2.2): intrusions, avoidance, maladaptive appraisals, hyperarousal and negative mood. Table 4.2 contains examples of the use of SIT in each of these domains.

Table 4.2 is presented to clients to illustrate the use of SIT. However it is not intended that clients adopt these examples verbatim. The coping self-statements arise from discussions with the client about their trauma and its effects and they are a collaborative endeavour. The self-statements are an end-product of Socratic dialogue and cognitive restructuring. They are then applied between sessions and their utility is examined at the next session and, if necessary, refined for further testing.

The domains tackled follow roughly the order as laid out in Table 4.1, item 4. At the outset intrusions and avoidance are tackled in tandem, as it is explained to the client that attempts to suppress the intrusions (avoidance) has the

**Table 4.2** Examples of the Application of SIT to the Domains of PTSD

| PTSD domain | Preparing for | Encountering | Coping with feeling overwhelmed |
|---|---|---|---|
| Intrusions | 'They are of the past, not today.' | 'They take my breath away, but if I stay focused they will sort themselves out.' | 'They are having a real tantrum, but if I continue to ignore them they will take care of themselves.' |
| Avoidance | 'I can never run fast enough to get away from the reminders, I just exhaust myself. I must gradually stop allowing myself to be bullied into avoidance.' | 'This situation just makes me want to run, I will stand my ground and see does anything terrible actually happen.' | 'I am feeling it is all too much, but that is just a feeling not a fact.' |
| Maladaptive Appraisal | 'I don't feel confident in doing anything since, but that does not mean I can't do things.' | 'I feel tongue-tied even with just relatives around, they will not know what I am thinking and feeling, just smile.' | 'I feel stupid, stay, they are not going to eat me alive.' |
| Hyperarousal | 'I am likely to overeact, I must use STOP and THINK.' | 'I can feel the anger at the dog barking at me, but would I have seen this situation as a threat before the incident?' | 'I am feeling overwhelmed, but in 30 minutes time will I think that there was a real and present danger?' |
| Negative Mood | 'I must not blame myself for things I could do nothing about.' | 'Just because it was hard trying to explain to Social Security why I can't go back to work doesn't mean I have to blame myself.' | 'It doesn't seem that anyone understands about my PTSD, but I understand because I'm suffering from it. There's no need to make it worse by blaming myself.' |

paradoxical effect of increasing them (Wenzlaff and Wegner 2000). To illustrate this point the PTSD Survival Manual (Appendix G) is pressed into service, and the client is asked not to think about the featured 'Orangutan'. Then after a brief pause the client is asked what they had just been thinking about/imagining.

Clients are very conscious that they are haunted by memories of their trauma, usually both when they are awake and when they are asleep. Consequently they are very receptive to learning ways to handle the intrusions that might make them of less felt relevance to today. Thus a client's symptoms of re-experiencing are made an initial target but so too is avoidance, as attempts to suppress thoughts/images of the 'Orangutan' will have shown that they produce precisely the opposite effect. Not only does cognitive avoidance increase intrusions, but so too does behavioural avoidance. It is explained that in the act of avoiding a place or situation, there is a greater consciousness of what is being avoided and why. Tackling a client's avoidance means not only that the client reclaims their life, but also that intrusions are rendered less frequent and less distressing. Avoidance is tackled by encouraging the client to gradually dare themselves to approach that which they have been avoiding, thereby conducting a behavioural experiment to test out whether their fears are grounded. Usually the first two sessions will be devoted to intrusions-avoidance and at subsequent sessions there will be at least some time devoted to these targets.

In the course of the initial sessions maladaptive appraisals inevitably crop up (e.g. 'I ought to be over this by now', 'I ought to have stopped it happening', etc.). These should be noted by the therapist but put on the agenda for tackling later – from about the third session onwards – so that sufficient space is given initially to intrusions-avoidance. These appraisals can be tackled by the therapist's use of Socratic dialogue, questioning the validity, utility and authority by which these negative automatic thoughts are held. The maladaptive appraisals inevitably lead to a negative mood, and clients can be taught to manage their mood using the thought record (MOOD chart) in the Survival Manual, Appendix G. Examining a client's MOOD charts inevitably reveals conflicts with significant others, often occurring because of irritability. This leads to a natural focus on hyperarousal and the distillation of anger management skills. Somewhat strangely, this hyperaousal often occurs alongside an emotional numbness and ways of problem solving this are also focused upon. Thus while the domains covered in the NTFCBT programme appear quite separate in Figure 4.1, there is a natural flow to tackling them.

For most PTSD clients their particular symptoms can be addressed in about 10 sessions (typically the first five consist of NTFCBT and the last five of TFCBT), but clients with more severe PTSD can take longer.

## SELF-INSTRUCTION TRAINING

Self-Instruction Training (SIT) may be understood as the development of metacognitive plans for handling each of the PTSD symptoms and is consistent with the metacognitive approach described by Wells and Sembi (2004). The components of SIT are shown in the left-hand column of Table 4.3.

Table 4.3 can be used with regard to any stressful situation. For example, you may have read the previous chapter, then seen a traumatised client and been dismayed that you seemed not to get a word in edgeways and were unable to conduct a thorough assessment, and are thus feeling embarrassed about taking the case to supervision. In preparing yourself for supervision (row one of Table 4.3), you might tell yourself, 'I've only just started seeing traumatised clients so I can't be

**Table 4.3** Generic SIT Form

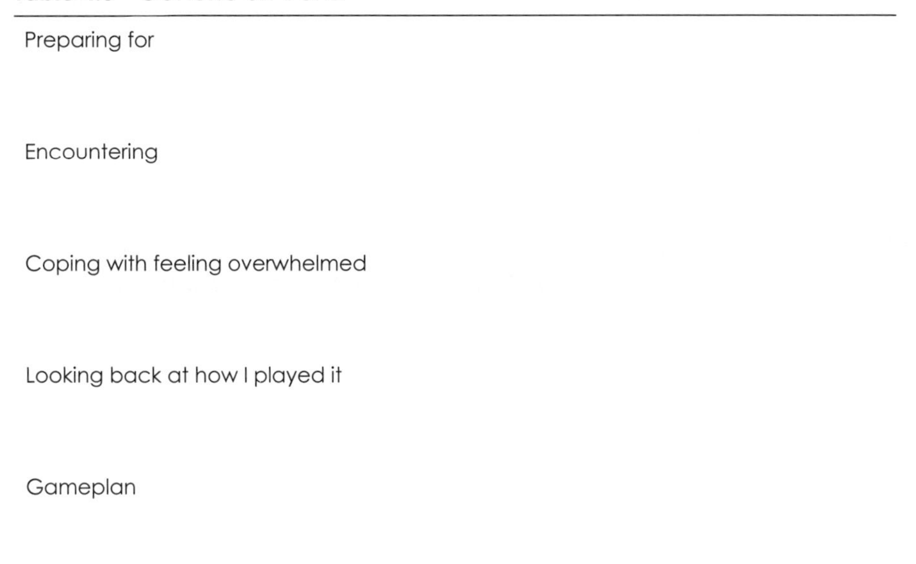

| |
|---|
| Preparing for |
| Encountering |
| Coping with feeling overwhelmed |
| Looking back at how I played it |
| Gameplan |

expected to learn the skills overnight'. However, you may be fearful of encountering your supervisor because he/she always knows something else that you should have read and the books just keep piling up, many unread. Accordingly, you might cope by asking your supervisor to model, using the strategies from the previous chapter, and you play the part of the client. You might anticipate feeling overwhelmed if your supervisor declines a role play and perhaps decide to tell yourself (fourth row down of Table 4.3) 'Medics don't attempt procedures without them being modelled. Why should I be placed in a different position? Perhaps I might ask a colleague to role play it.' The fifth row in Table 4.3 is a reflection on the effectiveness of your coping strategy and the bottom row, 'Gameplan', is a further refinement of your coping strategy.

Ongoing PTSD symptoms can be conceptualised as the absence of a plan for preparing for triggered symptoms (e.g. 'I hope I don't see any accidents'), the absence of a plan for encountering symptoms (e.g. 'This just takes me back to ...'), and the absence of a plan for coping with feeling overwhelmed (e.g. 'I can't stand this, when will it stop?').

The SIT can be used in relation to any of the PTSD symptoms. For example, if 'flashbacks' were entered in the first row of Table 4.3, after discussion, the client might decide to tell themselves 'It's normal to get flashbacks/nightmares because the incident was such a surprise, I am bound to go over and over it, but it doesn't mean that there is a real and present danger'. It can be explained to the client that the purpose of the second row is to enable them to get in the right frame of mind before encountering what they fear. The third row of Table 4.3 requires that the client, in consultation with the therapist and drawing on the prescribed reading, generates a coping self-statement for use when encountering a flashback, for example by noting the similarities to the trauma but also making a long list of differences.

Self-statements can be rehearsed and refined in a role play and/or imaginary rehearsal. However, the strategies used at the different stages of Self-Instruction Training need not be confined to verbal self-statements but may also use narrative and imagery which can often have a more powerful effect on emotion than objective appraisal. Thus, a client with PTSD following a road traffic accident might feel overwhelmed when they begin driving again, and while they might cope with such feelings by objectively appraising the situation with a self-statement such as 'The accident was the exception, one accident in 20 years of driving', the third row of Table 4.3 may need strengthening further by the inclusion of a narrative/imagery, e.g. 'My car is Dolores, she is very old, and I just need to coax her to safety. No one wants to hit an old woman.'

Further examples of coping self-statements are shown in Table 4.4.

**Table 4.4** Examples of Coping Self-statements for Particular PTSD Symptoms

| | Preparing for the stressor | Encountering the stressor | Coping with feeling overwhelmed | Looking back at how I played it |
|---|---|---|---|---|
| Insomnia | 'Tell myself before bed that my body will not let me go without the sleep I need.' | 'If I am not asleep in the next 20–30 minutes I will calmly get up and only go back to bed when really tired.' | 'I know it is 3 am and no one else is up but if I don't get angry and fuss over the sleep it will eventually sort itself out.' | 'I managed not to make sleep more difficult by getting agitated, except when I woke my wife up and we had a row as I was getting up.' |
| Irritability | 'Tell myself hassles are normal.' | 'Downgrade the threat level, others are not doing things deliberately, it is not the end of the world.' | 'I feel beside myself, go into another room, tell myself it will probably look like a molehill in a few minutes, not a mountain.' | 'Sometimes I managed to Stop and Think before getting angry, I am at least getting gradually better.' |
| Exaggerated startle response | 'Tell myself, so what if I'm jumpy, is it any worse than someone blushing or stuttering slightly?' | 'It's just my dodgy alarm, don't take the ringing seriously.' | 'Don't get angry with yourself or others, that just puts petrol on the fire.' | 'I'm beginning not to shout when people startle me, but in a car it is road rage. Maybe I should count the number of courteous drivers each trip.' |

**Table 4.5** Stages of Problem Solving

| |
|---|
| 1. Problem Orientation |
| 2. Problem Definition |
| 3. Generation of Alternatives |
| 4. Decision Making |
| 5. Solution Implementation and Verification |

The coping self-statements are not intended to be in a permanent state rather to be refined in they are light of experience. Thus, in practice, Table 4.4 would have an extra column to the right headed 'gameplan'.

## PROBLEM SOLVING

Meichenbaum (1985) advocates problem solving (Table 4.5) as a component of Stress Inoculation Training and this complements SIT.

Problem orientation (Nezu et al. 1989) refers to the frame of mind that the client brings to bear on problems generally. Introducing the metaphor of a turnstile helps clients conceptualise problem orientation (step 1 in Table 4.5), i.e. one experience through the turnstile at a time, and the distillation of a coping strategy for that experience/problem that will probably undergo refinement in light of experience. Implicitly, a problem orientation involves approaching problems rather than avoiding them. The message to be conveyed is that the PTSD symptoms can be resolved if addressed as a series of separate but interacting problems. The second stage of problem solving (step 2 in Table 4.5) involves a precise definition of the problem – a vaguely defined problem cannot be solved. Thus, for example, if a client's nightmares are being addressed it is important to define the target problem. Is the target just those nightmares that significantly disrupt sleep or other nightmares? Further, it is necessary to have baseline measures of the target problem, e.g. the frequency of nightmares that wake the client, the degree of distress once awake, and how long it typically takes them to get back to sleep. This tight definition of the problem enables both client and therapist to detect the often small and gradual improvements. For example, a client may notice a change in their distress on awakening before a reduction in the frequency of the nightmares.

The third stage of problem solving (step 3 in Table 4.5) involves the distillation of a wide range of options and should include what the client has been doing in the domain of the problem before the start of treatment. Thus the client's behaviour prior to treatment is given respect as a possible coping strategy, rather than being implicitly denigrated by the therapist as an inadequate response. Step 4 in Table 4.5 is decision making. It follows from the previous step that one option is to continue the coping strategy of pre-treatment, and the advantages and disadvantages of this in the short and long term are discussed.

The final stage of problem solving (step 5 in Table 4.5) involves distilling what would be a viable implementation of the treatment option and the use of a yardstick to determine the extent to which the chosen coping strategy has solved the problem. If the new strategy has not worked or worked only partially, the client returns to step 3 and the menu of options and chooses one of these, moving on to steps 4 and 5 to assess how well this further option has worked. Thus the client navigates through steps 3–5 of Table 4.5 until a satisfactory solution is found.

The problem solving should not, however, be construed as a wholly cerebral activity, for example most PTSD clients are very reluctant to begin encountering situations that they have been avoiding since the trauma. Nezu et al. (1989) have advocated a reverse advocacy strategy to help clients appreciate there is a viable different pathway. For example, a therapist role-played one client's concerns in the following dialogue:

*Therapist*: I can't go into the Big Store, something terrible is going to happen. I can't go to the cinema, something terrible is going to happen. I can't get on a train, something terrible is going to happen.

*Simon*: I thought you were going to say 'I can't go the loo, something terrible will happen!' But I know what you mean, it seems daft when you say it.

*Therapist*: Would it be easier if, as you approached things, you imagined me saying these things?

*Simon*: I could give it a try.

The reverse advocacy technique helps the client stand back from their difficulties, spot the maladaptive appraisals involved, and conceive a different strategy as a viable option. Thus while the cognitive restructuring in problem solving does involve a logical disputation, it should not be confined to a verbal, Socratic dialogue.

## SABOTEURS OF PROBLEM SOLVING AND COGNITIVE RESTRUCTURING

Almost a third of the items on the Posttraumatic Cognitions Inventory (PTCI) (Foa et al. 1999b), if endorsed, would likely sabotage problem solving (see Table 4.6).

**Table 4.6** Saboteurs of Problem Solving from the PTCI

1. I can't trust I will do the right thing.
2. I am a weak person.
3. I can't deal with the slightest upset.
4. I am inadequate.
5. My reactions since the event mean I'm going crazy.
6. I have permanently changed for the worse.
7. I can't stop bad things happening to me.
8. My reactions since the event show that I am a lousy coper.
9. I can't rely on myself.
10. Nothing good can happen to me anymore.

The aspect of problem solving that the above beliefs would most likely impinge on is the first stage of problem solving: problem orientation. Thus in order to enable clients to complete Table 4.5, it would be necessary to engage in cognitive restructuring, targeting the saboteurs of problem orientation.

It is important not to persist with the NTFCBT programme if a client is not responding to it and clients should be formally re-assessed after five sessions, and ten sessions. If PTSD is still present they should be stepped up to TFCBT. Even if the PTSD has not been resolved with the NTFCBT programme, there is inevitably an increased tolerance to discussing trauma-related material and the ground has been prepared for a TFCBT programme. The latter can be sold along the lines 'We have tried the outpatient approach. It was worth giving it a try but it has not really worked. Now we have to try the equivalent of an inpatient procedure.' In so doing, the stepping up is normalised.

## SUMMARY

1. Trauma-focused CBT (TFCBT) for PTSD is effective, but a significant minority do not recover.
2. There is some limited evidence that non-trauma-focused CBT (NTFCBT) for PTSD can be effective.
3. There can be difficulties in developing a therapeutic alliance in TFCBT as the therapist's focus is on the trauma and the client typically avoids conversations about the trauma and reminders. NTFCBT may make it easier to develop a therapeutic alliance.
4. NTFCBT and TFCBT can be used sequentially, the former socialising the client for the latter. If the front-end NTFCBT module resolves the PTSD, there is then no need to progress to TFCBT.
5. In some instances NTFCBT and TFCBT may be used simultaneously, with the former acting as a catalyst for the latter.
6. Stress Inoculation Training is a coping skills NTFCBT, composed of Self-Instruction Training (SIT), problem solving and cognitive restructuring.
7. Self-Instruction Training consists of the generation of coping statements covering: preparing for the stressor, encountering the stressor, coping with feeling overwhelmed, and reflecting on and refining of strategies. PTSD symptoms can be regarded as stressors to which SIT is applied.
8. SIT has to be interwoven with cognitive restructuring to develop coping self-statements. Excessively negative post-traumatic cognitions have to be challenged to provide 'space' for adaptive coping self-statements. The cognitive restructuring also facilitates problem solving, which is necessary in order to tackle the extensive hassles that accompany PTSD.

# Chapter Five

## TRAUMA-FOCUSED CBT

*Trauma-focused treatments for PTSD share a common assumption that the disorder arises from arrested information processing. Two treatment approaches have been developed to facilitate reprocessing: cognitive restructuring and prolonged exposure. Controlled trials conducted in research centres suggest that both approaches are equally effective. In routine practice difficulties have been noted with client compliance to prolonged exposure and surveys suggest that it is not popular with practitioners. PTSD acts as a 'prism', distorting a client's view of themselves, others, and their personal world. In this chapter a trauma-focused CBT (TFCBT) protocol based on cognitive restructuring is detailed to 'correct' these distortions. Implementation of the TFCBT protocol can be facilitated by using the Self-Instruction Training (SIT) strategies discussed in the previous chapter, but the latter are utilised purely as catalysts. In the TFCBT protocol, information processing is accelerated by having the client either write about their trauma or by using imaginal exposure. Memories, and in particular traumatic memories, are not fixed; rather they are updated every time they are retrieved. In treatment, cognitive restructuring is a vehicle for this updating. The function of memory appears to be to enable one to anticipate the future rather than remember the past per se. PTSD clients appear to make a model of future events from elements of a 'construction kit' of the trauma and can be taught to switch attention to a more adaptive model based on the much more prevalent non-traumatic events.*

TFCBT has traditionally focused on maladaptive appraisals of: the trauma itself, the way the client felt or behaved during the event, or, post-traumatic reactions. In addition, the TFCBT approach (e.g. Ehlers and Clark 2000) has assumed that the traumatic memory in PTSD sufferers is fragmented and poorly integrated into autobiographical memory. But more recent work (e.g. Lancaster et al. 2011) has

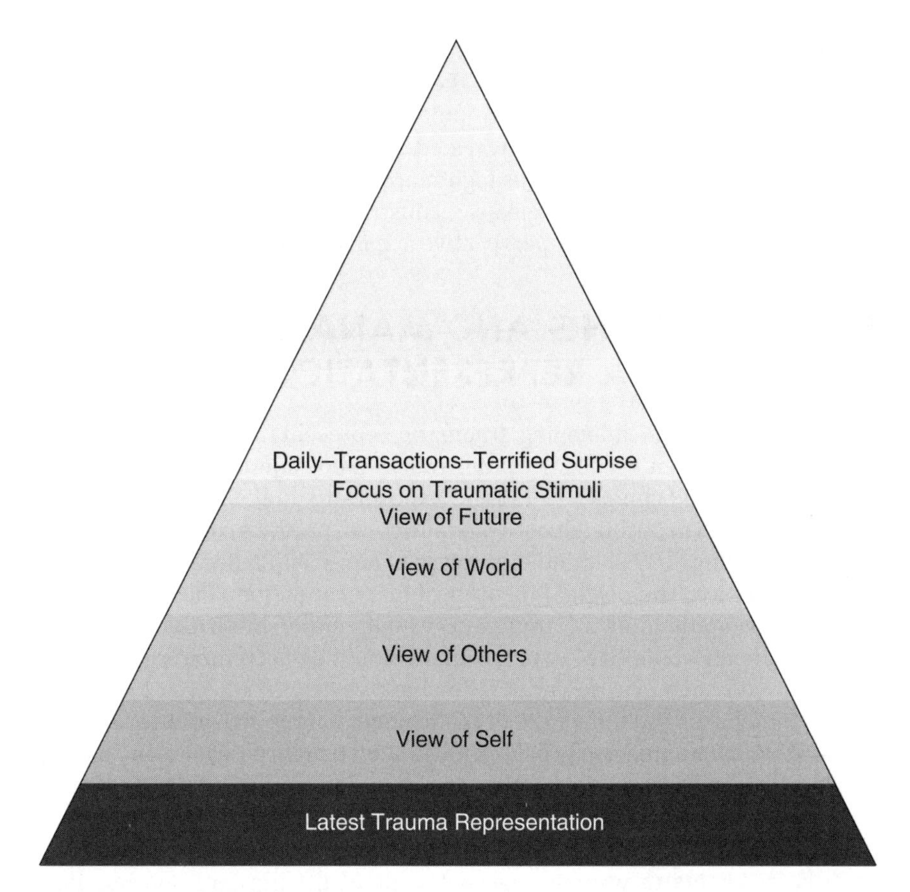


**Figure 5.1** The PTSD Prism

challenged this latter assumption, suggesting instead that the traumatic memory is dysfunctionally integrated, defining a PTSD sufferer's identity. Thus for sufferers, the trauma has become a prism (Figure 5.1), through which life is viewed.

It is explained to clients that we all look at life through a camera, with certain lenses and settings that we use almost without thinking. For example, some people who are prone to depression tend to zoom in on the negative in a situation and dwell on it. The PTSD sufferer operates with a particular prism in their camera, which is tinted by their trauma. The operation of the prism is then explained further, thus: 'Clients are disturbed not so much by the trauma but by their latest construction of it'. For example, one PTSD client was involved in a fire and was banging on a window to get out but in his flashback his children were on the other side of the window distraught, even though they were not in fact present. Thus the latest trauma representation is at the foot of the prism and operates to constrain the view of self (e.g. 'I've let the children down by not being able to play with them the way I used to'), others (e.g. 'My partner just sees me as a liability now'), the future (e.g. 'I can't be enclosed now, can't work, can't provide, no future'), and the world (e.g. 'I didn't see this coming, anything can happen, anytime'). It is further explained that the trauma prism automatically focuses the sufferer's attention on perceived traumatic stimuli (Vythilingham et al. 2007) and a client operates in a state of terrified surprise in which, for example, he smells the smoke from the fire in his nightmare and rushes out of the house with his children. Effective treatment means reconstructing the different layers of the prism by developing a different perspective at each level.

## RECONSTRUCTING AND MANAGING THE LATEST TRAUMA REPRESENTATION

TFCBT has focused on managing traumatic representations in two different ways: through written accounts of the trauma alongside cognitive restructuring (e.g. Resick and Schnicke 1993) and exposure to audiotapes of the trauma (e.g. Foa et al. 1999b). Although both modalities can produce comparable results, Scott and Stradling (1997) found high levels of non-compliance with audiotapes in routine practice. The original theoretical justification for TFCBT was that by repeated presentations of the traumatic stimuli, either in written form or on audiotape, clients would habituate (i.e. there would be decrements in response) to the traumatic memory. However, following a review of studies of expressive writing, Pennebaker and Chung (2011) concluded that the activation of emotions associated with a trauma can provide only limited benefits. Beyond any habituation processes, some form of cognitive change is also important.

One advantage of having a client write about their trauma is that it is possible to titrate the dose. Thus, although the recommendation from Resick and Schnicke (1993) is for clients to write a page a day about the incident and its effects, for clients expressing serious misgivings they can be invited to write initially just a paragraph a day or even a sentence a day. Some clients can initially only countenance writing in the presence of the therapist or their partner. For clients with literacy problems, they can dictate their trauma and have their partner or friend transcribe it – this was found to be effective with traumatised refugees who dictated details of their trauma over four sessions and the therapist then handed them their 'biography' (Neuner et al. 2004). Another variation on these processing methods has been to have the client write a full account of the trauma once and read it aloud three times a day for homework (Maercker et al. 2006).

The trauma representation may be much richer in imagery than the verbal content and associated with a range of sensory experiences, such as stomach turning, heart racing, etc. The client's reaction in such circumstances is often that the image speaks for itself; there is no story to it and as such the image persists unchallenged. For example, one soldier was besieged by an image of the severed head of a colleague coming towards him. He had had to pick up the head because nobody else would and put it in a bag. But as he began to write about the incident, initially with great distress, he realised that his colleagues were not being callous; they knew the person who had been killed whereas he was new and did not know him. After two weeks of writing most days, he concluded that perhaps the head coming towards him was to say 'thanks' for treating him with respect. Ideally, such reconstructions should come from the clients themselves, but if the therapist is allowed access to what is written, by questioning the client in the style of the TV detective Columbo – of bemused/befuddlement (Socratic dialogue) – alternative interpretations of the 'image' can take place.

The active ingredients involved in writing about a trauma remain to be delineated, but necessary requirements are: (i) that ultimately a comprehensive account of the trauma is provided – it is commonplace for clients to initially present a sanitised version of events, leaving out significant details often because including such detail makes them 'real'; (ii) that the writing of the account of the trauma should be an emotional but manageable experience – if there is little or no emotion there is a danger that important aspects of the trauma are not being acknowledged and the associated emotional experiences cannot then be labelled and modified. At the other extreme, if emotion is overwhelming, this reduces the likelihood that the client will again write about the trauma. If in the writing the client begins to feel overwhelmed they can moderate the intensity of distress by telling themselves 'this is just a memory, it is not happening now'; and (iii) that ultimately a more adaptive appraisal of the trauma and its sequelae emerges, e.g. 'You can't go on worrying about what might never happen'.

Writing about a trauma is a form of imaginal exposure whose aim is reconstruction, but imaginal exposure can also be used to help a PTSD client manage intrusions. In the latter context, the client can be asked to revisit the memory of the event as vividly as possible, talking about it in the present tense, out loud, with eyes closed and focusing on their thoughts, feelings, sensations and what they might want to do. The therapist notes the signs of strong emotion and associated thoughts/images and discusses them afterwards with the client. After this, the SIT 'grid' is imposed on the narrative/imagery. The 'grid' consists of: (a) distilling what the client could say to themselves in advance of deliberate recall of the trauma (e.g. 'I am choosing to recall it, I am in charge not it') or the preparatory statement might be gleaned from comments/images in the imaginal exposure (e.g. 'I fear it is going to swallow me up, but it doesn't. It's as though I've got a life jacket on going down a rapid'); (b) a coping self-statement on encountering the trauma in imagery, derived from the imaginal exposure (e.g. 'It does take my breath away when I "see" the scene, the chaos, but it is only like a cold plunge'; (c) a coping statement when feeling overwhelmed, derived from the imaginal exposure (e.g. 'This smell, takes me right back, I want to run get a gas mask but it is not needed'). After distilling the coping self-statements, the client is asked to commit to visualising their trauma in the session, but first to apply the preparatory coping self-statement first out loud, then covertly. Then they bring on the trauma and, when their stress reaches a moderate level, apply the encountering coping self-statement and then, when the stress rises further, apply the 'overwhelming' coping self-statement. The client can then be invited to try the deliberate recall with SIT grid three times a day. This deliberate recall is somewhat similar to the interoceptive exposure treatment for panic disorder devised by Barlow et al. (1989), in which the client deliberately induces panic attacks so as to learn not to be afraid of them. It is important, however, that the coping self-statements in the deliberate recall are not used to block the traumatic memory. Rather, the coping self-statements are taught as a commentary as the trauma unfolds on a screen and the client is in the audience. In this context the SIT is simply a catalyst for the TFCBT – a catalyst simply speeds up a chemical reaction, it is not involved in the formation of a new compound. The coping self-statements usually need refinement in light of the client's experience of using them.

In exposure-based treatment for PTSD (see, for example, Echiverri et al. 2011), the client repeats the imaginal exposure over and over in the session for 45–60 minutes. Then the therapist and client will process the latter's experience of the reliving for 15–20 minutes, particularly focusing on unhelpful beliefs and how their experience of the distress changed. For homework clients are asked to listen to the tape of the imaginal exposure daily. However, while this has been efficacious in controlled trials, its effectiveness in routine practice has been questioned (Scott and Stradling 1997).

## RECONSTRUCTING THE VIEW OF SELF, OTHERS AND THE WORLD

An extreme trauma can have a profound effect on the victim's view of self, the world and the future, and in cognitive processing therapy (Galovski and Resick 2008) these larger belief systems were addressed in the second phase of their PTSD treatment programme. This approach is adopted in the protocol described in this chapter. The PTSD Prism leads to a particular construction of the view of self, the world and others, but as Figure 5.2 indicates, by the bi-directional arrows, these can be reconstructed in CBT.

Clients with PTSD almost invariably report that they are 'not the same person' since their trauma and this is given as an example of the negative view of self in Figure 5.2. The other examples of negative cognitions of self, others and the world are not meant to be exhaustive but illustrative. It is therefore necessary to individualise Figure 5.2 by eliciting the salient cognitions on either 'face' of the prism for each client. The therapeutic task is to reflect back these cognitions (the inward arrows in Figure 5.2) in Socratic dialogue and to test out their validity using behavioural experiments. The therapist can challenge the validity, utility or authority by which a view is held. Beginning therapists tend to persist with one line of questioning, e.g. validity, beyond a point that it is producing any return rather than deftly switching to another line of questioning. Switching between the three different dimensions of questioning is as much an art as a science.

Guilt is often an associated symptom of PTSD, resulting in low self-esteem. This guilt often arises because the person believes that they should have played the trauma differently. In such circumstances it is useful to take the client 'frame by frame' through the alternative scenario and the unfolding likely consequences. While the outcome may be different, it is often not better; it is just a different set of consequences. For example, one client, a firefighter, was called to a building that was ablaze. He went into the building to discover a man unconscious and he had to make a decision whether to revive him *in situ* or to drag him out

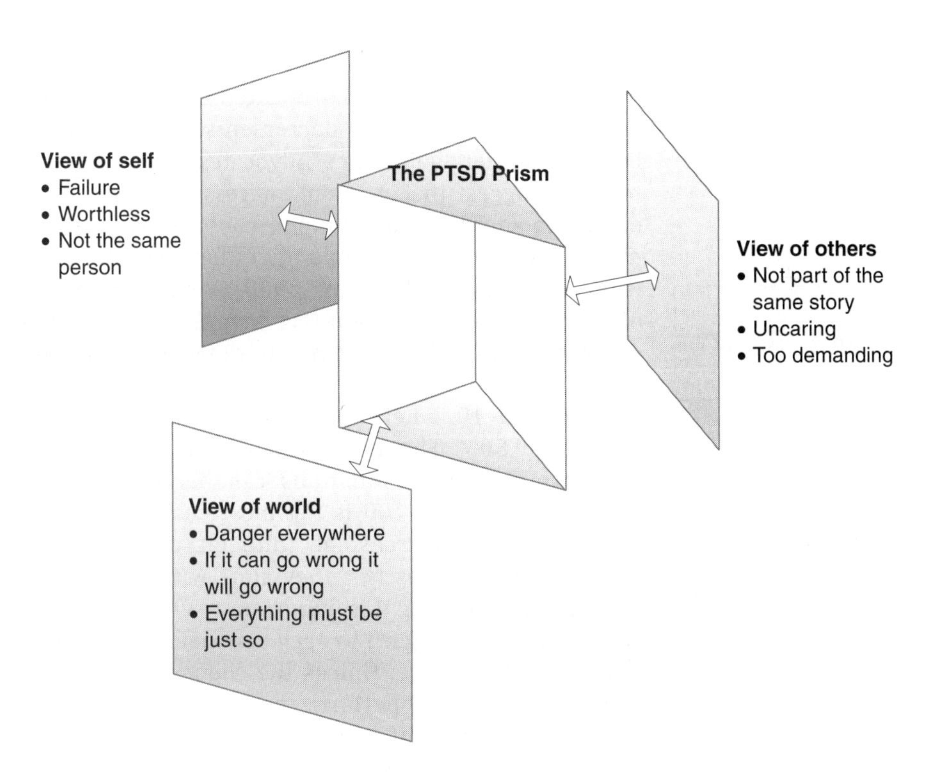


**Figure 5.2** Reconstructing View of Self, Other and the World Post Trauma

first. He opted for the former, but the man died. The firefighter was coping until, several days later, one of his bosses commented that he should have dragged him out first. In therapy, the focus was on what would likely have happened if he had taken the alternative course of action. The firefighter concluded that he was 'damned if he did and damned if he didn't'. This case also illustrated that in emergency situations there is a call to immediate action and this is very different from later sitting back in safety debating the pros and cons of a situation and choosing a particular course of action. During therapy the firefighter concluded that appropriate action at the time of the incident was in a different 'time zone' from a decision that might be made 'now'.

In the proposed *DSM V* (American Psychiatric Association, in press), a negative mood is one of the diagnostic symptoms. Feelings of guilt are common following trauma and can be easily construed as evidence of guilt, thereby lowering mood. True guilt, unlike trauma-related guilt (TRG), requires deliberate intent and it is the latter that predominates in PTSD, although true guilt may be present in sufferers who have perpetrated a crime.

The PTSD client's view of the world as dangerous is countered by *in vivo* exposure, that is by the client gradually daring themselves to encounter what they fear. In TFCBT two different rationales for the efficacy of this approach have been presented. The first, a cognitive one, is that clients learn experientially

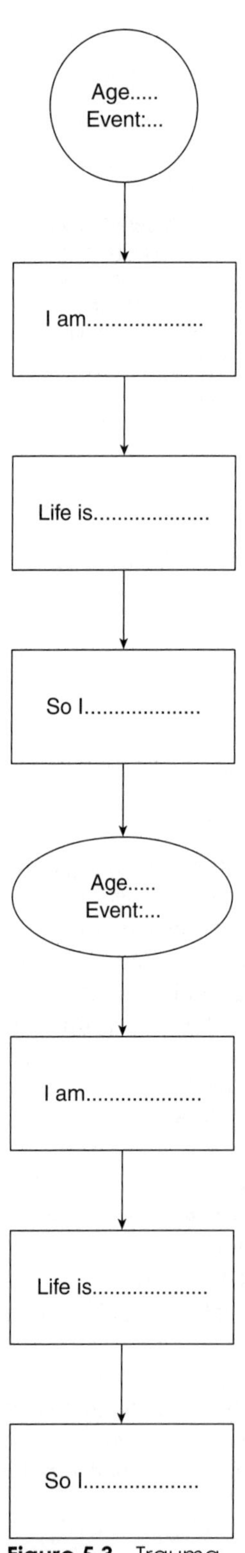

**Figure 5.3** Trauma History

that their fears are not realised, and the second, a behavioural one, is that by repeated exposure to that which is feared there are decrements in responsivity, i.e. that the client habituates. Advocates of the cognitive position suggest that it is only necessary to stay long enough in a feared situation to disconfirm the next prediction (i.e. the goal is to tolerate rather than eliminate fear; see Craske and Barlow 2008), while supporters of the behavioural position (e.g. Echiverri et al. 2011) recommend that the client stay in the feared situation until their SUDS (subjective units of distress, rated on a scale 0–10, where 10 is extreme distress) have reduced by 50%. The jury is still out on which is most appropriate. Feared situations can be ranked on a scale 0–100, where 100 is the most challenging, and clients take on increasingly difficult challenges as treatment progresses (i.e. they start with the easiest challenges). However, it is important to check a client's self-efficacy with regard to each task before it is set as a homework exercise. Unless the client believes they have the capacity to perform the task and that it will make a worthwhile difference they are likely to be non-compliant with the homework.

## RECONSTRUCTING VIEW OF FUTURE

PTSD clients do not have graphic recall of positive events pre-trauma. It is as if they define their life as beginning and ending with the trauma. The therapeutic task is to enable clients to see the trauma as just one chapter in their autobiography and that earlier chapters describe life pre-trauma. The danger is that life pre-trauma is described in over general terms as 'something I've lost' rather than as specific discrete events, the like of which may occur again and feature in subsequent chapters of their autobiography. The construction of a future is, however, particularly problematic where the extreme trauma is seen simply as confirming a negative view of self, the world or others. In such circumstances it may be necessary to ask the client whether you can both visit the origins of such a perspective, which may have its roots in child abuse. A trauma history can be constructed using Figure 5.3.

Early adverse events can be reconstructed by asking the client 'If you knew then what you know now, would you have had a different "I am" statement? If so, how?' Then, descending Figure 5.3, the therapist asks whether they would have had a different view of the world ('Life is...'). Descending further, they ask whether this would have resulted in different actions ('So I...') and, finally, they ask whether there would have been a different response to subsequent adverse events, including their recent trauma. This prepares the ground for an imagined visit to their younger 'traumatised' self and attempts to comfort them using language and a non-verbal approach (e.g. a hug) that is informed by an adult understanding of what happened, but is pitched at the developmental level they were operating on at the time. It can be explained that there can be two selves – X1, the younger self, and X2, the adult self – and the latter has to soothe the former. This can be done symbolically by suggesting that the client, say, hugs a cushion as a representation of the earlier self. It may be that it was in fact this earlier self, X1, that tended to be often activated even before the trauma that has led them to therapy. In reconstructing a negative early view of self and the world, the client may become more open to the possibility that the future is not necessarily wholly negative.

For adult survivors of abuse, revisiting the episodes of abuse in detail is likely to be essential, but this should be done in the second phase of a CBT protocol (Cloitre et al. 2010), after the client has learnt skills for managing intense emotion, impulsiveness and irritability in the first phase SIT programme.

Where there are multiple extreme traumas, the conventional wisdom is to focus on the worst trauma, treat this, and only treat other intrusions if they are still a problem after focusing on the worst trauma.

## RECONSTRUCTING THE VIEW OF TRAUMATIC STIMULI AND ATTENTION CONTROL

PTSD clients are hyper-alert for anything that vaguely resembles their trauma, thus an assault victim might be re-traumatised by the sight of someone of the same build as their assailant. Confronted with such triggers, it can be suggested that the client specify in what way it is similar to the trauma but then detail a long list of ways in which there are differences, e.g. 'I saw the face of my assailant, I can only see this person's back, it is daylight, there are lots of people around', etc. The stimuli discrimination can be likened to playing the childhood game of 'Spot the Difference', where at first glance two pictures appear the same, but on closer examination there are many differences. In PTSD clients' focus is almost automatically on potential trauma-related stimuli, for example the victim of a road traffic accident is very alert for the presence of bad drivers, but operates without acknowledging the number of courteous drivers. The Venn diagram in Figure 5.4 illustrates that it is important to differentiate the reminder from the trauma.

However, for complete contextualisation, the client also needs to switch attention to possible signs of safety, e.g. the number of courteous drivers counted each trip or that the rest of the city is today prepared to go into a large department store. One way of helping clients become aware of the inappropriateness of their safety behaviours is to suggest that they ring the local radio station and advocate that everybody engage in the same safety behaviours! It can be

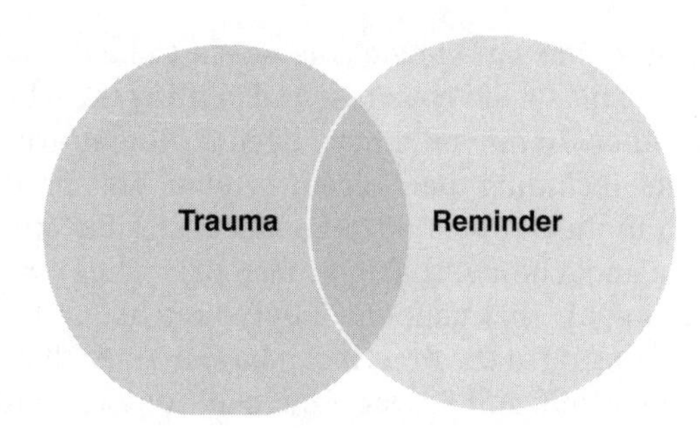


**Figure 5.4** Differentiating the Reminder from the Trauma

conceded that embarrassment might be a partial explanation of a failure to persuade the public to engage in these 'safety' behaviours but, in the style of Socratic dialogue, the therapist can lead the client with the question, 'If you really believed there was a real and present danger to the public, would you not take action?'

## RECONSTRUCTING DAILY TRANSACTIONS – GETTING OFF THE TREADMILL

PTSD clients function with one foot in the present and one in the past and are therefore not fully present with family, friends or at work. Their demeanour is one of terrified surprise, as if haunted by the ghost of the trauma. The inevitable hassles of life are badly handled and, as a consequence, their social and occupational functioning is significantly impaired (see Figure 5.5).

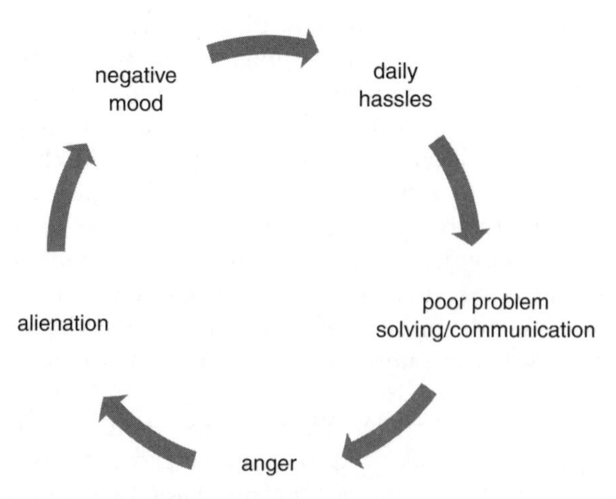


**Figure 5.5** The Treadmill of the PTSD Sufferer

The inevitable hassles of life are poorly handled. For example, a medical expert asks the client to tell them what happened to them, the client perceives a slight (e.g. 'Haven't you bothered to read my notes?'), anger results, followed by alienation so that not only may the medical expert feel alienated but also an accompanying relative sees the client's reaction as extreme, and this in turn serves to maintain their negative mood. A major issue is that PTSD clients often ruminate about those they perceive as responsible for the trauma, which serves to lower their mood and produce a simmering anger. In addition, they often get angry with themselves as a consequence of their displays of anger. Treatment therefore also has to focus on breaking the circle in Figure 5.5. Strategies for breaking the vicious circle at each of the ports of entry are described below:

1. Daily hassles – the common response of PTSD sufferers is to see hassles as beyond their resources, often having delegated tasks such as opening the post or managing finances to their partner. If such tasks are not delegated, they are often left untackled. The problems then grow in size, with dire consequences, such as the disconnection of the energy supply or the repossession of the home. In this context, the PTSD sufferer fails at the first stage of problem solving (problem orientation) by not locking on to problems. Client engagement in the problem-solving process can be enhanced by having clients visualise the likely consequence in six weeks, six months, etc. if they continue on their present path and contrasting it with the likely consequences if they put all their tasks in a queue, with their most important first, and let each one through a 'turnstile' at a time, celebrating the completion of the task before letting the next one through. Clients often need reassurance that it is normal to feel that there are too many tasks in the queue and few get through them all.
2. Poor problem solving/communication – PTSD clients are frightened by reminders of their trauma but this happens against a background emotion of feeling scared, which in turn makes it difficult to focus on the task in hand. Training the PTSD client to focus on the task in hand is a way of marginalising the 'scared' feeling, so that it becomes a fear that they are not afraid of. The steps for problem solving have been outlined in Chapter Four and clients can be taught to stay in problem-solving mode using the mnemonic TIC/TOC. TIC stands for 'task interfering cognitions', e.g. 'I can't face opening this letter from the solicitor', and TOC for 'task oriented cognitions', e.g. 'I could just read the letter once, then go and make a cup of tea and think it through'. When stressed, clients are encouraged to switch from TIC to TOC, hence TIC/TOC.

PTSD clients have a particular problem with interpersonal problem solving in that they often mind-read, for example assuming that others understand what they can or cannot do since the trauma without them having explicitly stated their limitations, resulting in fraught exchanges with friends and family. Communication becomes more fraught because the PTSD sufferer jumps from problem to problem. It is useful to teach clients to create a special time, usually with a partner, when they will problem solve a particular issue, stick to that issue and avoid mind-reading. However, the problem-solving process can be sabotaged by all-or-nothing thinking, in which the client sees either a perfect solution to a problem or no solution. Part of the problem-solving process is teaching clients that most solutions are at best partial solutions and are usually solved incrementally. Without following these ground rules for communicating and problem solving, the client is likely to continue to display outbursts of anger.

3. Anger – PTSD clients are often very angry. This anger can relate to those whom the client believes are responsible for their trauma, to what they are unable to do physically or emotionally since the trauma, to a perceived breaking of the rules, or a combination of these 'justifications'. As a result of ruminating about the misdeeds of others in 'causing' the trauma, the client can develop a simmering anger that is activated whenever anything does not go exactly as they wish. In some instances the client becomes a 'control freak', insisting that tasks are done exactly the way he or she would do them, e.g. insisting that the weekly shopping is put away exactly as they would do with jar labels facing outwards. The origins of such a response may lie in emotional avoidance – a commitment to never again experience the helplessness that occurred at the time of the trauma – combined with magical thinking – 'If everything is just done my way and care is taken, disaster can be avoided'.
4. Alienation – the anger of the PTSD client can lead to alienation from others (see Figure 5.5), affecting not just friends and family, but also work colleagues and professionals. In some instances the anger is a strategy to avoid conversations about the trauma. The alienation from others is likely to be enhanced for the PTSD client by an emotional numbness, which in turn results in a failure to approach others, most visibly in not visiting or contacting them, but also more subtly in not demonstrating affection with hugs or sitting daydreaming for hours without communicating. For the sake of a client's relationship with their partner in particular, it is important to stress that feelings of emotional numbness (Figure 3.4) and the wish to isolate oneself (Figure 3.3) are a normal responses to extreme trauma and are not to be taken as an indicator of 'not being in love'. Nevertheless, partners are often concerned about how long they can go on putting up without expressions of 'interest or caring'. Thus both the partner and the client need to be involved in the problem-solving process to address these difficulties. In this context, it is important to make explicit the ground rules for communication – a special time for communicating, one problem at a time, and no mind-reading and 'chipping away' at a problem. For example, the client's partner may assume that the absence of demonstrations of affection means 'deep down you don't really love me'. This could be flagged up as an example of mind-reading and a violation of one of the ground rules.
5. Negative mood – Low mood is an inevitable counterpart to PTSD and may be sufficiently severe to warrant an additional diagnosis of depression. The low mood may relate to ruminating about the incident or its effects. The MOOD chart in Table 5.1 may be used as an antidote to rumination.

**Table 5.1** MOOD Chart

| Monitor Mood | Observe thinking | Objective thinking | Decide what to do and do it |
|---|---|---|---|
| Sitting in the kitchen, by myself, daydreaming about the effect of the incident, when partner's sister visits. | I just can't be bothered with her, talking about trivia, why did she have to come now? | It's not the end of the world, could just ask whether they would like me to make a tea or coffee, I don't have to sit with them. | I'll make a drink for them and ask about my brother-in-law. |
| | | | |
| | | | |
| | | | |
| | | | |
| | | | |
| | | | |

Tracking mood is a necessary precursor to identifying the thoughts/images that are involved in shifts in mood. These thoughts/images can be in the form of powerful intrusions in that they grab the person's attention, somewhat in the way pain can be all-consuming, interrupting normal life. The illustration in Table 5.1 shows how, by using the MOOD framework, the client has noted their inevitably negative first thoughts. Thus, the M of MOOD stands for 'monitoring mood'. The first O stands for 'observe thinking' and encourages the client to stand back from these thoughts so as to come up with better second thoughts. The second O, 'objective thinking', leads to a plan of action, and the D represents 'deciding and doing', whose implementation short-circuits rumination. In addition, the client has bypassed the anger and alienation ports of Figure 5.5. The MOOD chart is therefore a multi-functional device for reconstructing daily transactions.

Sarah had been working at a betting shop for seven years. She had been there two years when she was the victim of an armed robbery at closing time. Fortunately, she was in a back room at the time and heard a commotion outside at the counter. She peered out of the open door and saw a man in a balaclava with a gun screaming at her female colleague, Amber, who was letting the robber come behind the counter. She slammed the dividing door closed and, trembling, she activated the alarm, but then there was a pounding at the door. She could hear screaming but couldn't make out the content. Sarah panicked about whether she had done the right thing, and thought 'What if they

*(Continued)*

*(Continued)*

shot Amber, shot the door open and shot her?'. It seemed an eternity before the police arrived a few minutes later and she pondered that the least that would happen was that she would be disciplined by her bosses, because they had been told 'Don't be a hero, its only money, just hand it over', but she froze, putting her hands over her ears. After this incident she experienced flashbacks and nightmares and was off work for three weeks. On returning to work she was fearful when she saw new customers and at closing time. Just walking along the street she would scrutinise males to try and identify the robber, even though she never saw his face, and wondered whether the robber might be after her. Technically, she fell just short of meeting the DSM criteria for PTSD (she had just one less than the required number of avoidance symptoms), and therefore strictly met the criteria for a sub-syndromal level of PTSD. Indeed, her preoccupations were more with what could have happened than what did happen. However, had CBT treatment been available locally, she would probably have been treated as suffering from likely PTSD. In the event her condition resolved within twelve months without CBT.

Five years later she was again in the back room at work when she heard an 'almighty crash' and the shattering of glass; her colleague Amber was again behind the counter. Sarah presumed it was another armed robbery and it brought back vivid memories of the robbery five years ago. In fact, a car had skidded off the road, driven by a young female, accompanied by two other females and had crossed the narrow pavement through the shop window. Initially she could not see Amber and presumed that she had been killed. The girls in the front seat were covered in blood and unconscious, while the rear-seat passenger was screaming. She remembered staring at the scene in disbelief. Amber had been cut by flying glass and she wrapped her arm in a towel, but the blood oozed through. Sarah managed to open the rear passenger door and tried to soothe the back-seat passenger, but didn't know whether getting her out could cause a spinal injury or whether the car might blow up. Just then, with considerable relief, she heard the sound of the emergency vehicles arriving. Sarah suffered from PTSD after this incident, but the intrusions (i.e. flashbacks/dreams) were as much of the armed robbery as the serious road traffic accident. The therapist therefore decided to tackle the flashbacks and dreams of both incidents using the SIT programme and the following exchange took place at the second treatment session. But no sooner had Sarah sat down than she was in tears:

*Therapist*: What was going through your mind just then?
*Sarah*: Knowing that I'm going to have to talk about it, I nearly didn't come.
*Therapist*: What I had in mind at this stage was not so much talking about it as looking at better ways of playing the flashbacks and dreams.
*Sarah*: I just want them to go away.
*Therapist*: What strategies have you tried to make them go away?
*Sarah*: I just busy myself. I'm exhausted cleaning and I know it is stupid but I squeeze my eyes tight.
*Therapist*: Why is that stupid?
*Sarah*: It's like I did as a little girl when I heard my parents rowing.

The above dialogue illustrates that although it is important for the therapist to have an agenda, if the client's pressing concerns are not addressed they can easily default from treatment, particularly from a PTSD treatment that is trauma-focused. Further, the therapist has encouraged the client to elaborate on the futility of present coping strategies as a necessary prelude for canvassing an alternative approach. The therapist gets alongside the client by suggesting that there might be better coping strategies rather than insisting that therapy is about re-living the trauma. The exchange continued:

*Therapist*: So you don't want to exhaust yourself cleaning?
*Sarah*: No.
*Therapist*: What else could you do when you get these unwanted visitors?
*Sarah*: I'd like to show them the door.
*Therapist*: What do you do when an unwanted relative visits?
*Sarah*: Mutter to my partner in the kitchen, keep the conversation brief, don't offer them a cup of tea.
*Therapist*: So you don't just show them the door, you have a gameplan?
*Sarah*: I suppose so, it's usually my younger brother who visits on the scrounge. There would just be a row if I threw him out and my mother would get on to me.
*Therapist*: So you have worked out a different way than showing him the door?
*Sarah*: I suppose I have but he is still a 'pain'.
*Therapist*: There is a special way of coming up with a plan that is a bit better than what you have been doing, but there will still be some discomfort with the flashbacks/dreams to begin with.
*Sarah*: OK.

In the above dialogue there is an implicit normalising of the client's flashbacks/dreams by suggesting that they can be addressed much as other everyday hassles, but that the initial and most attractive option for handling them is often not the best. The first phase of the SIT/TFCBT programme is concerned with teaching clients to interact adaptively with traumatic memories as opposed to re-living them. The therapist continues:

*Therapist*: What I would like to work out with you is what you might say to yourself before the worst flashbacks, what you might say and do when the worst flashback actually happens, then what you might say to yourself when feeling overwhelmed. Then you can see how it actually works out and we

*(Continued)*

*(Continued)*

might have to change it a bit to get it gradually better. [*The therapist then introduced Table 4.2 to document the coping statements in each of the domains.*] What would you put in the first row, for the worst flashback?

*Sarah*: The worst flashback is hearing the crashing of the glass, like the world has ended, then I see Amber covered in blood but she has been stabbed.

*Therapist*: Stabbed?

*Sarah*: Yes, that is what I imagined might have happened to her years ago after the robber was banging on the door.

*Therapist*: So the flashback is a mix of what did happen and what could have happened as well as a mix of the two incidents?

*Sarah*: Yes, it is like a dream, it terrifies me.

*Therapist*: Might it help to try telling yourself before there's a flashback that they are just daytime dreams?

*Sarah*: I could try that.

*Therapist*: What could you say to yourself when you are surprised by a flashback and are terrified?

*Sarah*: When they come for no reason it is not so bad, but when brought on by a reminder I go ballistic?

*Therapist*: Can you give me an example?

*Sarah*: Last week my partner dropped a glass in the kitchen and I was back there in the betting shop.

*Therapist*: At the last session we talked about your 'dodgy alarm', so what about telling yourself 'It's just a dodgy alarm' when 'alarmed' by a reminder?

*Sarah*: I could do that but I also need to remind myself where I am.

*Therapist*: How would you do that?

*Sarah*: Just tell myself I'm at home not in the shop.

*Therapist*: What about the third row, what to say when feeling overwhelmed?

*Sarah*: It will pass.

*Therapist*: That sounds good.

The above exchange shows that clients' flashbacks can be as much about what could have happened as what did happen and can be managed not only verbally but also by the use of imagery. Further, at this early stage in treatment the therapist has avoided putting any pressure on the client to disclose details of the trauma by focusing on the management of intrusions, yet somewhat paradoxically this results in disclosure.

As treatment progressed the therapist noted that Sarah was avoiding socialising, much to the annoyance of her partner, and in addition she was avoiding her best friend Amber. Initially the therapist tackled these difficulties by suggesting that Sarah gradually increased her dose of contact with others and this occurred with regard to family members but not with regard to Amber. In the fifth treatment session the therapist problem-solved why Sarah was avoiding Amber and the following dialogue took place:

*Sarah*: I feel terrible. I don't return her calls. She will want to talk about it and work. She's back at work and I'm not. I should be.

*Therapist*: How do you know that she will want to talk about it?

*Sarah*: I know she will.

*Therapist*: You thought I would want to talk about the incident and I didn't, how do you know Amber will not be any different, just wanting a better way of handling it all?

*Sarah*: Hmm. I do think about her all the time. I think I let her down at the robbery.

*Therapist*: But didn't you help her at the crash?

*Sarah*: I suppose I did, wrapping a towel around her arm.

*Therapist*: Why do you leave your camera on what you see as a mistake and not on what you did to help?

*Sarah*: I do dwell on the negatives.

In the above dialogue the therapist is engaging in Socratic dialogue, cognitive restructuring, to help the client come up with an alternative perspective. This restructuring can take place not only at the level of content, e.g. questioning whether her friend would want to talk about the incidents, but also at the level of process, e.g. her use of a mental filter, zooming in on the negatives and ignoring the positives. Socratic dialogue is as much an art as a science, with the therapist deftly moving from a focus on content to process and back. The exchange continued:

*Therapist*: You said you do dwell on the negatives and on Amber. Why not have a special time for these concerns when you, say, write a letter to Amber that you don't post instead of picking at these issues all day and making yourself ill?

*Sarah*: I wouldn't know where to begin.

*Therapist*: It doesn't really matter, so long as there is a time and a place. You could have a try now if you like?

*Sarah*: OK.

[*The therapist handed her pen and paper, Sarah began writing but almost instantly was in tears and stopped writing.*]

*Therapist*: What was going through your mind then?

*Sarah*: I've just written Dear Amber and I thought I've let her down ... it's too much.

*(Continued)*

*(Continued)*

*Therapist*: Do you let her down by stopping her from bleeding to death?
*Sarah*: I see what you mean.
*Therapist*: Just have a go at writing for a couple of minutes. You can stop if you feel overwhelmed. Usually we find that people come up with a slightly different angle about what is upsetting them after a week or two of writing for a couple of minutes a day.
*Sarah*: Sort of like pigeon-holing it?
*Therapist*: Yes, you can't not think about the incidents and their effects, they have had such a big effect, but you are saying there is a time and a place for them and I'm not having them interrupting everything.

In the above dialogue the therapist has moved seamlessly from a CS first-phase approach to a TFCBT second-phrase approach, in which the former has acted as a preparation for the latter, helping to prevent a premature discontinuation of treatment. At the sixth session the client brought into the session her completed homework assignment and the exchange continued:

*Therapist*: There's lots of guilt in this. For example 'I should have contacted Amber, what are friends for?' You might want to tackle these waves of guilt using the MOOD chart. [*The therapist introduces Table 5.1.*] So, in the first column you might put 'mood dipped thinking of Amber', in the second column, it sounds as if you have been thinking 'I've let her down'. What would you put in the third column, the objective thinking?
*Sarah*: I was a good friend after the first incident. I was there for her when she was off work after the robbery. It's only since the crash that I have been a waste of space.
*Therapist*: OK, so the final column is about stopping picking or ruminating after you have come up with better second thoughts and getting on and doing.
*Sarah*: I guess I could just text her.
*Therapist*: OK, that could go in the fourth column. You could also use the MOOD Chart for any dip in mood.

The above dialogue illustrates the interweaving of the various strategies in the SIT/TFCBT programme.

## SUMMARY

1. Trauma-focused CBT is an evidence-based treatment for PTSD. It has taken two forms: cognitive restructuring and prolonged exposure (PE). They have proven equally efficacious in controlled trials.
2. Prolonged exposure is unpopular with therapists in routine practice and questions have been raised about the acceptability of PE to clients in such settings.
3. PTSD clients have an exaggeratedly negative view of themselves, others, their personal world, the trauma and its consequences. Cognitive restructuring is designed to address this.
4. Cognitive restructuring involves Socratic dialogue – leading the client to question their trauma beliefs rather than the therapist directly challenging those beliefs. Beliefs can be challenged along three dimensions – validity, utility and authority – and using aids such as the MOOD thought record.
5. Writing about the trauma regularly and imaginal exposure to the trauma appear to involve cognitive restructuring.
6. Trauma-focused CBT (TFCBT) can be facilitated by Self-Instruction Training (SIT) and should involve training in problem solving.
7. Clients who have suffered prolonged childhood abuse can be taught to rewrite their script by revisiting the triad of 'Life is…', 'I am…', 'So I.....' at different points in their life and infusing them with the knowledge they now have as an adult. In this way an alternative story is distilled and made more available. The purpose of memory is to enable anticipation of future events and a reconstructed story may better do this.

# Chapter Six

# GROUP TREATMENT

*When there is a collective trauma, those affected often state that unless someone has been through the same experience, they cannot understand what they have been through. A group intervention for similarly traumatised clients can therefore do much to lessen isolation. But unfortunately there is also the risk of re-traumatisation from hearing the accounts of others' traumas. This risk is greater in a trauma-focused CBT (TFCBT) than in a coping skills non-trauma-focused CBT (NTFCBT) group. In this chapter a group coping skills programme is detailed which has at its core Self-Instruction Training (SIT). As in Chapter Four, SIT is used to target each of the PTSD symptoms. The therapist's teaching role can be easily derailed if group processes are not managed and the specifics of addressing process as well as content are detailed.*

A group treatment for PTSD is an attractive option, making better use of scarce therapeutic resources and lessening the sense of isolation felt by many trauma victims. Indeed, the early studies of cognitive processing therapy (CPT) for sexual assault victims were group-based (Resick and Schnicke 1992) and, more recently, Chard (2005) evaluated an adapted form of CPT, delivered in a group format for adult survivors of child sexual abuse. Scott (2011) has described a generic trauma-focused CBT intervention for PTSD, but noted that a perennial difficulty was that other group members may, without great care, be re-traumatised by other group members' difficulties. A group treatment that is based on coping skills is likely to be more acceptable to clients and may minimise the risk of re-traumatisation further. In this chapter a Group Coping Skills (GCS) approach is outlined.

## PREPARATION IS EVERYTHING

In some respects homogeneous PTSD groups, say a group of victims of road traffic accident victims, are better both for the client (ease of identification with other group members) and for the therapist (less need to adapt to the specifics of a particular client's trauma history), but in routine practice it is often the case that there are insufficient clients with one particular trauma to make a group viable. Thus there is, of necessity, likely to be a degree of heterogeneity in the composition of a group. There are, however, limits to this heterogeneity. For example, it would be inappropriate to have an adult survivor of childhood sexual abuse in a mixed group of primarily road traffic accident victims and clients who were the victims of man-made technological accidents at work.

Groups are an attractive option from a managerial perspective in that there is a 'greater throughput' of clients, and the therapist can come under pressure to admit 'all comers', but this can rebound badly. It only takes one group member with a serious personality disorder to disrupt a group. An example of the consequences of the failure to screen out such individuals in a PTSD group is given in Scott (2011). In the interests of brevity, the interested reader is referred to Scott (2011) for details of: the screening of group members, motivational interviewing for a group, addressing comorbidity using guided self-help manuals for depression and each of the anxiety disorders including PTSD – pertinent materials are freely available on the Routledge website. In this chapter the focus is on the content of a GCS programme and the management of group processes.

## CONTENT OF GROUP COPING SKILLS PROGRAMME

The remainder of this chapter will follow the group process session by session. A session-by-session group programme is outlined in Table 6.1. Details of the full cast of a PTSD group are summarised in Table 6.2.

**Table 6.1** Group Coping Skills Programme

| | |
|---|---|
| Session One: | Rationale for GCS programme – better ways of coping. Introduction to self-help materials. |
| Session Two: | Review of homework, refining the CS strategy that was applied. Targeting intrusions. |
| Session Three: | Review of homework, refining the CS strategy that was applied. Targeting avoidance. |
| Session Four: | Review of homework, refining the CS strategy that was applied. Targeting alienation. |
| Session Five: | Review of homework, refining the CS strategy that was applied. Further targeting, of the interpersonal aspects of PTSD: disconnection, increased irritability and emotional numbness. |
| Session Six: | Review of homework, refining the CS strategy that was applied. Targeting prejudice against self, others and the world. |
| Sessions Seven and Eight: | Putting it all together. |

**Table 6.2** Coping Skills Group Members

| Name | Thumbnail sketch |
|---|---|
| Bob | PTSD after assault at work |
| Wal | PTSD after accident on motorbike |
| Laura | PTSD after armed robbery at petrol station |
| Tom | PTSD after fire at home |
| Aidan | PTSD after pedestrian RTA |

# MANAGING GROUP PROCESSES

The delivery of effective individual CBT requires that the therapist is not only equipped with the technical skills specific to CBT but also has general therapeutic skills relating to empathy, warmth, etc. Both the technical and general skills are operationalised in the Cognitive Therapy Rating Scale (CTRS) (the scale and Scale Manual are available free from the Academy of Cognitive Therapy at www.academyofct.org). The CTRS has five items on Conceptualisation, Strategy and Technique and six items on General Therapeutic Skill (agenda, feedback, understanding, interpersonal effectiveness, collaboration and pacing). Thus the therapeutic relationship has always occupied an important place in CBT. However, in group CBT (GCBT) the therapist has not only to be able to relate to each group member, but also must be able to utilise their relationships with each other in a way that maximises therapeutic benefit. In addition, the therapist has also to synchronise effectively with a co-leader. Thus the GCBT therapist has need of a set of general group therapeutic skills. Scott (2011) has codified a set of General Group Therapeutic Skills in the General Group Therapeutic Skills Rating Scale (GGTSRS). A therapist's competence in these skills is a measure of how well they manage 'process', the sum of the interactions in the group. Thus to assess the competence of a therapist delivering GCBT, the GGTSRS can replace the first part of the CTRS, to make the latter applicable to a group modality. The headings of the GGTSRS are shown in Table 6.3.

**Table 6.3** General Group Therapeutic Skills Rating Scale Dimensions

1. Review of homework/agenda
2. Relevance
3. Adaptation
4. Inclusion
5. Additional disorders
6. Magnifying support and minimising criticism
7. Utilising group members as role models
8. Therapist presentation skills
9. Addressing group issues

Just as in individual CBT, the setting and review of homework is of key importance. One advantage of the group situation is that those members who have been successful in their homework can act as role models for those who have been less compliant with the homework assignment. However, it is tempting to ignore those in the group who have not completed their homework. Unless the difficulties of the non-completers are problem-solved at the outset this becomes a pattern and they will likely default. One possibility is that the homework set for the individual was not checked properly for relevance beforehand. For example, a client may have been encouraged to pass the scene of their trauma, but actually it was at a place that they very rarely went to anyway and the group members' preoccupation is, say, with horror (e.g. 'the state of the body I saw when it fell from the scaffolding and landed in front of me'). Some group members will invariably take in new material more easily than others and be more familiar with the use of pen and paper. Therapists may therefore have to depart from a didactic presentation of material and give some group members an analogous situation to which they can apply the new skills before trying to apply these themselves in their own context. For example, in teaching the Coping Skills framework the therapist might ask a struggling group member what sorts of things they would say to their son/daughter if they were fearful of going to the dentist. The group member's replies would then be slotted into Table 4.3 with a heading "dentist" on the first row. Then for the second row the therapists elicit from the group member what they would say to their son/daughter before they go the dentist, then on the third row write in what they would advise their child to say on arrival at the dentist. Then on the fourth row what they would advise their child to say to themselves when they have a strong urge to run out of the dentist's. In understanding how they might apply the framework to their child, they have a template for its application to themselves. Including all group members in the session is a constant challenge for the leader, particularly when the major concern of one group member (e.g. trauma-related guilt) is quite different from the largely fear-based concerns of the other group members.

The co-leaders may decide in advance about who will monitor and regulate the inclusion of the 'different' group members, ensuring that they are not, as it were, allowed to fade into the wallpaper. A similar differentiation of leaders' roles may be applied to addressing any comorbid disorders outside the group session. The feedback to group members on performance has to be given in such a way that the positives are first underlined before the difficulties are problem-solved. Not to magnify support and minimise criticism in this way runs the risk of setting up for a group member a resonance between a humiliating experience in a group situation at, say, school and the group experience. It can be that some group members are, by their attitude, creating a critical atmosphere and this will need to be addressed by the leaders for the sake of the group. Equally, some group members can be an asset and the leaders might wish to underline for others in the group the possible applicability of their coping strategies. Other group members are often, either for cultural reasons or because of shared experience of similar trauma, more credible sources of persuasion than the leaders. Finally, in the group situation the therapists are as much teachers as therapists and, to a greater extent than in individual therapy, attention has to be paid to visual aids and reading materials.

## SESSION 1

This session covers: an introduction to self-help materials such as the PTSD Survival Manual (see Appendix G) and *Moving on after Trauma* (Scott 2008); letting go of what doesn't work; business as usual or try something different?; getting there with 'baby steps'; the therapist's role play of 'the awkward customer' to illustrate the steps involved in Coping Skills (CS) – preparing for the situation, encountering the situation, coping with feeling overwhelmed; the selection of any situation that group members think they might apply to the three-stage approach and agreeing the homework assignment; and, finally, feedback on the session.

A group session in fact starts as soon as members begin assembling. In this more informal setting the therapist can often glean important information that may not be apparent in the preceding formal individual assessment interview. The following vignette illustrates this:

The co-leader for the group was alerted by his receptionist that Tom had arrived 30 minutes before the start of the session. After checking with Tom that he had the correct time for the start of the session, the latter revealed that he had made a dummy run to the Centre the day before (a Sunday) to check where he would park. Then Bob arrived, carrying a bottle of water. After checking in at reception, he nodded to the co-leader, whom he had seen at the assessment interview, and the latter introduced him to Tom. The following dialogue ensued:

*Bob*: You wouldn't think we were mad, would you?

*Tom*: Does PTSD mean you are mad?

*Co-leader*: Maybe in the next 20 minutes you could play 'spot the PTSD sufferer' from all the people that come and go. I'll organise tea and coffee and come back to see how you have got on. What would you like?

In the above exchange the therapist has followed the lead of one of the group members, with regard to normalisation of symptoms, and instead of didactically explaining the normality of PTSD symptoms sets up a behavioural experiment to test out whether the PTSD sufferer is truly distinguishable from others. The group context makes it particularly easy to address the issue of normality. The exchange also illustrates how group members can act as therapists to each other. Further, the informal dialogue highlights the extreme use of safety behaviours by PTSD sufferers which is often not verbalised by them because it has become automatic.

Welcoming group members with the offer of a drink implicitly builds a bridge to a 'safe zone' where, domestically, one offers a drink to a visitor. Safety is a major issue for PTSD sufferers, particularly where there has been interpersonal violence. (With this in mind, one might not include a woman battered by her male partner in a mixed sex group as one or more males might inadvertently act as a reminder.)

The first session begins with the distribution of the self-help guide, the PTSD Survival Manual – Revised, and a recommendation of *Moving on after Trauma* (Scott 2008). It is emphasised that in using this book the reader is encouraged to identify a person with PTSD who has had a similar trauma, and copy what they have done to gradually get better. This emphasis on what the client can do now to get better is important as there is some evidence that spending too much time on psychoeducation leads to the disengagement of clients with a comorbid psychotic depression (Gottlieb et al. 2011) and highlights the need to make an almost immediate CS focus.

The use of coping self-statements to cope with PTSD symptoms is introduced via a role play between the leader and co-leader about an everyday difficult situation, 'a difficult customer'. The rationale for doing this is that group members have first a concrete non-highly-charged template to help them complete the self-instruction forms (see Appendix E). This example also carries an implicit normalisation of coping strategies in that they do not have to be significantly different from what an ordinary person does at their best. The following exchange took place at the second session:

*Leader*: Hmm, you have just started working here ... you need to know about Albert, otherwise known as the 'grump'.

*Co-leader*: The 'grump'?

*Leader*: Yes, he comes into the garage most days for his morning or evening paper. On a good day he will grunt at you, usually he just throws the money at you. On a bad day he will say something like 'what is wrong with your face?'

*Co-leader*: Sounds like a barrel of laughs.

*Leader*: I just thought I would let you know, so you are prepared and don't take it too personally.

*Co-leader*: Don't fancy meeting him.

*Leader*: Unfortunately you will do sooner or later.

*Co-leader*: I don't mind grumpiness but personal remarks will get me going.

*Leader*: That's what he wants, he likes to see if he can get someone going and then make a complaint to the big bosses. When he is getting you going you've got to tell yourself I'm not playing his game by rising to the bait.

*Bob*: Has he been to these sessions? My partner says I'm grumpy nowadays but my name is 'Bob', honestly, not 'Albert'.

*(Continued)*

*(Continued)*

*Leader*: He's just imaginary but [*laughing looking at Bob*] if the cap fits?

*Co-leader*: On the Self-Instruction Form, just write in what I was advised to say to myself in preparation for meeting Albert, that is the second row. [*This was followed by a general discussion as to what members had written on the first row.*] Now write down what I should be saying to myself when I meet him, that is on the third row. [*Again, this was followed by a general discussion as to what members had written.*] And finally, write down on the fourth row what I might need to tell myself when feeling overwhelmed by Albert. [*Again, this was followed by a general discussion as to what members had written.*]

The exchange continues:

*Leader*: The intrusions you suffer, the flashbacks/nightmares, are rather like being troubled by Albert. You hope they won't turn up but they inevitably do, and if you are not careful they can put you very much out of your stride. You can be bullied by them.

*Co-leader*: What I want us to look at now is how this can be applied to flashbacks/nightmares, upsetting reminders.

*Laura*: Talking about Albert going to a garage just turned my stomach. Just the mention of the word 'garage' brings all the robbery back.

*Co-leader*: That is the problem when you have been traumatised, the most innocent thing can transport you back. How could you prepare yourself for coming across these unexpected reminders?

*Laura*: I guess I just make myself really busy cleaning when I come across reminders?

*Co-leader*: So you don't have a way of getting yourself in the right frame of mind to handle reminders, just a strategy you use if you come across them?

*Laura*: No, I don't prepare myself. I just touch wood hoping there will be no reminder.

The dialogue above shows the therapist using a 'bottom-up' approach, using clients' experiences to teach material, rather than a didactic 'top-down' approach. This ensures that group members are actively processing (technically, centrally processing) what is being taught rather than peripherally processing material using a 'rule of thumb', such as 'It's all theory, you have got to sort out your own problems'. Further, the examples chosen are such that all group members can readily appreciate them, thereby facilitating inclusion. While therapists will have an agenda for a session, they will go with the flow of group members' concerns but use them to illustrate the teaching for the session. There is thus fidelity with flexibility. The exchange continues:

*Aidan*: I shouldn't be having these flashbacks now. It is eighteen months since I was knocked down.

*Leader*: You can fight against the intrusions and protest, but has that worked for anyone?

*Aidan*: Well no, but I can't stand them.

*Co-leader*: What we can look at is the better and worse ways of handling the memories.

*Aidan*: I know I drink too much just to get to sleep, otherwise the memories go round and round.

*Wal*: I had an accident on my motorbike because an idiot driver had been drinking, just cut right across my path. I had no chance, went over the top of the car, landed in the road, thought something is going to hit me but I was lucky. I tell myself I'm lucky to be alive but it doesn't make any difference.

*Co-leader*: So already we have come across some things you can say to yourself that don't seem very useful: 'Just hope for the best with flashbacks', 'get yourself busy', 'you are lucky to be alive'. What do you think would be useful to say to yourself to prepare for the intrusions, the flashbacks, nightmares and reminders?

The above exchange makes it clear that there are better and worse ways of handling the traumatic memory and that sometimes the approach suggested by common sense is actually ineffective.

## SESSION 2

This session covers a review of group members' first steps in applying a CS framework and the refinement of their strategy, not only didactically but also by role play. The normality of traumatic intrusions is stressed but it is explained that they are only maintained at a level of distress if there are maladaptive interactions with them. The new material to be introduced involves targeting intrusions, regarding them as a 'big bully' with whom a head-on collision or avoidance does not work but who can, with subtlety, be prevented from having the last word. It is stressed that a key feature of PTSD is the way in which the past is always present. The notion of keeping a balance between the vividness of the

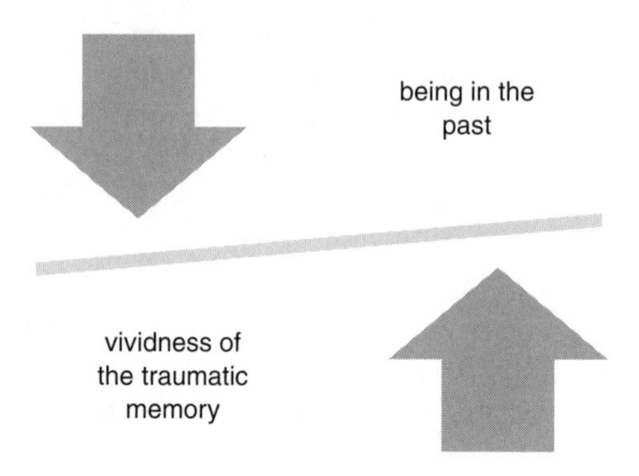


**Figure 6.1** Balancing the Past and Present

intrusions and a realisation that it is 'now' not 'then' can be introduced, using the see-saw balance (Figure 6.1).

Figure 6.1 illustrates that the more graphic the intrusions, the less sense the person has that they are in the present, and that there can be a balancing of the two by the person grounding themselves in the present, as the following exchange illustrates:

| | |
|---|---|
| *Tom:* | The coping statements were fine for flashbacks of the fire but I have real problems when I wake from a nightmare of the fire. I can 'smell' the smoke. |
| *Bob:* | Don't you have a smoke alarm? |
| *Tom:* | Yes, I had them put in after the fire. |
| *Bob:* | Well, they would be going off if there really was smoke, wouldn't they? |
| *Tom:* | I suppose so. |
| *Leader:* | It is as if you are sitting on the left hand of the see-saw when you wake from the dream – it is all very vivid. And the other end then tips you into being back there. You could balance the see-saw by, as Bob suggests, saying right now there is no alarm ringing. I wouldn't ring the Fire Brigade, it's now not then. |

The second session, as with all the subsequent sessions, ends with the therapist eliciting feedback on the session.

This session, as with all the subsequent sessions, begins with a review of the homework:

| | |
|---|---|
| *Wal:* | I tried preparing myself for the flashbacks by telling myself they are perfectly natural, as you always go over and over surprises. There is no law to say that they should have stopped by eighteen months after and that was OK for the ones that just popped into my head but not for others. |
| *Co-leader:* | How do you mean, 'not for others'? |
| *Wal:* | If I try to do something that I used to be able to do easily before the accident, such as lift something down from a shelf, I get really frustrated and it brings it all back and I'm in a real mood. |
| *Leader:* | Maybe we need to get you to apply the coping self-statements to the situations you find really frustrating so that they don't unlock the door to the memories? |
| *Aidan:* | I get frustrated like that, having to ask my thirteen-year-old daughter to tie my shoe laces for me since my injuries. I've robbed her of part of her childhood. |

The above exchange exemplifies one of the benefits of a group intervention, the ready identification with each other's difficulties and the consequent lessening of a sense of isolation. The dialogue continued:

| | |
|---|---|
| *Co-leader:* | So what could you say to yourself when you come across things you can no longer do or are very difficult? |
| *Wal:* | I think what I say is if it hadn't been for that ***** driver I wouldn't be in this mess. |
| *Leader:* | Does that work? |
| *Wal:* | No. |
| *Leader:* | What might be a better thing to say to yourself, say when you are trying to lift something down from a shelf? |
| *Wal:* | I should just ask my partner to give me a hand, but I don't like to – it's giving in and asking her makes it real that the accident has happened. |
| *Co-leader:* | So you sort of pretend that the accident hasn't happened? |
| *Wal:* | Yes, but it sounds weird when you put it like that. |
| *Laura:* | I know what you mean. That's why I don't like to talk of the robbery. If it's just in my mind, I can pretend it's not real. |

This dialogue indicates that acceptance of intrusions is not just a matter of accepting the discomfort that they bring, but also acknowledging that they relate to an event that happened. However, sometimes the intrusions are of something worse than what actually happened:

*Laura*: In my flashbacks I see myself lying in a pool of blood, dying alone.
*Leader*: I think we need to eyeball and accept what did happen but see the rest as being on 'fantasy television'. To tell it as it is, without this you can't move on, but 'fantasies' have a way of playing through your mind anyway. Provided you see them as just 'fantasy' there is no problem.

In the above dialogue the therapists are distilling an appropriate metacognitive approach to intrusions as a prelude for elaborating preparatory coping self-statements. The case has also been implicitly made that intrusions are mood dependent and that a dysphoric mood such as irritability accesses them and that the better management of such difficulties makes it less likely that the door to them is unlocked. The distillation of coping self-statements implicitly involves cognitive restructuring as it involves reaching agreement on the marginalisation of maladaptive self-talk and its replacement with adaptive self-talk/imagery/narrative. The exchange continues:

*Co-leader*: Wal, what would be a better way of approaching situations you can't physically manage as you used to.
*Wal*: I guess I've just got to eat 'humble pie'.
*Co-leader*: Hmm, I'm worried you would choke on the 'pie'.
*Wal*: Yes, I think I will still be fuming.
*Co-leader*: Could get gassed by the 'fumes'?
*Wal*: 'Pies', 'fumes', I'm not doing well.
*Leader*: You have to sort out what doesn't really work before you can move on to what might work.
*Laura*: Who's bothered if you can't lift something from a shelf by yourself? It happens to me all the time.
*Wal*: Yes, but I 'should'.
*Laura*: Why?
*Wal*: [*Deep intake of breath.*]
*Laura*: Oh God, we are not going to get this male thing, are we?!
*Wal*: Hmm [*blushing, moving uncomfortably*]. I need to start telling myself it doesn't matter if I need a hand, but I feel the accident has aged me twenty years.
*Tom*: I'm like that with my knee since I fell down the stairs with the fire. When the pain is bad I dream more of the fire.

The above dialogue shows that in a group, other group members can become quasi therapists to others in the group and can at times be more powerful sources of persuasion than the therapist. The therapists have allowed the dialogue to flow so that group members can provide support for each other (see Table 6.3, item 6). The exchange continues:

*Leader*: So how, Wal, could you play the frustrations differently?
*Wal*: Perhaps, as Laura says, I should tell myself that it doesn't really matter if I can't do something or it takes longer, there is no time limit.
*Leader*: So that the heading on the blank self-instruction form [*see Appendix E*] could be 'Frustration' and on the second row you could put what you have just said. On the next row what could you put to say to yourself when you actually meet a frustration?
*Wal*: Maybe 'It's bait, don't rise to it'.
*Leader*: OK, and on the next row when it is really getting to you?
*Wal*: Maybe 'Take a deep breath, do it all slowly and get some help'.
*Tom*: I could try the same when the pain in my knee stops me playing football with the kids in the park. If I can stop getting in a state, maybe these nightmares will ease.

# SESSION 3

This session begins with a review and troubleshooting of homework. The new material to be introduced involves targeting avoidance, which is viewed as a maladaptive response to the 'bullying intrusions', an adaptive response involves gradually daring to approach what is avoided, 'reclaiming your life'. The following exchange took place at the third session:

*Leader*: How have people got on with their self-talk since the last session?
*Laura*: I found myself using the 'bait' idea when I'm about to take off on my husband, usually for nothing.
*Wal*: [*Laughing*] I wouldn't like to be on the receiving end of your outbursts.

This dialogue illustrates how quite naturally members can extend the range of applicability of coping skills beyond those areas originally focused upon, often via a process of vicarious learning in the group. The therapist then invited group members to make a list of what they believed it was no longer safe for them to do. The session continued:

*Bob*: This is embarrassing, I've even got down to it not being safe to walk past young men coming out of the local pub after watching a football match. It's stupid, I know most of them and I was attacked in work by a colleague.
*Co-leader*: That could be your first 'baby step' dare. Stay on the same side of the road locally when young men are coming towards you. You could prepare for this situation by reminding yourself that you know most of them.
*Bob*: But I know when I see them I will want to cross the road.
*Co-leader*: What could you say to yourself to stop yourself?
*Bob*: It is just a fear that I don't need to be afraid of. Let's see how it goes.
*Co-leader*: So rather than do a 'runner', you are going to conduct an experiment and test out whether there is a real and present danger. Dares are just experiments to see whether you really do need to be as afraid as you initially feel.

The rest of the session is devoted to distilling appropriate behavioural experiments. For group members to follow through on such 'dares' each has to believe they have the capacity for the challenge and that the successful completion of it would make a worthwhile difference. Unless the therapist distils these aspects of group members' self-efficacy, there is likely to be non-compliance with the homework exercise. One advantage of the group format, however, is that each member sees others accepting 'dares' and a group norm about behavioural experiments is thereby cultivated, increasing motivation. Further, the 'dares' are facilitated by the generation of an internal dialogue of appropriate coping self-statements, and thus the session material builds on previous sessions.

## SESSION 4

The new material to be introduced involves targeting alienation. This can involve no longer confiding in or sharing with significant others but equally (and particularly with those from a collectivist culture rather than a western individualistic culture) perceiving that they are no longer discharging an interpersonal role, e.g. mother, grandparent, 'bread winner'. The session begins with a review of homework and a focus on the PTSD Survival Manual (see Appendix G). In Figure G.2 (The Brain's Alarm – Amygdala), the dares are conceptualised as the deliberate tripping of the alarm to collect experimental evidence that there is not a threat, thereby resetting the alarm – edging it anti-clockwise with each dare. Other dares are then negotiated for homework. The session then moves on to Figure G.3 in Appendix G, 'The PTSD Bubble'. The alienation from others present in PTSD is represented by being in a 'bubble'. The sufferer is in a state of 'terrified surprise', a 'war zone', while others, by contrast, are in a 'safe place'. The following dialogue ensued:

*Aidan*: I know what you mean, yesterday I was going the shops with my wife and I told her off for walking too close to the kerb. She told me she is not a four year old, we had a row and she went home.
*Tom*: Sounds a good way to get out of going shopping!
*Aidan*: Yes, but it spoilt the day.
*Co-leader*: What I would like to do is a slow-motion action replay of how it fell apart. That way we might discover how you might play it better next time.
*Aidan*: OK.
*Co-leader*: What went through your mind as you saw her nearing the kerb?
*Aidan*: I could 'see' her lying in the road injured, just like me.
*Co-leader*: It might be useful to think of having two TVs in your mind – one is Reality TV and one is Fantasy TV – and deciding which one what pops into your mind really belongs to. For example, you might have an idea that some absolutely gorgeous person fancies you. Now in my case I would put that on my Reality TV, but if it was the Leader here, he would definitely have to put it on Fantasy TV.
*Leader*: Thanks for that, really appreciate it.
*Bob*: [*looking at co-leader*] Do you think you need to attend a group for what you are suffering from?
*Co-leader*: [*laughing*] I'm probably beyond treatment.
*Aidan*: I can see what you mean.
*Leader*: Maybe your wife might find it useful to read the Survival Manual.
*Aidan*: I would have to choose my moment in suggesting it.

In the above exchange connectedness is modelled by the interaction of the therapists, clients' intrusions are normalised, and a coping skill is canvassed. Further, it is suggested that self-help material can start the building of a bridge between a group member and their significant others. Further steps for the completion of a 'bridge' are elaborated in the following exchange:

*Leader*: I remember you mentioning Aidan, at an earlier session, that you felt that you had robbed your daughter of her childhood because you got her to tie your shoe laces. Does she see it that way?
*Aidan*: No, she is the light of my life.
*Leader*: So you have a different story about how you relate to her and how she relates to you?

*(Continued)*

*(Continued)*

*Aidan:* Hmm, they don't square.
*Laura:* My Dad had severe arthritis, I wasn't bothered having to help him.
*Aidan:* With not working since the accident it has caused financial problems, I've let the family down.
*Co-leader:* Does your wife say you have let them down?
*Aidan:* No, she is usually very patient.
*Co-leader* So again, there is a gap between your story and those of others?
*Aidan:* Yes.
*Leader:* After a trauma people often develop a 'prejudice' against themselves, with a much more negative view of themselves than others have. Maybe in preparing to interact with others you can tell yourself not to give in to the prejudice against yourself [*there is a discussion of this in* Moving on after Trauma] but to look at yourself through others' eyes. Maybe actually, though my colleague could do with a bit of a prejudice against themselves when it comes to attractiveness!
*Co-leader:* [*laughing*] Not sure.

In this exchange the discrepancy between group members' views of themselves and those of others is explored and crystallised as a 'prejudice' rather than left as an abstract concept. It is suggested that it is this 'prejudice' that is largely producing disconnection rather than the behaviour of others, as the following exchange further underlines:

*Aidan:* After the incident on the pavement I made an excuse not to attend a family member's 50th birthday celebration.
*Leader:* Why?
*Aidan:* I wouldn't know what to say.
*Leader:* Before the accident, would you have been happy to go to such a celebration?
*Aidan:* Yes.
*Leader:* How was your wife about you not attending?
*Aidan:* Livid. I stayed in and got drunk.
*Leader:* Each of your safety behaviours – telling your wife she is too close to the kerb, backing away from attending a family celebration, drinking – is a step away from others that evokes criticism. I'll just draw what has happened [see Figure 6.2].

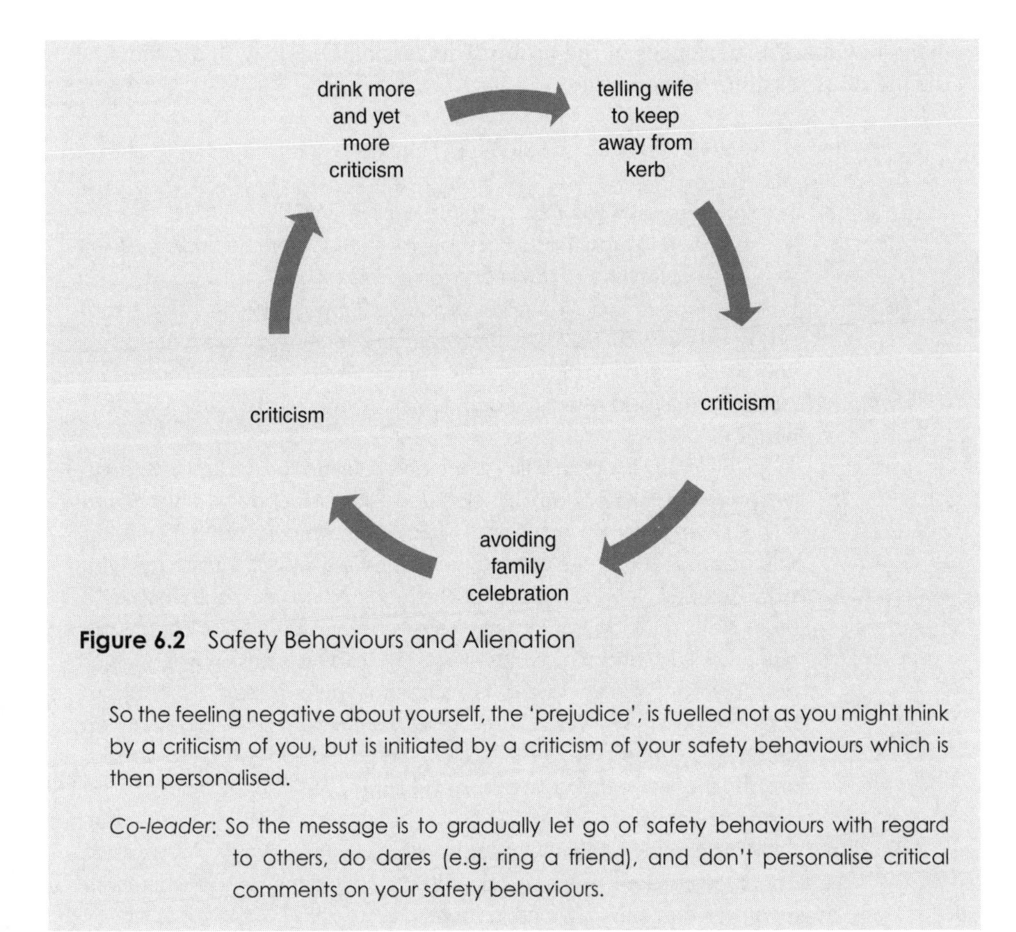


**Figure 6.2** Safety Behaviours and Alienation

So the feeling negative about yourself, the 'prejudice', is fuelled not as you might think by a criticism of you, but is initiated by a criticism of your safety behaviours which is then personalised.

*Co-leader*: So the message is to gradually let go of safety behaviours with regard to others, do dares (e.g. ring a friend), and don't personalise critical comments on your safety behaviours.

In the above exchange the therapists have been very conscious of the need in a group not to get sucked into the details of any one group member's difficulties, to the extent it excludes others (see Relevance – item 2 in Table 6.3) and to demonstrate good presentation skills (see Presentation Skills – item 8 in Table 6.3) to engage the whole group.

## SESSION 5

This session continues the focus on the aspects of PTSD that impinge directly on relationships: a disconnection from others, increased irritability and emotional numbness. The ways in which group members have established connections with each other in the group are used as a template for the re-establishment of relationships outside the group programme. The notion that only those who have been through the same trauma could understand is challenged experientially, using members' experiences of the group. The session begins with a review of the previous session's homework:

| | |
|---|---|
| *Leader*: | Who has been adventurous since the last session? |
| *Aidan*: | I have started to cross roads more, but it is stupid when the traffic is a long way off – I put my head down and run across. |
| *Leader*: | Well, you can only do the dares gradually. Perhaps the next step might be just to keep your head up, and the step after that to cross at the pace you did before the accident. |
| *Aidan*: | I still avoid the road where the accident happened, just outside my sister's house. |
| *Leader*: | That is probably the most difficult one because the flashbacks are likely to be quite vivid, and looking at the left-hand side of the see-saw [*see Figure 6.1*], the weight of the flashback will push it down and as the right-hand side goes up, your sense of today will almost disappear. What might you say to yourself when you feel overwhelmed outside your sister's home? |
| *Aidan*: | If I make it a Sunday afternoon there is always the smell of apple pie being cooked, and the accident was on a Saturday night when it was dark. I need to remind myself it is different – there is apple pie cooking. But it is not just that she will ask me how I'm getting on physically and then go on about when she arrived to find me on the floor without my shoes on, and she will go on again about how I came to have my shoes off and I've told her I don't ****** know! |
| *Co-leader*: | This is a general problem for people with PTSD. They avoid conversations about the incident, and consequently they avoid the people who might mention it and then relationships deteriorate. Today I would like us to look at ways of building bridges. |

In this exchange there is a review of all that has been taught previously but in such a way that it is made relevant (item 2 in Table 6.3) to all group members. Further, the therapists have shown flexibility in allowing a group member to express the details of their concern but in such a way as to allow fidelity to the teaching of the scheduled new material. In a group format the dangers of straying off-task are multiplied and there is an art to allowing such flexibility that each member feels that what has been addressed is relevant to them while at same time maintaining a fidelity to what has to be taught. One of the virtues of having two therapists is that if one of the therapists is struggling to maintain this balance, at any point the other can take over. However, this does require a rapport and respect between the co-leaders and a post-session debrief where such matters are discussed, as well as a discussion of any group member who appears to be consciously, or not, hampering group cohesion. The session continued:

*Bob:* I had a phone call from a colleague, Bill, at work. He wanted to meet up. He is a nice guy, but I just put him off.

*Co-leader:* Why?

*Bob:* It is as you say, I don't want to go into detail about it because it will bring it all back.

*Co-leader:* Will he push you to talk about it any more than those in the group have pushed you to talk about it?

*Bob:* Probably not, he's just concerned.

*Laura:* Like we all are Bob.

*Bob:* Thanks Laura.

*Leader:* Even if meeting Bill did act as something of a reminder, you have got a gameplan for handling flashbacks.

*Wal:* There is always a reminder, I was coming in here this morning and a couple of guys in 'high viz' jackets walked past. It took me back to the scene of the accident and I had to balance it out with where I am now.

*Leader:* So you told yourself it's the day of the wonderful coffee and company in the group, not the day of the motorbike accident surrounded by those in high viz jackets.

*Wal:* I could have said that, but what I actually said is 'Right now I'm really desperate to go the loo' and I wasn't thinking about the loo at the time of the accident!

*Co-leader:* Sounds just as good a thing to ground yourself. If someone is just being nosey about your trauma, you can use a one liner that you just repeat over and over without explaining yourself. For example, 'It was a bad do, I just want to move on'. We could role-play it if you like. Perhaps, Tom, we could look at how you would handle a nosey neighbour when you return to your property after refurbishment.

*Tom:* OK.

*Co-leader:* You will be OK for a bit of compensation, eh Tom!

*Tom:* I just want to strangle you! That comment just reminds me of why I don't want to meet people.

*Leader:* But how many people would say that?

*Tom:* I agree they are a minority. No one in the group has said it because you understand, we just want our lives back. I think I would just have to walk away if someone mentioned compensation. Even repeating a one-liner over and over wouldn't be enough.

In the above exchange group members have acted as role models for coping with both reminders of trauma and interactions with others. Further, the group is used as a template for suggesting that perhaps not all others are going to be a threat by their conversation. The session concludes by focusing on Figure G.4 in Appendix G, as in the following dialogue:

*Leader:* Looking at Figure 3 in the Survival Manual, if you wait until you feel like making contact with others, you will wait a very long time. You could commit to being a hermit or you could commit to gradually restoring relationships, the choice is yours.

*Laura:* The group has shown me that my own thoughts are such bad company, I'm better off with people. I've got to start making contact, perhaps see my Mum weekly as I used to.

This dialogue emphasises the experiential learning that occurs in the group. Rather than have to persuade a client that they would be better off contacting others, one of the group members has discovered this for herself from the group experience. In turn, this group member acts as a role model for making a commitment to 'bursting the bubble' (Figure 2 in the Survival Manual).

# SESSION 6

This session focuses on the way in which each group member's narrative and behaviour has varied at different stages in their life and that the current trauma perspective is not therefore immutable. Client's autobiographies can be summarised using Table 6.4.

**Table 6.4** Me Through the Lifecycle

| | As a child | Before the trauma | Since the trauma | Updating me with what I now know |
|---|---|---|---|---|
| I am ... | | | | |
| Life is ... | | | | |
| So I ... | | | | |

The following exchange illustrates the use of Table 6.4:

*Leader:* Laura you mentioned in the last session about your thoughts being 'bad company', what did you mean by that?

*Laura:* I've let everybody down, I'm not a wife for my husband, I've let my daughter down. Until the last session I wouldn't even join other parents in the playground picking my daughter up from school. Instead I would make a mad dash at the last minute so I wouldn't have to talk to anyone.

*Leader*: So Laura, looking at Table 6.4, what would you put on the first row 'I am ...' under 'Since the Trauma'?
*Laura*: Horrible.
*Co-leader*: How do you mean 'horrible'?
*Laura*: I've let myself go, put weight on, don't care about anyone, can be nasty.
*Leader*: Does everyone think that?
*Laura*: I think so.
*Leader*: What about others in the group?
*Laura*: I'm not sure.
*Bob*: [*laughing*] Yes, I think you are at least as bad as a mass murderer! Seriously though, I've really appreciated your support [*a chorus of approval from other group members*].
*Laura*: [*on the verge of tears*] Thanks ever so.
*Co-leader*: So how would you update your view of yourself under 'Updating me with what I now know'.
*Laura*: I think I would put that the old me is coming back, I've made a start at least.
*Leader*: Perhaps everyone could take a few minutes to complete Table 6.4 over coffee and we could chat about it afterwards. [...]
*Co-leader*: How did folks get on?
*Wal*: I never thought much of myself before the accident.
*Co-leader*: How come?
*Wal*: I think I under-achieved. As a teenager I got into trouble with the law, I was into motorbikes then. I can hear my father saying from the grave 'I told you so'. Then as an adult, I got it together, did a Law degree, but then found couldn't get into Law because of my stupidity as a teenager.
*Co-leader*: How were you as a child?
*Wal*: Didn't do well at school but, looking back, that was because I couldn't concentrate because of the constant rows between my parents.
*Co-leader*: If it was, say, Tom with this history, what would you say to him?
*Wal*: Poor ******.
*Tom*: I think anyone would struggle with all that going on. Maybe the wonder is that you did not end up in prison.
*Aidan*: At least you have tried. My childhood was great but if anything got difficult I just gave up. Better to have tried and failed than not to have tried at all.
*Wal*: My wife says I just beat myself up all the time.
*Co-leader*: Maybe for homework we could all update how we look at ourselves and whether there is any real evidence we are not performing important roles.

In this exchange group members challenge an individual member's exaggeratedly negative views of the self. Finally, members are invited to consider their view of the world (see Table 6.4, 'Life is ...') and their strategies (Table 6.4, 'So I ...') and reflect on whether they need updating.

## SESSIONS 7 AND 8

The final sessions of the group Coping Skills programme focus on the underlining and revision of previously taught material. An individual session is also scheduled to re-assess each member's diagnostic status and decide whether, largely on the basis of the significance of their intrusions, whether they should be stepped up to an individual trauma-focused intervention. It is recommended that if the group member is still upset by flashbacks in the sense that they have to stop what they are doing when they occur and become distressed, then they should be stepped up to a trauma-focused intervention. However, if it is the case that the member is now simply uncomfortable with flashbacks and they are not affecting functioning, then they would not be stepped up. At the individual re-assessment it is important to assess the frequency and intensity of nightmares. As a rough rule of thumb, if the nightmares have reduced to say one or two a month but the person either does not wake or wakes only briefly, they would not be stepped up to a trauma-focused intervention, but they would if the frequency and intensity were greater. Where nightmares are an ongoing issue, the rationale given for stepping up the group member to an individual intervention can be: 'If we look at how you can sort out the memory of the trauma in the day, you won't be troubled about it in the night, you only dream of what is not sorted in the day'. Group members may also be stepped up to an individual intervention if the group member's negative view of themselves and/ or guilt persists. Group members that are stepped up for individual interventions can be socialised into this by reading in *Moving on after Trauma* (Scott 2008) about the alternative ways of handling intrusions and a 'prejudice' against self.

The seventh session began:

*Leader*: How did people get on updating the view of themselves, the world and their coping strategies [*Table* 6.4]?

*Bob*: It is really hard, I'm back at work now, though the guy that assaulted me has been dismissed. I'm furious that I was also automatically suspended and the Manager was totally unsympathetic. Now they want me to 'bust my guts' for them the way I did before.

*Co-leader*: But because work has treated you badly should you be avoiding other things, such as going to watch rugby?

*Bob*: I can see what you mean – I've let it spread.

*Laura*: I've let it spread as well. I'm still avoiding going the pub.

*Co-leader*: You can think of the 'danger zone' as a dot, a little circle, a medium circle or a big circle. When you are fearful, ask yourself 'Am I magnifying the size of the danger zone?' Even if you conclude that you are magnifying the size of the danger zone, you may well still be fearful but you can tell yourself that 'This is a fear that I don't need to be afraid of', which is basically what you said to yourself as a child when you started jumping into a swimming pool, and from repeated 'dares' your fear subsided.

In the above dialogue there is a recap of important earlier material regarding behavioural experiments ('dares'), but it is integrated with newer material on challenging an exaggeratedly negative view of the world. The exchange also involves the therapists engaging in cognitive restructuring to distil possible coping self-statements that might be used by group members.

## SUMMARY

1. Group treatment can lessen isolation, but there is also a risk of re-traumatisation. This risk can be minimised using a coping skills approach.
2. Each of the PTSD symptoms can be targeted using Self-Instruction Training.
3. Self-help materials can be used both as a teaching resource and as a reference for clients beyond the group session.
4. Groups should be as homogeneous as practicalities and concerns for privacy allow. Clients with a significant personality disorder should be offered individual treatment instead.
5. Therapists need to be as aware of group processes as the content of a session.
6. Competence in managing the group process can be reflected in paying attention to:
   i. The review of homework/agenda
   ii. Relevance
   iii. Adaptation
   iv. Inclusion
   v. Additional disorders
   vi. Magnifying support and minimising criticism
   vii. Utilising group members as role models
   viii. Therapist presentation skills
   ix. Addressing group issues

# Chapter Seven

## DUAL TREATMENT OF PTSD WITH COMMONLY ASSOCIATED DISORDERS

*PTSD is often only part of the story of a client's difficulties, but it tends to 'hog the limelight', so much so that other disorders may not be identified or are undertreated. In general, the more disorders from which a person suffers the more they are impaired. In some instances other disorders may resolve just by focusing on the PTSD but this cannot be taken for granted. Interventions for PTSD sufferers should comprehensively cover all their difficulties. Common comorbidities for PTSD include depression, panic disorder, substance abuse and borderline personality disorder. In this chapter the interplay between PTSD and each of these common comorbidities is discussed. A case example is then described illustrating the treatment of a PTSD client with all these common comorbidities. The case example highlights the role that supervision can play in the management of a client with multiple comorbidities.*

Among PTSD sufferers, comorbidity is the norm, with three out of four suffering from additional disorders (Kessler et al. 2005). The pathways by which one disorder affects another remain largely to be determined. From a clinical point of view, some degree of reciprocal interaction appears the most likely scenario. For clients with PTSD and comorbid disorders interventions are therefore probably best targeted at all the disorders. PTSD may or may not be the principal disorder (i.e. the disorder the client regards as causing most impairment) from which a client is suffering. Whether or not PTSD is the principal disorder, they do wish for treatment for all their disorders (Zimmerman and Mattia 2000). Although it can be the case that targeting one disorder, such as PTSD, can result in the resolution of an accompanying disorder, this fortunate scenario cannot be assumed. In this chapter the focus is on the dual interventions for PTSD and depression, panic disorder, substance abuse and borderline personality disorder.

## DEPRESSION

Most clients with PTSD also suffer from depression. The depression may be compounded by trauma-related guilt, in which the person blames themselves either for surviving the trauma or some other aspect of it, even though nobody else blames them. A depressed person has increased access to past negative memories, thus if they have experienced an extreme trauma they are likely to brood on it and the treatment of the depression will need a focus on depressive rumination (Scott 2009). Though PTSD and depression share many common symptoms, they are nevertheless distinct disorders.

Depression is commonly associated with major negative life events but they are neither necessary nor sufficient to cause the disorder. Often depression develops following a traumatic physical injury and has its onset when the individual realises they are never going to return to their previous level of physical functioning. As a consequence, they may be unable to discharge important occupational or social roles. Champion and Power (1995) have suggested that the loss of an overvalued role may lead to depression and that the mechanism involves a vulnerability (distal) factor and a triggering (proximal) factor. While roles may be valued and give a sense of achievement or pleasure, if they are central to the person's identity, defining who they are, they constitute a vulnerability factor for depression. In the event of a trigger that is pertinent to the overvalued role (e.g. loss of a job), depression may ensue. The vulnerability and triggering factor need to match, operating rather like a 'key' and 'lock'.

## PANIC DISORDER

Panic attacks may occur at the time of the extreme trauma or shortly afterwards (e.g. on arrival at hospital) and may continue; equally, they may not develop until several months later. Sometimes the link between the panic attack and the trauma is fairly clear, such as a person gasping for breath in a smoke-filled room who later becomes alarmed when they are a little breathless. More often, the link between the two is less clear. Scocco et al. (2007) have found that in the year preceding the onset of panic disorder 92.7% had experienced a role transition, 85.5% interpersonal deficits, 74.5% a role dispute, and 38.2% had suffered the loss of a relative or significant other. It may be that post trauma an individual's capacity to discharge roles is affected and this in turn affects relationships leading to panic disorder, but it may take some time for the interpersonal consequences to reach a crescendo.

The association between panic attacks and a fear response becomes easier to understand when viewed from a neurobiological perspective. Neurobiologically, the brain's amygdala is involved in the fear response (LeDoux 1998) and in panic attacks.

The overlap between PTSD and panic disorder can be understood in biological terms as both involve the amygdala in the brain, which post trauma becomes hypersensitive. In PTSD this hypersensitive alarm is triggered externally by any perceptual match to the trauma or in panic disorder by any unusual but not abnormal bodily sensation that is interpreted catastrophically (Clark 1986; Scott 2009). Thus the PTSD/panic disorders can be regarded as the 'other side of the same coin'.

## SUBSTANCE ABUSE

Trauma plays a significant part in the development of alcohol use disorders, even among those without PTSD. Fezner et al. (2011) found that childhood trauma, assaultive violence and learning of trauma positively predicted the presence of alcohol use disorders. For those with PTSD, childhood trauma and assaultive violence both predicted alcohol use disorders (Fezner et al. 2011).

However, it cannot be assumed that trauma victims who are, say, drinking more than they did pre-trauma are necessarily motivated to tackle their drinking. If the therapist and perhaps the client's relatives see the substance use as a 'problem' and the client does not, it is likely to be fruitless to devote therapeutic efforts to the abuse/dependence. The starting point with such comorbidity has to be an assessment of the client's motivation to change and the likely saboteurs of change. This process can be begun by administering the Readiness Ruler (Figure 7.1).

While 25–42% of people in addiction treatment programmes have a current diagnosis of PTSD (McGovern et al. 2009), historically PTSD has not been addressed for fear of stimulating or exacerbating re-experiencing symptoms and risking jeopardising early and unstable periods of abstinence. But McGovern et al.'s (2009) work suggests that there can be a successful dual focus. Interestingly, at least for drug abusers, changes in PTSD symptoms pre-date changes in drug use (Hien et al. 2010), calling into question the conventional wisdom of insisting that clients are drug/alcohol-free before commencing treatment.

Please indicate on the ruler below how ready you feel to change your drink/drug behaviours:

<table>
<tr><td colspan="3">No</td><td colspan="4">Maybe</td><td colspan="3">Yes</td></tr>
<tr><td>1</td><td>2</td><td>3</td><td>4</td><td>5</td><td>6</td><td>7</td><td>8</td><td>9</td><td>10</td></tr>
</table>

If you indicated a 'No' or 'Maybe' number above, what is it that puts you off?

**Figure 7.1** Readiness to Tackle Drink/Drugs

Distress tolerance, the perceived ability to withstand emotional distress, appears to mediate the relationship between PTSD and alcohol use (Vujanovic et al. 2011) and does so to the same extent as emotional regulation difficulties. These authors also found that while distress tolerance and emotional regulation difficulties were correlated, they were not so highly correlated as to indicate that they are the same construct. Potter, Vujanovic and Marshall-Berenz (2011) found that distress tolerance also played a mediating role between PTSD and marijuana use. These findings suggest that targeting distress tolerance and emotion regulation difficulties may be beneficial for cases of comorbid PTSD and substance use disorders.

## BORDERLINE PERSONALITY DISORDER

Almost a third of clients with borderline personality disorder (BPD) have been found to be suffering from PTSD (Pagura et al. 2010). In a study by Zimmerman and Mattia (1999), 70% of BPD clients met diagnostic criteria for three or more Axis I disorders in *DSM IV*.

In *DSM IV TR* (American Psychiatric Association 2000) borderline personality disorder is characterised by abrupt changes in mood, impulsive behaviour, inappropriate anger, self-harm behaviours, relationship problems and identity disturbance. Emotional dysregulation is thought to be the central feature of BPD (Linehan 1993). The diagnosis and cognitive therapy for BPD can be assisted by use of the BPD scale (Butler et al. 2002), which reflects the specific cognitive content of the disorder. Emotion regulation difficulties have been found in both BPD and PTSD (Tull et al. 2007).

There is some evidence (Huband et al. 2007) that teaching problem-solving skills to clients with a personality disorder can improve functioning. Interestingly, this teaching was delivered in a group format, in a *Stop and Think!* programme. The programme was based around six questions: (1) Bad feelings? (2) What's my problem? (3) What do I want? (4) What are my options? (5) What is my plan? (6) How am I doing? The questions reflect the steps in problem solving outlined by D'Zurilla and Nezu (2007): problem orientation, problem definition, goal setting, the generation of alternatives, decision making and evaluation. Further, the gains appear to be achieved via an improvement in negative problem orientation (McMurran et al. 2008).

## ADDRESSING COMORBIDITY

Weerasekra (1996) has suggested that the important components of case formulation can be summarised under four headings (the 4Ps): predisposing factors, precipitating factors, perpetuating factors and protective factors. The constituents of case formulation are expressed in tabular form in Table 7.1 with regard to a client traumatised by child abuse and involvement in a serious road traffic accident as an adult:

**Table 7.1** Components of Case Formulation – Case Example of Deirdre

| | **Individual** | **Environmental** |
|---|---|---|
| **Predisposing Factors**: sexual abuse aged 9 to 11 by older brother, suicide of mother | Borderline Personality Disorder and Panic Disorder | Estranged from family of origin, difficulties in relationships, sister has severe mental illness |
| **Precipitating Factors**: recent road traffic accident, in which a front seat passenger and driver were thrown through windscreen suffering severe brain damage | PTSD and trauma-related guilt, depression and alcohol abuse | Conflicts with neighbours over alcohol abuse |
| **Perpetuating Factors**: avoidance of travelling as a passenger, avoiding going out by self, cognitive avoidance of memories of childhood and adult trauma | Disconnection from others, concern that no longer regarded by daughter as 'safe' to mind granddaughter | Husband joins her in excessive drinking |
| **Protective Factors**: commitment of husband, son and daughter | A desire to relate to granddaughter | Interest in crafts and craft classes |

Background information: Deirdre attended her initial assessment appointment with her husband Mark, following her involvement in a serious road traffic accident. She was being given a lift home from a Craft class by a neighbour's daughter, Karen. It had begun snowing lightly, the car skidded out of control, hit a kerb, somersaulted and she was thrown through the windscreen. Fortunately Deirdre had her seatbelt on. Deirdre remembered seeing Karen's head hit the road and thought that she was dead. The car toppled over a few times and ended on its roof, she got out through her window and tried to crawl towards Karen. Eighteen months after the incident Deirdre's physical injuries had largely healed but Karen had been left with severe brain damage.

## First Interview

The first interview begins by encouraging the client to tell their story of their current difficulties, with the therapist asking clarifying questions. The interview is initially open-ended. The client may have arrived with a relative or friend and can be invited to choose whether they want this person to accompany them into the interview room. While this invitation enhances the therapeutic alliance, there is a danger that the client may be inhibited in the presence of the relative/friend. On the other hand, the other person can provide additional information. This is highlighted in the following exchange:

*Therapist*: Were you abused as a child?
*Deirdre*: [*Hesitated and turned to look at her husband, Mark.*]
*Mark*: Go on tell.
*Deirdre*: [*Silence.*]

| | |
|---|---|
| *Mark:* | I didn't know for years. I was furious that she didn't tell me. I wanted to kill her brother. |
| *Therapist:* | Was it often or just occasional? |
| *Deirdre:* | Often when my parents were out. Why do we have to go into that? It's the car crash. |
| *Therapist:* | If you have been through physical or sexual abuse, you can struggle getting on with others, maybe drinking, and then if something really bad happens you might struggle even more than most. Knowing about abuse gives a more complete picture and we can look at skills for not only handling memories of the car accident but also those from earlier traumas. |
| *Deirdre:* | I just blank it all. |
| *Therapist:* | Does that work? |
| *Deirdre:* | No. |
| *Therapist:* | In therapy we look at better ways of handling past memories. I see from the notes that you have had contact with the mental health services since your teenage years. Did anyone ever ask you whether you were abused as a child? |
| *Deirdre:* | No, they just talked about panic attacks, relaxation exercises, breathing into brown paper bags and all that ****! |
| *Mark:* | We are that close to breaking up. |

In the above exchange it is questionable whether the client would have been more or less forthcoming in the absence of her husband but it does highlight the importance of routinely asking about abuse and the rationale that can be given for such seemingly 'intrusive' questioning. Further, the presence of the client's husband aids the detailing of the environmental aspects of the case formulation (see Table 7.1).

The open-ended part of the interview suggested a number of diagnostic possibilities and use of the CBT Pocketbook (Scott 2011) confirmed the presence of PTSD, panic disorder with severe agoraphobic avoidance, and depression.

## AT SUPERVISION

The therapist was, however, concerned at the felt 'complexity' of this case and took it to supervision. The supervisor identified that the supervisee's comfort zone was depression and the anxiety disorders and suggested that the therapist may be missing additional diagnoses of substance abuse and borderline personality disorder. To determine the presence/absence of substance abuse/dependence the supervisor suggested that the therapist use the Structured Clinical Interview for *DSM IV* (SCID) Axis I disorders (First et al. 1997a) and assess for borderline personality disorder using SCID for Axis II disorders (First

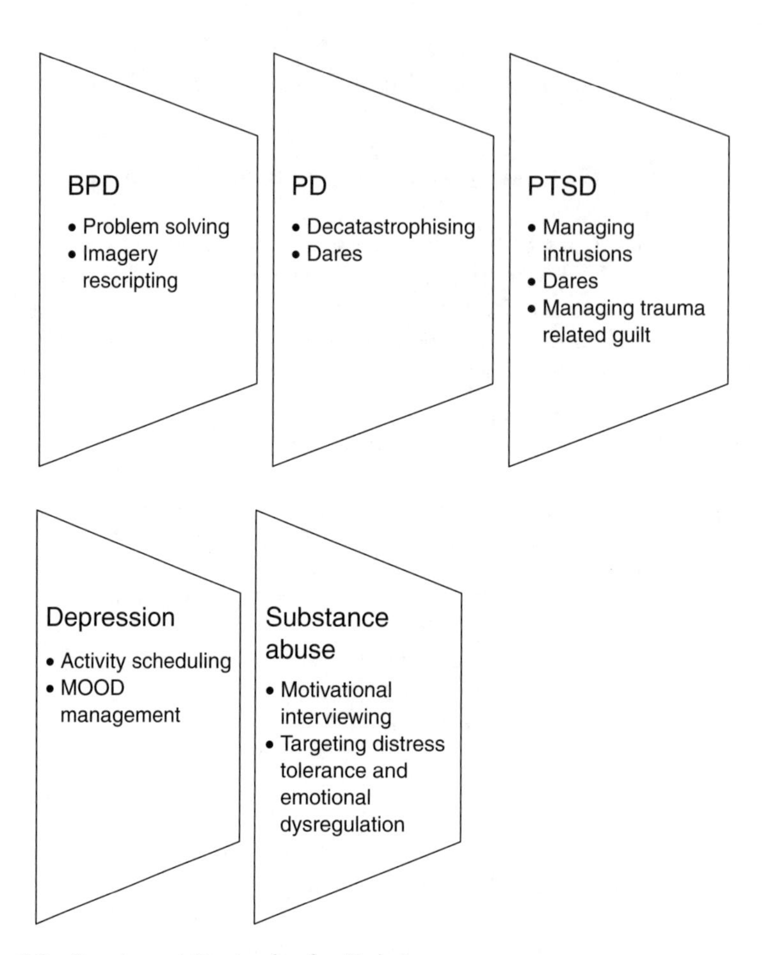


**Figure 7.2** Treatment Strategies for Deirdre

et al. 1997b). (These disorders were in fact confirmed at the next interview.) The supervisor also pointed out that clients with Axis II disorders can evoke much stronger emotional reactions in the therapist than clients with only Axis I disorders and relationships can be more fraught. The therapist was much relieved by this as she had felt criticised by the client but assumed that was wholly due to her prior bad experiences with therapists working on her panic attacks. The supervisor suggested that while prior negative experiences might partially explain the client's negativity there could well be more to it than that. The therapist confessed that she half hoped the client would not turn up to the next session! The supervisor normalised this feeling in working with such clients. The rest of the supervision session was devoted to mapping out the possible treatment strategies with regard to this client (see Figure 7.2).

These considerations indicate that there should be a dynamic reciprocal interaction between assessment, treatment and supervision, and that assessment is not necessarily confined to the first interview or to Axis I disorders, much less to depression and anxiety. The supervisor suggested that the therapist might benefit from reading Smucker and Niederee (1995) on Imagery Rescripting (IR), in which the adult client might visit the child self and soothe her with the knowledge she now has as an adult – this strategy is often appropriate with BPD clients but can equally be appropriate with PTSD as result of child-related trauma.

## SESSIONS 2–4

In weaving together the treatment strategies, the therapist has to be mindful of the self-efficacy of the client with regard to each strategy. There are two aspects of self-efficacy: (a) the extent to which the person believes the actions will result in a worthwhile difference; and (b) the extent to which the client believes they have the capacity to take the actions. In the interests of developing a therapeutic alliance initial treatment strategies should focus on implementing those coping skills for which there are high levels of self-efficacy. At the same time the therapist has to be aware of factors which may impinge on treatment efficacy and on which the client may be ambivalent or opposed to working, such as substance abuse.

The therapist began the second session by stating that she would like to ask some further questions to get a more complete picture of the client's problems and whether there was anything the client would also like to put on the agenda. The following dialogue ensued:

*Deirdre*: I'm fed up that Myra [her daughter] will not let me look after the baby by myself.

*Therapist*: How come?

*Deirdre*: Myra rang me from her work asking me if I could pick up Mandy [aged three] from nursery, because she was vomiting. I had had a few drinks but I couldn't just leave the baby, so I collected her. When I got her home she carried on awful, 'I want my Mum'. I finally settled her but then I needed to settle myself so I had a couple more drinks. When Myra came to collect her she went ballistic because she could smell the drink!

The therapist used this opportunity to ask the client the SCID questions about substance abuse (First et al. 1997b) and confirmed that the client tended to binge drink rather than that she was alcohol dependent. Nevertheless, it had caused problems with her daughter and neighbours and that, of late, her husband would join her in the drinking if not at work. The therapist was unsure of Deirdre's motivation to tackle her drinking and asked her to complete the Readiness Ruler exercise (Figure 7.1). The following dialogue ensued:

*Therapist*: I noticed you put a 4, which is in the 'maybe' region for wanting to tackle your difficulties in drinking and you put that your 'demons will overtake me if I am stressed and don't have a drink'. How do you know that they will?
*Deirdre*: I just think that it will all be too much.
*Therapist*: What will happen when it is all too much?
*Deirdre*: They might cart me off to hospital or I might kill myself the way my mother did.
*Therapist*: If you hadn't drank after you brought Mandy home from nursery, what would have happened?
*Deirdre*: Probably Myra would still be talking to me and she would let me have Mandy.
*Therapist*: So you have a horror video of what will happen if you don't drink but the reality video of what would happen if you don't drink seems a bit different.
*Deirdre*: Hmm, it doesn't square.

In the above exchange the therapist is using the motivational interviewing technique of juxtaposing contradictory information and leaving it to the client to resolve the cognitive dissonance in their own time and, by so doing, is hopefully moving the client along the motivational ruler. Unless the client owns the problem of substance abuse (the 'yes' area), they are unlikely to tackle it and therapeutic strategies for altering alcohol intake are likely to go unheeded. Further, in addressing a substance abuse difficulty, the client is likely to vary in their position on the ruler, i.e. their motivation will wax and wane and the therapist needs to adapt to the client's level of motivation. The dialogue continued:

*Therapist*: When people have been traumatised one of the things that affects whether they take a substance to soothe themselves is their Distress Tolerance, that is their belief in the ability to withstand the discomfort of not taking the substance. You can think of a person as being like a tree – winds/hassles blow all the time but the tree just sways from side to side. Sometimes there is a storm and the tree bends more from side to side, but it is very rare that any one tree is uprooted. It is as if you believe that if there is any wind you will be uprooted?
*Deirdre*: I have just run for cover when there is any distress, tried to soothe myself with yoga or relaxation exercises.
*Therapist*: How would you feel just practising letting yourself blow in the wind?
*Deirdre*: That is the opposite of what I've been doing for over 40 years!
*Therapist*: I know, it's just that the old way doesn't seem to have worked, so maybe we could experiment with something new.
*Deirdre*: Maybe I could cross-stitch a tree to remind me?

*Therapist*: Might be worth a try? One of the problems in depression is that people stop doing what they used to do. There is no investment so there is no return. Doing some cross-stitching would also be the start of investing again as well as a way of reminding yourself that it may not be true that the 'wind will uproot you'.

In the above exchange there is a focus on tackling one of the mediators between PTSD and substance abuse, Distress Tolerance, but the latter is translated into an easy-to-understand graphic image of the need to and the likelihood of bending like a tree in the wind. Further, there is a natural flow into tackling another comorbid disorder, depression, but again using an easy-to-grasp metaphor of the need to invest for a return. At the third and fourth interviews the client's ability to apply these metaphors was monitored, her motivation to tackle substance abuse increased, and the client agreed to postpone drinking until after she had watched an evening soap on TV.

# SESSION 5

This session focuses on intrusions and in earlier chapters both trauma-focused and non-trauma-focused approaches to their management have been delineated. It is something of a puzzle that differing methods appear to produce comparable results even within trauma-focused interventions, for example cognitive processing therapy and prolonged imaginal exposure. In the present state of knowledge it seems to be appropriate to use the treatment strategy that is most acceptable to the client and for the therapist not too push their preferred intervention. Sometimes the strategy that the client finds most acceptable is surprising, as the following exchange indicates:

*Therapist*: I would like to look at better ways of handling the flashbacks of both the child abuse and the accident, how does that sound?

*Deirdre*: I just run away, but it is like running away from my shadow. I can't do it.

*Therapist*: What else could you do?

*Deirdre*: Stop running like a headless chicken and face the enemy.

*Therapist*: Maybe we could get you to do that by giving you some special things you could say to yourself when the memories pop in.

*Deirdre*: I'm tired of talking to myself, trying to soothe myself.

*Therapist*: It wouldn't really be about trying to soothe yourself but about the coping statements you make, so you better handle the flashbacks, reminders and dreams.

*Deirdre*: Same thing.

*Therapist*: Hmm.

In the above dialogue the therapist has reached something of an impasse. She had assumed a coping skills approach to the client's childhood and adult trauma would most commend itself to the client and would be least threatening, but felt that she had hit a wall in conveying the rationale for it. Feeling somewhat frustrated, she decided to take the matter to supervision and switched the client's attention in the fifth session to the client's panic disorder. The exchange continues:

*Therapist:* You mentioned facing the enemy, what about facing the panic symptoms in this session and practising a 'see if I care approach'?
*Deirdre:* OK.
*Therapist:* I would like you to stand up and breathe deeply and quickly until I tell you to stop, OK?
*Deidre:* OK.
*Therapist:* [*after 90 seconds*] How are you feeling now?
*Deirdre:* A little light headed.
*Therapist:* OK, carry on a little longer. [*After a further 40 seconds*] How are you feeling now?
*Deirdre:* Terrible [*and about to sit down*].
*Therapist:* No don't sit just yet. Tell me what are you feeling?
*Deirdre:* Like I am going to faint, lose control.
*Therapist:* Anything else?
*Deirdre:* Heart racing, sweaty.
*Therapist:* I didn't let you sit down because I wanted to show you that nothing happens if you don't use this 'safety behaviour'. I would like you to practise deliberately bringing on the panic attacks at home so that you can train yourself to tolerate them.
*Deirdre:* I could only do that with my husband present, just in case.
*Therapist:* In case what?
*Deirdre:* Don't know, I was OK doing it when you were present but I would need my husband present at home.
*Therapist:* But I did not alter the chemicals going around your body?
*Deirdre:* No.
*Therapist:* Seems the other people are 'armbands' that you wear when having panic attacks but you could probably swim without them? You might want to read the Panic Disorder Survival Manual [*as well as the PTSD and Depression Manuals (Scott 2011)*] to look at the steps that you can take to better manage the attacks.

In this dialogue the therapist has shown flexibility by addressing another relevant topic when she became stuck. She has made a mental note to address the difficulty, surrounding the management of intrusions in supervision, rather than insist that the client take a particular approach to managing intrusions, risking a rupture of the therapeutic alliance.

## AT SUPERVISION AGAIN

The supervisor was pleased that the therapist was keeping to the treatment strategies outlined at the previous supervision session (see Figure 7.2), albeit that matters had come to an impasse in addressing the PTSD intrusion symptoms and there was yet to be a focus on the BPD. The therapist expressed her irritation with the client for being dismissive of her attempt to teach her coping skills to manage intrusions. The supervisor pointed out that it is almost the hallmark of clients with BPD that they have difficulty in relationships and not to take the abruptness too seriously. The therapist added that the client had upset one of the receptionists when the latter told her she was not allowed to park in front of the building. The supervisor helped the therapist explore other items on the menu for helping the client process her memories of the trauma. They included making an audiotape of the traumas and listening to it over and over until her level of distress (SUDS – Subjective Units of Disturbance) reduced by half, an imaginal rehearsal of the trauma involving halting at the 'hot spots' until her SUDS reduced before moving on, and writing daily about the trauma and its effects. Further, the supervisor suggested that these options might be presented within a problem-solving framework to additionally illustrate the key features of problem solving, as ineffective problem solving was a key feature of both BPD and PTSD. But the therapist raised the question as to whether just tackling the intrusions from the accident might not be sufficient. The therapist opined that it would probably not be as the intrusions of the abuse pre-dated the accident. So as not to overload the client, the therapist decided to tackle the accident-related intrusions first and then re-assess the level of abuse-related intrusions. For a thorough exposition of Supervision in CBT see Scott (In Press).

## SESSIONS 6 AND 7

At session six the therapist canvassed the treatment options for managing the intrusions, but the client did not respond, maintaining a fixed stare. The therapist thought that she was not adequately explaining herself so repeated the rationales for each of the treatment options. She was just beginning to feel frustrated and suppressed the urge to ask 'is anyone at home?' when she realised that what she was witnessing was likely to be an expression of the client's difficulties with the first step in problem solving – problem orientation – so she changed tack, as follows:

*Therapist:* Sometimes people see life's problems as so jumbled up together that they conclude that it is not worth even starting on them, they turn away. It is rather like continually closing the door on the state of your teenage son's bedroom – eventually it's a health hazard. When people do this with life's problems, we describe them as having difficulties in problem orientation. They can in fact solve problems as well as anyone but they never get started.

*Deirdre:* Sort of like burying your head in the sand?

*Therapist:* I wouldn't quite put it like that.

*Deirdre:* I would, it is being an ostrich!

*Therapist:* OK, if you don't want to be an ostrich and are going to be problem oriented, we can go on to the second stage of problem solving – problem definition. If you make the problem vague or 'fuzzy' it does not get sorted. It is rather like asking the untidy adolescent son to 'just change your attitude' instead of saying 'I want your room tidy by the weekend or there is no pocket money on Saturday'. You are troubled by memories of the accident and abuse. What would a realistic goal be for them?

*Deirdre:* I'd like them to just go, but it is unrealistic. If they could just become a bad memory that would do.

*Therapist:* OK, it sounds that you are saying you would settle for them just making you uncomfortable rather than upset, is that right?

*Deirdre:* Yes, that would do.

*Therapist:* The next step in problem solving is considering the options, the options are …

*Deirdre:* Yes, I heard you before.

*Therapist:* [*feeling somewhat put out*] The next step in problem solving is looking at the advantages and disadvantages of each option and choosing an option. What would you go for?

*Deirdre:* If I am going to stop being an ostrich, this eye-balling what upsets you sounds the right thing but it also sounds *****.

*Therapist:* The choice is yours. I could take you through the accident, get you to pause at points that really get to you and stay there until you become more relaxed then carry on. We could tape it and you could then listen to the tape each day at home.

*Deirdre:* I think I would want my husband present when I listen to it.

*Therapist:* Fine, the next stage in problem solving is to try out your chosen strategy to see how it works and, if it is totally not working, to try something else from the menu of options. But usually we have to just alter the chosen strategy a little. Typically, it takes two to three weeks of daily listening to the tape to get sufficiently bored that the memories make you uncomfortable rather than upset.

*Deirdre:* OK.

In the above exchange the therapist has not only obtained the client's agreement to prolonged imaginal exposure but has also taught the principles of problem solving, which can later be utilised in other contexts, such as managing memories of child abuse. However, the therapist has had to work hard at not being derailed by the client's manner. Afterwards the therapist reflected that the client's approach is typical of clients with BPD who have a penchant for black and white thinking – they are either an 'ostrich' or they are able to face the memories. This same dichotomous thinking results in the abrupt mood changes that are characteristic of BPD. At the seventh session the client reported that her nightmares of the accident had increased in frequency and that rather than use the tape she was just taking herself through the incident and pausing at 'hot spots' to 'catch her breath'.The following exchange took place:

*Therapist:* Flashbacks/nightmares do usually get worse before they get better. It is like going into hospital with a back injury and they put you on traction and you are in such pain that you begin to think that you are sorry you agreed to the hospitalisation, but it is a temporary thing before you get better.
*Deirdre:* You should have told me this!
*Therapist:* Sorry.

The above exchange illustrates a common dilemma for therapists. Clients often react negatively to the prospect of prolonged exposure and there can therefore be a tendency to downplay or not mention a deterioration before an improvement, but this can have a deleterious effect on the therapeutic relationship. For clients with BPD, 'trust' is often a major issue and this omission can have more serious consequences than usual. The dialogue continued:

*Therapist:* What were the 'hot spots' you stopped at?
*Deirdre:* When her head hit the floor I thought she was dead. I eye-balled that but then thought stupid ***** she didn't die, but then I thought of meeting her in the supermarket. She was in a wheelchair with severe brain damage being pushed by her mother. I just wanted to run.
*Therapist:* Why did you want to run?
*Deirdre:* I feel so guilty. She is the same age as my daughter [*at this point she burst into tears.*]
*Therapist:* What did you do wrong?

*(Continued)*

*(Continued)*

| | |
|---|---|
| *Deirdre:* | Nothing, but I still feel guilty. |
| *Therapist:* | Does Karen's mum blame you? |
| *Deirdre:* | No she is very nice, but deep down she probably does. |
| *Therapist:* | How do you know she does deep down? |
| *Deirdre:* | I just feel it. |
| *Therapist:* | Does that make it true? |
| *Deirdre:* | No, I suppose not. |
| *Therapist:* | Guilt feelings are common in these extreme situations. It is what we call trauma-related guilt, a bogus guilt. Unfortunately, with trauma-related guilt you can't just cut it out. The more you do, the worse state you get in, but you can train yourself to take such feelings with a 'pinch of salt'. |
| *Deirdre:* | I could do with doing that over other things as well. |

In the above exchange the therapist has used Socratic dialogue to challenge the client's trauma-related guilt (TRG) and there is a hint that the client has begun transferring the coping strategies for dealing with this to matters related to her childhood abuse. This gives the therapist permission to suggest that TRG is common following child abuse and may be handled in a similar way to such feelings arising from an adult trauma. Thus, although the treatment strategies depicted in Figure 7.2 are for different disorders, there is in practice a natural interweaving of the strategies, as opposed to sequentially addressing one disorder in full and then another.

## SESSIONS 8–12

At the eighth treatment session the client gave the therapist a sealed letter which she said was about the child abuse but asked the therapist not to read it until after the session. When the therapist read the letter it detailed the client's sexual abuse by her older brother. At the ninth session the following exchange took place:

| | |
|---|---|
| *Deirdre:* | Did you read it? |
| *Therapist:* | Yes, the body is like a machine, if you press certain buttons certain things happen. It is the responsibility of the person pressing the buttons. |
| *Deirdre:* | He should have known better, but then so should I. |
| *Therapist:* | At age 9 to 11, particularly in those days, would you have known any better? |

*Deirdre*: I suppose not, but it still affects me as an adult. I can't let my husband initiate sex. I have to. If he does, it brings it all back.
*Therapist*: Although you are an adult now, it sounds like there is a little girl inside getting very upset in those types of situation. Maybe she just needs soothing.
*Deirdre*: I hate her.
*Therapist*: Sounds like she is pretty bewildered. If, God forbid, it happened in years to come to Mandy, how would you comfort her?
*Deirdre*: I think I would kill whoever did it.
*Therapist*: But you wouldn't kill Mandy?
*Deirdre*: No, not at all.
*Therapist*: Could you write a letter to the 9–11 year-old Deirdre comforting her?
*Deirdre*: I could give it a try, but I might want to rip it up.
*Therapist*: That's fine, I don't have to see it, but if you want to show it to me that's fine to.
*Deirdre*: OK.

In the above exchange the therapist is updating the memory of the child trauma with information the client knows as an adult so that when the client retrieves it, it is less toxic and loses the power to sabotage adult interactions. Imagery re-scripting involves accessing traumatic childhood material and soothing the child with a compassionate image. In the above instance in the tenth session, the client imagined wiping away the tears of the younger version of herself, taking her by the hand into the garden and weeding it together, enjoying the feel and smell of the soil, the fragrance of roses and the smell of freshly cut grass. The rescripting image is a form of emotion regulation, an important treatment strategy in view of the part that emotion dysregulation plays in both BPD and PTSD. Emotion regulation strategies can be explained to a client as a way of singing in tune with others rather than striking discordant notes and alienating others.

## TRANSDIAGNOSTIC MUDDLE

When there is multiple comorbidity, there is a temptation to bypass an elucidation of the factors involved in the development of each disorder and the interaction between disorders by taking refuge (van Bilsen and Thomson 2011) in an allegedly simpler transdiagnostic approach. This 'transdiagnostic approach' supposedly identifies the key processes that cut across conditions and these become the treatment targets. However, in our present state of knowledge, this is a case of 'telling more than we know'. The result is exemplified in a case example presented by van Bilsen and Thomson (2011) of a client with PTSD, substance abuse, borderline and antisocial personality disorder. Their recommended treatment centres around attentional processes, memory processes, thought processes and behavioural processes, without an evidence-based protocol for any one disorder in sight (van Bilsen and Thomson 2011: 11–15). The putative processes are so vague with respect to the different disorders that almost any intervention could be justified and treatment is likely to be idiosyncratic, hindering the development of an evidence base. Such transdiagnostic approaches fail to capitalise on Beck's CCSH – Cognitive Content Specificity hypothesis (Alford and Beck 1997).

The following exchange from a supervision session highlights the pitfalls of a transdiagnostic approach:

*Supervisee*: I have got this really complex case.
*Supervisor*: How do you mean 'complex'?
*Supervisee*: There's lots going on.
*Supervisor*: How do you mean 'lots'?
*Supervisee*: PTSD, substance abuse, maybe personality disorder.
*Supervisor*: How is that 'lots'?
*Supervisee*: Well, I've got to look at the underlying causes and tackle those.
*Supervisor*: Would you expect a medic to take that approach if you had cancer, heart disease and diabetes?
*Supervisee*: Well, no.
*Supervisor*: What's the difference?
*Supervisee*: Well, its simpler to do it transdiagnostically.
*Supervisor*: It is always simple to create a rule of thumb to speed up conceptualisation and the treatment of clients, such as '5 foot 5 inches and above get intervention "X", those below intervention "Y"'. The question is whether there is an evidence base supporting the rule of thumb?
*Supervisee*: What else could I do?
*Supervisor*: Have a look at Figure 7.2 for the conceptualisation of a similar sort of case and the specific interventions that flow from it.

There is no empirical evidence that where there is comorbidity, even extensive comorbidity (as discussed above), that it is not possible simultaneously to interweave disorder-specific protocols. This is not to say that considerable effort may not be needed to delineate the terrain of the client's difficulties, but this can stop comorbid clients having to go through a revolving door of therapeutic endeavours.

## SUMMARY

1. The norm is that if PTSD is present, it is only part of a client's difficulties.
2. The more additional disorders that a PTSD client suffers from, the greater the overall impairment.
3. Clients should be screened for a wide range of disorders. Reliable assessment involves asking questions about each symptom that comprises a disorder.
4. It cannot be assumed that simply tackling PTSD will result in a resolution of the additional disorders.
5. Common comorbidities with PTSD are depression, panic disorder, substance abuse and borderline personality disorder. There are evidence-based CBT protocols for each of these disorders.
6. Example treatment strategies for:

   i. PTSD – managing intrusions, dares and managing trauma-related guilt

   ii. Depression – activity scheduling, MOOD management

   iii. Panic disorder – de-catastrophising and dares

   iv. Substance abuse – motivational interviewing, targeting distress tolerance and emotional dysregulation

   v. Borderline personality disorder – problem solving and imagery re-scripting

7. There is no empirical evidence that it is not possible to interweave evidence-based CBT protocols for different disorders when clients present with comorbidity.
8. There is no empirical evidence that a transdiagnostic approach to PTSD and associated disorders is any more effective than a diagnostic approach. It remains to be elaborated as to which transdiagnostic treatment strategy works with which transdiagnostic process.
9. Supervision is particularly important in dealing with clients with PTSD and significant comorbidity and should include role-playing the difficulties encountered.

# Part Two

## PRINCIPAL DISORDERS OTHER THAN PTSD

# Chapter Eight

## SUB-SYNDROMAL PTSD AND PHOBIAS

*Emotional disorders exist on a continuum and it is necessarily somewhat arbitrary to decide that having 'x' number of symptoms or above of a disorder means that the disorder is present, but having, say, 'x-1' symptoms means that it is not present. This has led to use of the term 'sub-syndromal' to describe the situation in which a person falls just short of the requisite number of symptoms for a disorder. In the case of PTSD, sub-syndromal cases are almost as common as cases of the full condition. Clients with sub-syndromal PTSD deserve attention as sufferers are almost as impaired as those with full PTSD and a small minority of the former progress to the latter, 'delayed PTSD'. Sub-syndromal PTSD itself shades into a specific phobia and the CBT treatment strategies for both are considered in this chapter.*

Sub-syndromal PTSD is not officially recognised in *DSM IV TR* (American Psychiatric Association 2000), however it is proposed that it is given a diagnostic status in *DSM V* (American Psychiatric Association, in press) as a subtype of adjustment disorder: 'acute stress disorder/post-traumatic stress disorder subtype' (Strain and Friedman 2011). PTSD, sub-syndromal PTSD and a trauma-related phobia arguably exist on a continuum of trauma responses and, as such, the cut-offs are somewhat arbitrary. From a clinical point of view the PTSD programme described in Chapters 3–7 may be appropriate not only for PTSD but also for severe sub-syndromal PTSD. 'Severe' may be defined as having at least two of the following symptoms of hyperarousal: difficulty falling or staying asleep, irritability or outbursts of anger, difficulty concentrating, hypervigilance or an exaggerated startle response (these are the hyperaousal symptoms specified in the ICD–10 (World Health Organisation 1992) criteria for PTSD), as well as the person being very upset at reminders. Case examples of the application of the PTSD programme to severe sub-syndromal PTSD are described in this chapter. For the milder sub-syndromal PTSD or phobia, trauma-focused CBT (TFCBT) (phase two of the PTSD programme) is unlikely to be necessary and may result in a re-traumatisation of the client and premature disengagement from treatment. For this population, the first phase of the PTSD programme, Stress Inoculation Training including behavioural experiments, is likely to be more appropriate. There can, however, be some movement between categories along the continuum. For example, it is not uncommon for a client with a phobia undergoing exposure treatment to initially develop many PTSD symptoms and it may be necessary to revert to a programme for the latter.

Clients with a sub-syndromal level of PTSD should not be regarded as below the threshold of concern. Cukor et al. (2010) found that almost 10% of helpers after the World Trade Center disaster suffered sub-syndromal PTSD. While 75% of these subsequently recovered 12.5% did not, and the remaining 12.5% developed full PTSD. In a longitudinal study of motor vehicle accident (MVA) survivors, Buckley et al. (1996) found that all those who developed delayed onset PTSD had an initial diagnosis of sub-syndromal PTSD. Interestingly, they were significantly lower in social support and had more overall distress than those with sub-syndromal PTSD who did not develop delayed onset. In practice, the full PTSD programme has been applied to those with PTSD and those with more severe sub-syndromal PTSD, and Maercker et al. (2006) found that 67% of this composite group of MVA survivors no longer met diagnostic criteria at post CBT treatment. There were nine clients with sub-syndromal PTSD pre-treatment (Maercker et al. 2006), only two of which were still sub-syndromal at the end of the CBT programme, with the other seven having fully recovered. By contrast, there were twelve clients with full PTSD pre-treatment: two clients had sub-syndromal PTSD at the end of treatment, three still had full PTSD, and seven had fully recovered. Comparable results were found by Blanchard et al. (2003) in an earlier study of road traffic accident victims, on the same diagnostic populations, using a CBT protocol.

The conventional wisdom is that phobias are easily treated, but the evidence base is less compelling. Choy et al. (2007) cite only eight studies that included a control condition and these studies addressed only a limited range of phobia subtypes (i.e. animal phobia, water phobia, height phobia, flying phobia and claustrophobia). When a phobia is triggered by a trauma, the person may in addition suffer disturbing intrusions as reminders and this may require an approach that goes beyond the usual exposure treatment for a phobia. Handley et al. (2009) treated clients with a travel phobia following the London bombings of 7 July 2005, differentiating phobics from phobics + distressings intrusion. Those with an uncomplicated travel phobia were treated using *in vivo* behavioural experiments to test out their fears, while those additionally troubled by intrusions had elements of PTSD treatment included. By the end of the treatment all ten clients who had completed treatment had overcome their travel phobia.

Sub-syndromal PTSD and a trauma-induced specific phobia are overlapping constructs (Figure 8.1). Sub-syndromal PTSD sufferers and those suffering the full disorder are, by definition, disturbed by intrusions of the trauma. By contrast, sufferers from a phobia, if distressed by flashbacks at all, are likely to do so only

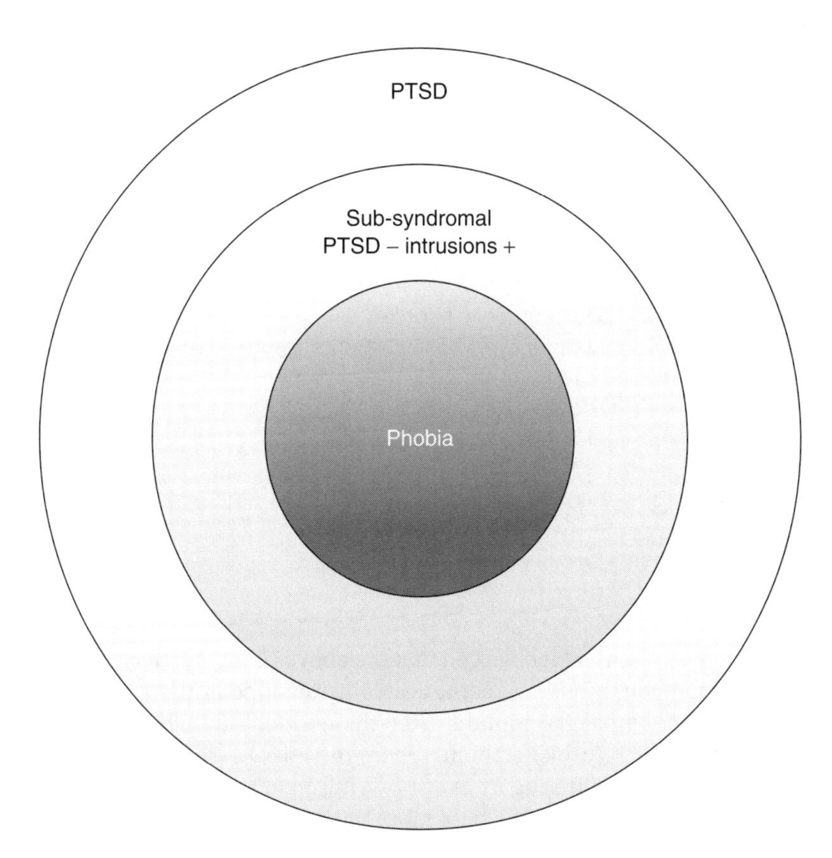


**Figure 8.1** Diagnostic Overlap between PTSD, Sub-syndromal PTSD and Trauma-related Phobia

on encountering reminders. Thus the programme described in the previous chapters for full PTSD are likely to be applicable to varying degrees to those with sub-syndromal PTSD and those with a phobia.

The following case example illustrates the approach taken.

Maria was at home in a back room downstairs, with her two children, Andrea (aged 13) and Andrew (age 5) asleep upstairs, when she heard the screeching of brakes and an 'explosion' as a car crashed through the front of her house. Glass flew everywhere. She remembers being 'frozen', hearing screams from the car and then her daughter screaming at her and holding her son's hand. She told them to go out the back door to a neighbour's house. When she looked at the teenagers in the car the two front-seat passengers were covered in blood. One was making no sound at all and the other a

*(Continued)*

*(Continued)*

strange sound. The backseat passengers were screaming, but then got out of the car and ran off. She came to the appointment with her husband, Mike, who had been on shift work on the night of the accident. It emerged that he felt slightly guilty that he had not been there for the family at the time of the accident. The following is an extract from the initial assessment interview:

*Therapist*: Have you been unusually irritable?
*Maria*: [*looking at her husband*] You had better ask him that.
*Mike*: Snappy, I'd say.
*Maria*: I'm a lot better than I was, though. I'm OK in the house of a day and I don't get the nightmares so much. I'm worse, though, when you are on nights. If I hear those boy racers and I have to look out of the front window.
*Mike*: But you won't stay in the front room.
*Maria*: Well, no.

From the initial assessment it emerged that the above client met diagnostic criteria for PTSD for about four months after the accident. Her appointment with a therapist did not take place until nine months after the accident, by which time she had moved back into her refurbished home. From the initial assessment it transpired that she was currently suffering from a sub-syndromal level of PTSD. The content of the client's preoccupation was now more with what could have happened – 'I could have been in the front room with the kids and we could have all been killed' – rather than what did happen – 'Seeing the front-seat passengers, heads drooped like dolls'. Clients with a sub-syndromal level of PTSD may usually be spared the discomfort of a trauma-focused approach because the trauma itself tends not to be the focus and a coping skills approach may well suffice. The exchange continued:

*Maria*: I won't stay in bed by myself, the kids are in with me.
*Therapist*: What, when Mike is at home as well?
*Mike*: Oh yes.
*Maria*: I know I shouldn't. They are very clingy. I have to push my daughter to go to school and she doesn't play out with her friends like she used to. Andrew keeps saying he has got a sore tummy before school.
*Mike*: You've got them a nervous wreck.
*Maria*: [*in tears*] No I haven't. I've got to look after them. You weren't there!
*Mike*: So it is my fault now! I can hear the kids creating mayhem in the waiting room, I had better go and sort them out.
*Therapist*: Bring them both in. There are some useful strategies both you and they might like to try.

The above exchange illustrates how the whole dynamics of a family can be affected by a trauma without any one of them currently suffering from full PTSD. The therapist has flexibly used the session to involve all family members in treatment. The session continued:

*Andrea*: It's not my fault, he just wanted to come in [*a reference to Andrew, who instantly went over and snuggled into his mother*].
*Maria*: It's OK, it's OK.
*Therapist*: Andrew, can you do some 'dares'?
*Andrew*: [*Looking up*] Hmm.
*Therapist*: Would you dare to go over to my window, look out and see if there are any dinosaurs coming?
*Andrew*: There are no dinosaurs coming!
*Therapist*: Are you sure?
*Andrew*: OK, I'll go and see [*and he proceeds to the window. After a minute says ...*] ... there are none there.
*Therapist*: Maybe they are coming over the top of the buildings opposite?
*Andrew*: [*laughing*] They are not.
*Therapist*: When you go into your Mum's bed, is it because you think the dinosaurs are coming?
*Andrew*: No.
*Therapist*: Then what is coming?
*Andrew*: Nothing.
*Therapist*: You dared to go to my window, could you do other dares like staying in your bed like a big boy, and for each dare you could have a star.
*Andrew*: A big star?
*Therapist*: Yes. [*then turning to Maria*] One of the key features of treatment is getting people to gradually dare to do what they are avoiding.
*Maria*: I know, I should let the kids play in the front room. But I just imagine us all being killed.
*Therapist*: Maybe a dare might be to all play a game of snap in the front room. Just small dares to begin with.
*Maria*: I suppose I could, but I just imagine the worse.
*Therapist*: Is imagining the worst any different from imagining the dinosaurs are coming?
*Maria*: The worst could happen.
*Mike*: But it has never happened in the ten years of living there and the Council have put bollards outside now.
*Therapist*: What you could do is practise switching attention from the horror video of what could have happened to a reality video of what would most likely happen outside your house tonight.
*Maria*: People coming out of the local club after closing shouting their goodnights to each other as if they all had hearing difficulties. It's a miracle one of them wasn't hit passing by.

In the above exchange the therapist has used another family member to model appropriate coping strategies ('dares') and in addressing a child's need has done so at the appropriate developmental level. Further, the distinctive feature of the sub-syndromal PTSD – a pre-occupation with a 'horror rather than reality video' – is addressed.

The therapist noted that Andrea had been silent throughout this exchange and asked her whether she would like to talk about how she had been affected either by herself or with one or other of her parents present, and she elected to talk with just her father present. It emerged that she had suffered from separation anxiety disorder since the incident. She felt that she needed to be around her mother to protect her but was also fearful of going to school because a brother of the driver of the car was in the year above her. The therapist arranged for her to be seen by a therapist from the Child and Adolescent Mental Health Team. At Maria's third treatment session the following dialogue took place:

*Maria*: I'm still in a lather of sweat when I hear the screech of brakes outside.
*Therapist*: Do you get an image at the same time?
*Maria*: Yes, if it is night time and I can hear the 'explosion' and see the glass flying everywhere.
*Therapist*: So what would be the actual story with the last car that screeched its brakes?
*Maria*: I don't know, probably a young guy showing off with his girlfriend.
*Therapist*: So not as young as those in the accident?
*Maria*: No.
*Therapist*: Do you think this guy with his girlfriend would have jumped the next set of lights or been involved in an accident?
*Maria*: Probably not.
*Therapist*: So in preparing for the next time you hear the screeching of brakes you could play a video of a guy showing off with his girlfriend passing your house, stopping at the traffic lights and not being involved in an accident.
*Maria*: OK.
*Therapist*: I'd like to write this in the second row of the Self-Instruction Training Form [see *Appendix E*]. The third row is for what you say to yourself when you actually come across the reminder. What could you put there?
*Maria*: I could give him a name, tell myself 'Pat is passing' and he's just wanting a good night out with his girlfriend. He's not trying to kill me and the kids.
*Therapist*: OK. What about the fourth row when you are feeling overwhelmed?
*Maria*: I just need to tell myself, don't be daft there's bollards there now. I wouldn't ring the emergency services right now so I can't really believe there is that much danger.

The focus in the above exchange is on refining the client's coping skills rather than a direct focus on the trauma. At subsequent sessions the coping skills approach was applied not only to reminders, but also to the client's irritability and fear of sleeping alone. The coping skills are reviewed and refined at each session. Only if they bear no fruit is there a switch to a trauma-focused intervention. The client's son had a simple phobia about sleeping alone and this was tackled by having other family members gradually getting him to dare to do what he had been avoiding, which is the core element of treating a phobia.

## SUMMARY

1. Clients who have disturbing intrusions of trauma but have either too few avoidance or too few hyperaousal symptoms have been labelled as suffering from a sub-syndromal level of PTSD.
2. While clients with sub-syndromal PTSD are less impaired than those with full PTSD, they are nevertheless significantly impaired and deserving of therapeutic attention. A small minority of those suffering from sub-syndromal PTSD go on to develop full PTSD – 'delayed PTSD'.
3. CBT treatment of those with the severest sub-syndromal PTSD should resemble that for full PTSD, but for others a non-trauma-focused CBT approach is recommended.
4. While CBT is of demonstrated effectiveness with specific phobias, there has been little research on the effectiveness of the treatment of trauma-induced specific phobias.
5. The treatment of trauma-induced specific phobias should follow the standard behavioural exposure protocols for specific phobias. However, it may also be necessary to draw on some of the strategies used in non-trauma-focused CBT for PTSD.

# Chapter Nine

## PROLONGED DURESS STRESS DISORDER

*Symptoms of PTSD can rise from prolonged stressors, such as bullying at work or caring for a relative with a progressive neurological disorder, that are not extreme enough to qualify as triggers for PTSD. This symptom profile has been termed prolonged duress stress disorder (PDSD). For example, a victim of bullying at work might suffer flashbacks/ nightmares of the bullying and avoid the workplace. The difference between PTSD and PDSD may be a question of degree. Treatment of PDSD can profitably reflect the treatment of PTSD.*

Some clients, while they have not been exposed to 'earthquakes' as such, have, as it were, experienced repeated storm damage from, say, prolonged bullying at work or caring for a relative with a progressive neurological disorder and may show all the symptoms of PTSD but without the extreme trauma. Scott and Stradling (1994) have termed this condition prolonged duress stress disorder (PDSD). Marsh (2003) found that both PTSD and PDSD imagery elicit physiological responses but these are more readily and more strongly evoked by the former than the latter. These findings suggest that the physiological differences between PTSD and PDSD may be only a matter of degree. Although PDSD is not recognised in *DSM IV TR* (American Psychiatric Association 2000), it is proposed that in *DSM V* (American Psyciatric Association, in press) the category of adjustment disorder be reserved as referring to stress response syndromes, one subtype of which is a response to non-traumatic stressors (Strain and Friedman 2011). It seems likely, therefore, that PDSD will be subsumed under an adjustment disorder subtype. Such cases can be treated within a PTSD framework but empirical evidence for the efficacy of this approach awaits research. The following case illustrates a CBT approach to PDSD.

Nuala worked at a GP surgery as a receptionist/administrative assistant. She enjoyed her contact with the public but after being there a few weeks she began to be bullied by the Practice Manager and to a lesser degree by the Assistant Practice Manager. On several occasions she complained to the Senior Partner who was 'very polite and nice' and told her on one occasion not to take the Practice Manager too seriously – 'Her bark is worse than her bite' – and on another occasion that 'She is good with her kids'. She worked at the surgery for a year and towards the end of that period was vomiting in the toilet at work. At assessment Nuala recalled several incidents, and said that the first time she was harangued by the Practice Manager was when she told her she could not help with the end-of-year accounts on a particular day because they were very short staffed in reception, and was told emphatically and with a pointed finger 'You do what I tell you to do'. She was then told off for wearing too much make up – 'You look like a tart'. The Assistant Manager met her in the toilets, saw her crying and said 'If you don't like the heat in the kitchen, get out'. Nuala was referred to a CBT therapist after being off work for nine months. She had dreams of the Practice Manager almost every night which would feature her scolding her with a pointed finger, but sometimes the dreams were in other locations than the surgery. Nuala reported that the Practice Manager's voice was constantly in her head and she could not bear to utter the name of the Practice Manager and referred to her simply as 'K'. Her husband, who accompanied her to the interview, said that her name was in fact Katrina. From a symptom point of view she met the diagnostic criteria for PTSD and since going off sick would not go out alone. Technically, Nuala's job was still open. Nuala had no previous psychiatric history.

This client was given a copy of *Moving on after Trauma* (Scott 2008) and it was suggested that she read about Bob, who also suffered from PDSD after being bullied at work. At the next session the following dialogue ensued:

*Therapist*: How did you get on reading about Bob?

*Nuala*: Like Bob's manager, 'K' is still bullying me even though I'm not at work. I'm letting her intimidate me into not going out and maybe like Bob I should just get angry, say 'I'm not having it', and get out there.

This exchange illustrates that though in CBT emotion is usually changed via cognitions and behaviour, it is also possible to replace one emotion with another, in this case sadness with anger. Reading about someone else who has undergone similar tribulations and successfully taken active steps to overcome them lessens isolation and increases the sense of self-efficacy. The dialogue continued:

*Therapist*: Getting out there, with gradual dares, sounds a great idea, but if you do it too quickly it can backfire.
*Nuala*: No, I don't think that I will ever go back to the surgery.
*Therapist*: How might you start joining in with life?
*Nuala*: Maybe just ringing friends. I should ring my sister but she's a physiotherapist and she will just go on at me for not having made a formal complaint. She means well but ...
*Therapist*: Sounds a bit like 'K'?
*Nuala*: That's what it feels like when she starts, but I know she is not. Any raised voice just sets me off.
*Therapist*: So if a person isn't absolutely nice they are put in the 'K' box? Forgive the pun, but the 'OK' box is left empty. You might get people into the 'OK' box by noting a similarity with 'K' – say, a raised voice – but spelling out the differences.
*Nuala*: Should have done this last night. My husband was getting a dish out of the oven and burnt himself, said some expletives and I just shouted at him for shouting. I wasn't bothered that he had burnt himself. I don't know how he puts up with me. He does belong in the 'OK' box.
*Therapist*: Did anything else strike you from reading *Moving on after Trauma*?
*Nuala*: Yes, the way I 'stew' on what happened.
*Therapist*: One way of not stewing is to postpone thoughts of 'K' to a special time when you spend a few minutes a day writing her a letter that you don't post. After a few weeks it becomes boring and you don't dream about what has become boring.
*Nuala*: I don't know that I would dare to. I suppose somehow I think she would 'get me', I know it is stupid.
*Therapist*: We could do an experiment to see if she does get you, because of daring to write, say, a description of what she looks like here and now. Here's a piece of paper.
*Nuala*: I can't.
*Therapist*: Not even a few words.
*Nuala*: OK [*she begins to write*].
*Therapist*: What have you written?
*Nuala*: 'Forty and frumpy'.

The above dialogue illustrates the need to titrate the dose of exposure treatment with PDSD as much as with PTSD. Similarly, as with the treatment of PTSD, behavioural experiments are used in the treatment of PDSD as a more compelling way of contradicting negative predictions than persuasion. At the next session the following exchange took place:

*Therapist*: How did you get on writing about what happened and its effects?

*Nuala*: When I was writing I realised how much I've let everything slide. I don't do any baking with the grandchildren, don't go the shops. It's stupid the way I have let myself go. I went with my husband, Tony, back to the Cardiac Rehab Unit for his check up and I saw a notice there for volunteers, so I took a form, filled it in while waiting for his appointment, and handed it to the lady who said they would telephone me for an appointment to see what sort of things I might do. When I came out I couldn't believe what I had done. Tony said I nearly gave him another heart attack!

*Therapist*: Great, because it had been as if you saw working at the surgery as the only route to happiness and now you are saying there are other routes to a sense of achievement and pleasure, making cakes with the children, voluntary work. It's gradually daring yourself to do things again.

*Nuala*: Yesterday the grandchildren stayed over. We were going to have breakfast but then I realised we had run out of bread so I went the shops. Mary who works there said she had not seen me for 18 months and we had a great chat for one and a half hours. The kids were starving when I got home with the bread!

*Therapist*: Seems the more you do, the better you feel.

*Nuala*: Yes.

The above dialogue indicates the need to address the depression that is an inevitable concomitant of the PDSD by activity scheduling. Further, the daily scheduled writing about the prolonged non-extreme stressor is an antidote to depressive rumination.

## SUMMARY

1. Clients can meet the symptom criteria for PTSD without experiencing the objectively extreme trauma required in the DSM criteria, for example as a result of prolonged bullying or caring for a relative with a progressive neurological disorder.
2. Both PTSD and PDSD imagery evoke a physiological response but it is stronger in the former. The difference between the disorders may be a question of degree.
3. PDSD can be treated using either a trauma-focused CBT approach or non-trauma-focused CBT protocol.

# Chapter Ten

## CHRONIC ADJUSTMENT DISORDER

*An adjustment disorder diagnosis is used to describe a person destabilised by an identifiable stressor. Historically, it has been a 'dustbin category', to be used only when no other disorder has been identified. Unsurprisingly there has therefore been little research on the effective treatment or measurement of adjustment disorder. Yet clients commonly present with adjustment disorders, from a wide variety of stressors, such as needlestick injury or loss of a job. In this chapter the CBT treatment of a person with a chronic adjustment disorder is illustrated.*

Inappropriate use of an adjustment disorder label can mean that clients miss out on evidence-based CBT treatments for specific mood and anxiety disorders. In a study of 145 non-psychotic clients attending community clinics, Shear et al. (2000) found that 58 had been diagnosed as having an adjustment disorder using a routine open-ended psychiatric interview. By contrast, when the 'gold standard' SCID (First et al. 1997a) was used, only five met criteria for an adjustment disorder. (The SCID asks one or more questions about each symptom that comprises a disorder and specifies the criteria for judging whether that symptom is present at a clinically significant level.) In addition, the SCID identified 22 sufferers from PTSD while the routine interview identified only one. An adjustment disorder diagnosis can be nothing more than a convenient label if it is used simply to describe social or occupational impairment following an identifiable stressor. In fact, *DSM IV TR* (American Psychiatric Association 2000) stipulates that this diagnosis should not be used unless it is first established that the person is *not* suffering from another Axis I disorder such as depression or PTSD.

It seems likely that in *DSM V* (American Psychiatric Association, in press) adjustment disorders will be reconceptualised as stress response syndromes, clients with sub-syndromal PTSD will be referred to as suffering from adjustment disorder, an acute stress disorder/post-traumatic stress disorder subtype, while clients suffering debility following non-traumatic stressors would constitute another adjustment disorder subtype (Strain and Friedman 2011). Historically, there has been a dearth of research on adjustment disorders, but with the advent of specific subtypes in *DSM V* this may change resulting in more specific treatment protocols.

The following example of a client's debility following a needlestick injury would probably be classified as an adjustment disorder in both *DSM IV* and *DSM V*. While there has been no randomised controlled trial of the efficacy of CBT for adjustment disorder, it is possible to utilise CBT strategies in treatment and these are made explicit in the following example.

Marina was employed as a cleaner for a local bus company. She put her hand down the side of a seat as she readjusted it and pricked her right thumb on a needle and it bled. She went with a colleague to rinse the wound and then to her Manager, who advised her to go immediately to the organisation's Occupational Health Service which was based at the local hospital. Marina was referred to a CBT therapist by the OH service four months after the incident. She complained of irritability, tension, sleep disturbance and agitation, and no longer had a physical relationship with her husband for fear of HIV transmission. Though she had many of the symptoms of generalised anxiety disorder (GAD), she lacked the defining characteristic of GAD uncontrollable worry about a wide range of matters. The focus of her worry was simply on the possibly dire consequences of the needlestick injury and she was considered to have been suffering from an adjustment disorder. However, OH informed her that she could not be given the all-clear with regard to possible infection until a point six months after the injury. Thus the needlestick injury constituted a chronic stressor lasting six months, and rather than being given a diagnosis of acute adjustment disorder she was given a diagnosis of chronic adjustment disorder. She did not have flashbacks or nightmares of the needlestick injury itself, though she was very cautious in her work and was alarmed when the OH nurse told her that they see a cleaner a month with a needlestick injury. The initial evaluation of Marina was not confined to diagnosis but also included questioning about her relationships and history. She was grateful for the detailed diagnostic questioning as it allowed her for the first time to express the breadth of her difficulties and the questioning about her symptoms made her feel more 'normal', while at the same time illuminating further relationship problems.

The treatment of clients with a chronic adjustment disorder is similar to that of clients with PTSD in that it begins with a normalisation of their responses, as in the following exchange:

*Therapist*: If you had had a needlestick injury and were skipping down the street that would be weird.

*Marina*: I know, but I don't want to be bothered with my husband or family. It is not fair to them. I just go off into my own world, then get cross when I'm interrupted.

*Therapist*: Maybe they would be better company than your own thoughts.

*Marina*: I just go over and over what might happen, then get busy to distract myself. I got in a state when I thought my right thumb was swollen. When I went to see my GP he said it looked OK to him. I came out reassured, but by the time I got home I thought he wasn't that interested as his last words were 'You can get needlestick injuries very easily in this job'. So I went and saw Occupational Health again and by the time I got there I was in a state. That is how they came to send me to you.

In this dialogue the therapist has used cognitive restructuring to help re-frame the client's interpersonal cognitions but the origin of the interpersonal difficulties appears to lie in rumination on a worst-case scenario. The exchange continued:

*Therapist*: If something is likely, it is probably worth worrying about. How likely is it that you have been infected?

*Marina*: I will not know for another two months.

*Therapist*: So two months' time is when you can be certain whether you have been infected or not, but at this moment what are the odds?

*Marina*: My husband went on the internet about it and he says it is very unlikely.

*Therapist*: What did Occupational Health say at the last visit?

*Marina*: They were very nice and said don't worry so.

*Therapist*: So despite reassurance from your GP, husband and Occupational Health you still agonise about the worst case?

*Marina*: Yes.

*Therapist*: Sounds like seeking reassurance doesn't work?

*Marina*: No.

*Therapist*: I think that you might be addicted to seeking reassurance and that is making it worse?

*Marina*: Well, what else do I do?

*Therapist*: It is a question of finding something reasonably convincing to tell yourself but then not picking at it to try to reach the impossible, the feeling of absolute certainty. Put your right thumb alongside the left. Is the right thumb any bigger than the left?

*Marina*: No.

*Therapist*: What do you make of that?
*Marina*: I suppose my right thumb cannot be infected if the right is no bigger than the left.

In the above dialogue the therapist has identified intolerance of uncertainty as a therapeutic target. It has also become apparent that the client has bypassed her critical analyses of the situation by a reliance on the views of others around her – peripheral processing. The therapist has used Socratic dialogue to ensure she is centrally processing the data as peripheral processing does not result in lasting change (see Petty and Cacioppo 1986). Over the first three sessions the therapist introduced the client to strategies that are particularly useful for clients with adjustment disorders: the use of a worry time technique to contain the amount of time she spent thinking of the consequences of the trauma, a traffic light routine for the management of anger, and investment in pre-injury activities. The fifth treatment session took place three weeks after she had received the all clear with regard to possible infection, when the following dialogue ensued:

*Marina*: Although I'm so relieved that I have been given the all clear, things are still not right with my husband.
*Therapist*: How is that?
*Marina*: We are still in separate bedrooms.
*Therapist*: Why is that?
*Marina*: I think it has just become habit now.
*Therapist*: What stops you saying you are moving back?
*Marina*: I think he thinks I am dirty.
*Therapist*: How do you know he thinks that?
*Marina*: I just do, he's been so irritable.
*Therapist*: What other explanations might there be for his irritability?
*Marina*: I have been a 'cow' and he's just retaliated.
*Therapist*: You might find it useful to read about mind-reading and jumping to conclusions in *Moving on after Trauma* (Scott 2008: 98), and you can also read about another person there with an adjustment disorder and how they handled it.

The above dialogue illustrates that a chronic adjustment disorder does not immediately resolve when the chronic stressor comes to an end, but that there may be ongoing debility that needs addressing. Technically, according to *DSM IV TR* (American Psychiatric Association 2000), a diagnosis of adjustment disorder cannot be made if the debility persists for six months beyond the stressor or if it is a chronic stressor for no more than six months after the chronic stressor is at an end.

## SUMMARY

1. The key feature of an adjustment disorder is debility following an identifiable stressor. However, it is a diagnosis of 'last resort' and clients must not meet diagnostic criteria for another disorder.
2. Adjustment disorders are likely to be reconceptualised in *DSM V* (American Psychiatric Association, in press) as an umbrella term for stress response syndromes. Subtypes of the disorder are likely to be specified, which may stimulate research on treatment which has been virtually non-existent.
3. CBT treatment of an adjustment disorder can usefully draw on elements of non-trauma-focused CBT for PTSD as well as depression protocols.

# Part Three

## SPECIAL POPULATIONS

# Chapter Eleven

# WORKING WITH TRAUMATISED CHILDREN

*The debility of children and youths following trauma can be easily missed by both parents and therapists. Many of the symptoms of PTSD, such as flashbacks, are internal, so that unless the child/youth is directly asked about them, disorder can go undetected. While parents are a useful source of information they have been found to be unreliable for assessing the diagnostic status of their child. The therapist also has to be aware that children show their distress in different ways at different ages. Children's appraisals of their initial symptoms predict PTSD and are therefore a prime target in CBT interventions. Parents can influence the course of a child's symptoms and therapy should be construed as a collaborative endeavour between the child, parent and therapist. In this chapter, the management of this triadic relationship is illustrated together with a developmentally appropriate way of conducting cognitive restructuring.*

Children's maladaptive appraisals play a mediating role between initial post trauma distress and the development and maintenance of PTSD (Meiser-Stedman et al. 2009a). The types of appraisal that play this pivotal role are embodied in the Child Post-traumatic Stress Cognitions Inventory (Meiser-Stedman et al. 2009b) and fall under two headings: 'disturbing and permanent change' and 'feeble person in a scary world'. For younger children it appears that cognitions focused around their vulnerability to further trauma are more salient, while for older children/youth it is the sense of having been irreparably damaged that appears more critical. However, it is not yet clear whether the same sets of maladaptive cognitions would also operate in children exposed to natural disasters or witnessing the horrors of riot or war. Nevertheless, the modification of maladaptive appraisals, of one type or another, is likely to be a needed central focus for CBT with children suffering from PTSD.

## FAMILY OR CHILD FOCUS?

In general, a child's behaviour is very much influenced by that of a parent and parental depression has been found to be associated with the development of PTSD in children. Parents may fuel PTSD in their child by seeing worry as a virtue and encouraging avoidance and hypervigilance (Meiser-Stedman et al. 2006). It is thus crucial to involve parents in treatment and ensure they are facilitating the therapeutic process rather than giving contrary messages. Unfortunately, if a parent was also subject to the same trauma as the child, it can make it doubly difficult to utilise that parent as 'the therapist in the community'. A parent's view of their child's functioning post trauma is often very different from that established by a diagnostic interview with the child alone (Shemesh et al. 2005), as parents may not always know the extent of subjective distress and range of emotions that are experienced by the child. Further, parents may assume that because they are suffering from PTSD following a trauma that their child must be also. The discrepancies between parent and child reports are particularly marked for 12–19 year olds. It is essential, therefore, that the child has the opportunity to fully verbalise their distress unencumbered.

From a logistical point of view it is tempting to assess and treat the family as a homogeneous entity but this is fraught with difficulties, including divergent trauma responses, developmental differences, and relationships that may be less than supportive. However, a parent will inevitably attend a treatment session with a child and there will be certain commonalities (e.g. living in temporary accommodation following a house fire) so that a mix of individual and family group (or subgroup) sessions may be the most appropriate. It is recommended that each affected family member undergoes an individual assessment, albeit that at least one parent will be present when a child is assessed. With the agreement of family members, this can then be followed by a psychoeducational 'group' session in which the PTSD Survival Manual (see Appendix G) is introduced. Because of the likely age disparity in family members, the material to be taught makes use of the 'pictures' in the Manual and a group discussion is elicited after presentation of each picture, for example asking a child not to think about the 'Orangutan' in the Survival Manual illustrates easily the futility of cognitive avoidance. The teaching and discussion helps other family members to be able to understand what might be happening with parents/siblings. The 'group' session also teaches family members appropriate coping strategies and this in turn can affect the quality of support they give within the family. The psychoeducational group session can then be followed by individual sessions. Parents can also be recommended to read *Moving on after Trauma* (Scott 2008) to help understand how their expression of traumatisation may well be different from their child's.

## DEVELOPMENTALLY APPROPRIATE MANIFESTATIONS OF PTSD

Clarifying whether young children have been traumatised has been a difficult endeavour because some of the symptoms of PTSD, for example emotional numbness, present a major diagnostic problem in that the young child may not experience such a symptom or lack the verbal capacity to report it. Thus the apparent much lower rates of PTSD in young children may be more a reflection that the *DSM IV* diagnostic criteria are not developmentally sensitive enough rather than that young children are especially protected against the slings and arrows of outrageous fortune. The proposed *DSM V* diagnostic criteria for children less than 6 years are shown in Appendix I, Table 1 and for children 6 years and over in Appendix I, Table 2.

The thought of children suffering long-term psychological debility is emotionally very challenging for clinicians as well as parents and both may bypass a critical evaluation of the child with a rule of thumb that it 'will have washed over them, they are too young, and in any case they haven't said anything'. If a family has been subjected to a trauma, a child may wish to protect an affected parent by not mentioning the trauma. Unfortunately, from the range of traumas studied, such as bushfires, hurricanes, and motor vehicle accidents, spontaneous recovery from PTSD symptoms is not the norm (Pine and Cohen 2002), albeit that only a significant minority of those traumatised suffer from PTSD in the first place.

### Case Example

Martin, aged 10, was referred to the Child and Adolescent Mental Health Team (CAMHT) via his GP. Martin's mother, Agnes, was concerned that his school were complaining of his aggressive behaviour to other children and she found him clingy and verbally aggressive to her boyfriend. Agnes was herself undergoing CBT for PTSD with a counsellor from a local charity. Martin had two older brothers, Christopher (aged 15) and Karl (19). Christopher had had some help from the CAMHT which arose from his non-attendance at school. Mum had had concerns about Karl's withdrawn behaviour, but Karl had steadfastly refused to talk to anyone about his difficulties and he lived in his own flat away from Mum and his siblings.

The history reported by Mum was that her husband, Dan, showed no problems when they first got together and married, and he was a respected and well liked accountant. However, when she became pregnant with Karl, he became increasingly controlling, specifying what she should eat, and insisting that food was put away in cupboards just as he wished. Then when Karl was a toddler he began to show jealousy if she spoke to any man, including her male cousins. She kept his behaviour secret, partly out of loyalty to her husband and partly out of a feeling that she would not be believed by others as he was

*(Continued)*

*(Continued)*

so charming and respectable, and she became more and more depressed. There were many arguments and he broke her jaw. She was insistent to medical staff that she had simply fallen, her husband apologised, and matters improved over a six-month period. Then one evening she was late home and he accused her yet again of having an affair and she was subjected to further violence. He insisted that she drove him to violence and she was responsible for breaking up the family, that he was the true victim. Finally, she pressed charges against him and he was imprisoned for 18 months. On his release he was granted only supervised access to his children. He was busily contesting this, insisting that as he had not harmed the children he had a right to unsupervised access. At the time of his referral Martin had not seen his father for three years.

Martin reported that his father used to whisper in his ear and on one occasion had said 'I am going to kill Uncle Sam' (his mother's cousin). He was very upset by this. He had also whispered to Martin to be naughty when he saw Uncle Sam. Martin said that he was scared that if he did not do this Dad 'would come to school and get me'. He said that now he 'hears' Dad whispering to be naughty to Mum's boyfriend John, and because he is whispering 'be naughty, I do silly things like hit my brothers'. When Martin was asked had he told anyone outside the family about it he said: 'I don't want to talk about it because it's bad news. I think that if I told friends it would be bad luck for them and they might want to stay away from me.' He said that he was scared Mum and John would send him to his Dad's for Christmas.

A diagnostic interview was conducted using the *DSM IV TR* criteria and revealed that he had intrusive images of his father whispering in his ear and that if this occurred when he was in school it would stop him working for two minutes. (He thus met the criteria for a flashback in *DSM IV* and the proposed *DSM V*.) In view of his age, Martin believed that there was a very serious physical threat to his Uncle Sam and therefore met the gateway stressor criteria for PTSD. He said that he had bad dreams of being left alone in the house and nobody coming to help him, and insisted that this had happened to him when he was six years old (but it was doubtful whether these dreams were related to being told of his father's intent to kill his uncle, and in terms of *DSM IV* criteria this would be insufficient for endorsement of the dreams symptom. However, in the more developmentally appropriate proposed *DSM V* criteria he possibly would meet the dream criteria, in that for young children dreams do not necessarily have to have a recognisable content and these had persisted at least since his father's departure from the home). Martin met the cognitive avoidance criteria in both *DSM IV* and *DSM V*, but his rationale for avoiding talking about his father's behaviour would not be at all obvious to an adult and illustrates the need with children to have them explain the basis for their behaviours as it often involves magical thinking, which can be a later therapeutic target. The only other *DSM IV* avoidance symptom that Martin appeared to be suffering from was emotional numbness, which he described as 'empty a lot of the time, for a long time'. Thus in terms of the *DSM IV* criteria Martin had insufficient avoidance symptoms for a diagnosis of PTSD but with regard to the proposed *DSM V* criteria (see Appendix I.2) he had sufficient symptoms. With regard to hyperarousal (Cluster E in Appendix I.2), the following symptoms were identified: (i) Martin's Mum reported that at least once a week he would leave his own bed and get in bed with her, complaining of the pictures in his head; (ii) Martin was bad tempered at home and in school; and (iii) would look out of windows to check if Dad was coming. Martin had sufficient hyperarousal symptoms within both the *DSM IV* and proposed *DSM V* criteria. Using the *DSM IV* criteria, Martin would be regarded as suffering from a sub-syndromal level of PTSD but using the proposed *DSM V* criteria would be regarded as suffering from full PTSD.

Mum was also asked to complete the Eyberg Child Behaviour Inventory (ECBI) (Eyberg and Ross 1978), in which a parent indicates which of 36 difficulties they regard as a problem. The severity of each difficulty is also rated. The ECBI chiefly measures child non-compliance, though there are items related to stealing, lying, and bed wetting. Agnes identified 14 problems with Martin, twice the number most parents report with children of the same age, but these were confined to not doing what he was told.

## INITIAL SESSIONS

In treating a child it is necessary to ensure that not only is the child motivated but so too is the parent, as the latter is needed to act as a quasi-therapist in the community. This can be particularly difficult in cases were the parent has significant problems themselves and, as in the above case, is also undergoing treatment elsewhere. By the same token, however, the parent's self-esteem can be enhanced if they are empowered with skills to help their child. The following exchange took place between the therapist, Martin and his Mum at the first treatment session:

*Therapist*: *[looking at the PTSD Survival Manual; see Chapter Three, Figure 3.2]* Sometimes when very bad things happen, the alarm in your brain instead of staying over here to the left flips to the right and you feel as if you are in a war zone, feeling something bad is going to happen any time. So you might keep checking out of the window.

*Martin*: That's what I do.

*Therapist*: Do you find anything when you look out?

*Martin*: No.

*Therapist*: If you were in class and the fire alarm kept going off and each time everyone was marched into the playground, even in the rain and snow, what would you think?

*Martin*: Stupid school, shouldn't take any notice.

*Therapist*: Just like the school alarm may be faulty, you seem to have a faulty alarm. What would it be like if you tried to take no notice?

*Mum*: I could do with not taking notice of my alarm going off.

The above exchange illustrates the importance of using visual aids with children, avoiding abstractions and adopting detailed graphic imagery. A bonus of having a traumatised parent at the session with the child is that they can be an *in vivo* model of a taught coping strategy. The session continued:

*Therapist*: Martin, do not think of this picture [*pointing to the Orangutan*]. Now close your eyes. [*Therapist pauses for 15 seconds*] What were you thinking about when you had your eyes closed?
*Martin*: The funny monkey.
*Therapist*: Right, that is what happens when you try not to think of something, you think about it. So if you try not to think of Dad, you think about him.
*Martin*: Something bad might happen if I don't think about him.
*Therapist*: Were you thinking of your Dad this morning?
*Martin*: No, I was playing on my X Box.
*Therapist*: So nothing happened when you weren't thinking of your Dad?
*Martin*: No, can I play on your computer?
*Therapist*: Well, if first of all you draw me the faulty alarm, and the funny monkey and colour them in and I will print them off and you can take them home.

The above dialogue illustrates that it is possible to do cognitive restructuring with a child but it has to be kept as concrete as possible. Concepts such as cognitive avoidance are not taught directly, rather they are implied by tangible examples. With children, more effort than usual has to be spent on developing a therapeutic alliance with engagement in seemingly off-task behaviours, but if the therapist has media that excite the child's interest, such as a Tablet PC that allows drawing and printing and the translation of handwriting into text, this can be used by the child to underline what is being taught. But problems are not necessarily confined to PTSD and in the above case example it is his behaviour problems at home and in school that are more directly impinging on Mum. In engaging Mum as a quasi-therapist, these behavioural difficulties also need to be addressed. The first session continued:

*Therapist*: You've done a good drawing of the faulty alarm and the Orangutan, Martin. We can print them off now. [*Pause*] Have a draw now while I chat to Mum. [*Turning to Mum*] ...What I tried then with Martin was to apply Grandma's Law – 'When you have done ... then you can ...' – and it seems to be working. There's a whole set of strategies like that that we could look at and put in a Parent Survival Manual, just like we have got this PTSD Survival Manual, and you can write in it, say, how it worked out using Grandma's Law between the sessions and we can gradually adjust the strategies to get them right.
*Mum*: Surviving all the kids has been an ordeal.

*Therapist*: It's been a lot to cope with, but hopefully with the strategies you learn from the other therapist and from what you learn here we can make a definite difference.
*Mum*: I've got to give it a try.
*Therapist*: Martin, you've done some good drawings here. When you get home from school why don't you have a special time when you do some drawing and writing about whatever has been bothering you?
*Martin*: I could do.
*Therapist*: Would you bring them in for me?
*Martin*: OK.
*Therapist*: Maybe Mum could keep you going with a chocolate biscuit while you are doing it?
*Mum*: OK.
*Therapist*: [*Looking at Mum*] Just track what Martin is doing, don't take over. We can leave the questions until the next session.
*Mum*: Fine.

The second session begins, as with all succeeding sessions, with a review of homework. In these early sessions the therapist's focus is on distilling the child's trauma narrative. Clients want treatment for all their difficulties but it is inevitable sometimes that there is a division of labour between organisations. The danger is that some of the problems are not addressed and this may make progress impossible, or if progress is made relapse soon follows. Even within an organisation there can be zealots for PTSD or ADHD/Asperger's Syndrome and strategies for these problems may be applied indiscriminately without a comprehensive and thorough evaluation. In the case example part of the subsequent sessions were devoted to a behavioural parent treatment programme consisting of teaching, planned ignoring, positive reinforcement, time out and contracts, which are detailed in Scott (1989) and evaluated in Scott and Stradling (1990).

## MIDDLE SESSIONS

The focus in the middle sessions, as with adults suffering from PTSD, is on the reconstruction of the trauma narrative. But this reconstruction has to take place in a developmentally sensitive way, as illustrated by the following dialogue:

*Therapist*: The pictures you have drawn seem to be about your Dad coming to get you. He is in a van and you are just standing by the side of the road. Is that right?
*Martin*: Yes.

*(Continued)*

*(Continued)*

| | |
|---|---|
| *Therapist:* | Do you have any wolves where you live? |
| *Martin:* | [*with astonishment*] No! |
| *Therapist:* | Do you have any friend who is younger than you that you like to play with? |
| *Martin:* | My cousin Martha, she is four. |
| *Therapist:* | If you told Martha the story of the Big Bad Wolf, would she get scared? |
| *Martin:* | She might do, she would go running to her Mum and I would get into trouble. |
| *Therapist:* | Is there someone you play with who is older than Martha? |
| *Martin:* | Martha's brother, Isaac, he is six. |
| *Therapist:* | Would Isaac get scared if you told him the story of the Big Bad Wolf? |
| *Martin:* | No. |
| *Therapist:* | So when you are a bigger boy the story doesn't scare you, because you know it's just a story? |
| *Martin:* | Yes. |
| *Therapist:* | And if they said on TV a wolf had escaped from the zoo, what would you think or do? |
| *Martin:* | They would find him. |
| *Therapist:* | Would you keep looking out of the window and not go out to play? |
| *Martin:* | No. |
| *Therapist:* | Maybe you have turned Dad into the Big Bad Wolf, made a story about him and frightened yourself? [*At this point in the interview Martin cuddles up to Mum who soothes him.*] Could you think of your Dad the way Isaac thinks of the Big Bad Wolf? |
| *Martin:* | I could try. |

At succeeding sessions the child's ability to create and adopt an alternative narrative is reviewed. CBT is usually thought of as involving the identification of individual maladaptive thoughts and their modification but it can take place at the level of a story. This 'chunky' CBT is particularly appropriate with children. However, the MOOD chart (see Table 5.1) is sufficiently simple that it can be used with older children and treatment involves flexible movement from the micro to macro level. The following exchange took place at the fifth session:

| | |
|---|---|
| *Therapist:* | Martin, I noticed in the pictures you did you are always by yourself? |
| *Martin:* | Don't like being by myself. |
| *Therapist:* | What is going to happen if you are by yourself? |
| *Martin:* | Something horrible. |

Here there has been a shift in the child's narrative. The focus is no longer on the perpetrator of the trauma yet there is still a sense of vulnerability. The session continued:

*Therapist:* Martin, do you ever make things out of construction kits?
*Martin:* Sometimes I make cars.
*Mum:* You get the glue everywhere.
*Therapist:* When bad things happen you end up with a construction kit of pieces. [*Pointing to Figure 7 in the PTSD Survival Manual – Revised (see Appendix H)*] And then when you think of things that might happen you build something out of those pieces [*pointing to Figure 8*] but it is a mess, the pieces don't really fit together and you just get angry. You stick more and more glue on but it just gets more and more of a mess. Maybe when you think of things that might happen, you travel back in time, pick up the feeling you had when you thought Dad was going to kill Uncle Sam, and you travel forward with this feeling and this causes you to feel bad now.
*Martin:* Like in a Time Machine in Dr Who?
*Therapist:* Yes, when you are frightened you could say I've just gone back in my Time Machine and landed in the wrong place. I need to go back in my Time Machine to another place, pick up some good things, like Mum has never let me down, my Uncle Sam and cousins are always around, and then go forward to now. These are part of a proper construction kit [*pointing to Figure 9*] and with these pieces you can build something proper [*pointing to Figure 10*]. Maybe you could draw about the Time Machine and show it going back to different places and to now?
*Martin:* OK, I could be Dr Who.

The above exchange draws on the work of Schacter et al. (2007), which suggests that the brain is a prospective brain and that a main purpose of memory is to enable the future anticipation of events. In PTSD the mental time travel appears to be to the trauma rather than to the accumulation of instances that have been non-traumatic. It is important that the child is actively involved in the process of reconstruction and that the sessions are not didactic. One of the ways of ensuring this is by getting the child to draw and write. But older children can often deal with a degree of abstraction, as the following exchange illustrates:

*Mum:* He got really upset when John was staying overnight.
*Therapist:* What were you thinking, Martin?
*Martin:* Don't know.

*(Continued)*

*(Continued)*

| | |
|---|---|
| *Therapist:* | Do you ever watch slow action replays of a goal scored on a football game? |
| *Martin:* | Yes, I support Liverpool. |
| *Therapist:* | So if you weren't sure how Stephen Gerard had scored a goal you would watch a replay? |
| *Martin:* | Yes. |
| *Therapist:* | Well, when you suddenly feel unhappy it is like a goal has been scored against you, and you need to watch a replay of it to see how the ball got in the back of the net, then when you have found this you can do something else. |
| *Martin:* | Teacher told me not just to run after the ball but stay in defence. |
| *Therapist:* | So teacher came up with a better way for you to play? |
| *Martin:* | Yes. |
| *Therapist:* | Well, we can do the same with your first thoughts and come up with better second thoughts. [*The therapist then introduces and explains the headings in the MOOD chart (see Table 5.1)*]. |

In subsequent sessions the child's use of the MOOD chart is examined. It is also useful for the child and parent, if possible, to explain the MOOD Chart to the class teacher so that he/she can ensure that the child is using it there. Teachers in Years 4 and 5 may find the MOOD chart a useful tool for all the class.

## FINAL SESSIONS

The last three sessions should be planned with longer gaps between them, partly to lessen any dependence on the therapist but also to give the child ample opportunity to practise their new-found skills in a variety of settings. In these last sessions the focus is on a consolidation of learning and the distillation of a relapse prevention strategy. Given that the last three sessions are spread over a two- to three-month period the unexpected often happens and this can be used to underline previous learning, as the following dialogue at the penultimate session illustrates:

| | |
|---|---|
| *Mum:* | [*looking at Martin*] He's not happy, I'm not happy. |
| *Therapist:* | Why is that? |
| *Mum:* | His father has dropped his request for unsupervised access and now wants supervised access. I don't want any access, but my solicitor said it would be difficult for the Court to refuse supervised access unless an expert witness could testify it was harmful, but because of government |

cutbacks it is unlikely they would fund an expert. My therapist keeps insisting I write and talk about what his Dad did to me but I can't bring myself to do it and so I have stopped going to the sessions. I just left a message saying I have got a lot on at the moment. Martin is miserable as well.

*Therapist*: How do you feel about seeing your Dad with other people around?

*Martin*: Don't want to.

*Therapist*: Did you use the MOOD chart for trying to sort out the best way of playing this?

*Martin*: No.

*Mum*: I don't think I have helped. I've been too upset.

*Therapist*: Maybe if we run all this through the MOOD chart, we might come up with a better way of playing it. Shall we try that?

*Mum*: OK.

*Martin*: OK.

*Therapist*: So if we write in the first column of the MOOD chart that the upset is having to go to supervised access, what would we put in the second column? What would be so bad about that?

*Mum*: It would bring back all the memories.

*Martin*: Yes.

*Therapist*: And what would be so bad about all the memories coming back?

*Martin*: It will make bad things happen.

*Therapist*: You could write that in the second column. Now the third column – so if I think now about when I fell over in the school playground when I was ten and had to go to hospital, will that make me fall over when I go and make us a drink.

*Martin*: No.

*Therapist*: So does getting a memory of a bad thing make it happen?

*Martin*: No, it's just that I've gone in my Time Machine back to the bad thing and then forward with it. I need to get in my Machine and travel somewhere else and take that forward.

*Therapist*: Where could you travel to?

*Martin*: Playing with Martha and Isaac.

*Therapist*: So when you think of meeting your Dad with others around, including your Mum, you will get a bit frustrated because you will start off using the faulty construction kit, but then you could go back to thinking of playing with your cousins and forward to thinking of playing with them after you have seen him.

*Martin*: That's good.

*Therapist*: So in the third column on the MOOD chart you could say a better way of playing 'going to meet my Dad' is to switch my attention from the model I've built with the faulty kit to a model from a proper kit about playing with your cousins. You will be carrying two kits to the meeting so

*(Continued)*

*(Continued)*

just keep switching to the kit that works. Finally, in the fourth column, you might decide I've got my gameplan for the match, so no point in keep on going over it.

*Martin*: I should have used MOOD for this. We have been using it in class, though.

*Therapist*: [*Turning to Mum*] What we have done is to work on a coping strategy for reminders. It is also possible to swork on coping strategies for other things, such as dreams or situations you avoid, so you can have a coping skills approach to PTSD and you can see how far you get with this. It then may or may not be necessary to go on to the trauma-focused approach you have been doing with your therapist.

*Mum*: I could give that sort of thing a go.

The above exchange illustrates how in the final sessions the materials that have been taught are integrated and applied to 'hot' issues that make the learning memorable. The dialogue also highlights the importance of focusing almost as much on the parent when treating the child, as the former needs to be functioning sufficiently to perform a quasi-therapist and nurturing role to help ensure the maintenance of treatment gains.

## SUMMARY

1. Unless children and youths are directly asked about all the possible symptoms of debility, their distress is likely to go unrecognised and, at best, will be inappropriately treated.
2. Care has to be taken not to over rely on a parent's summary judgement of their child's difficulties.
3. The expression of post-trauma symptoms varies with the age of the child.
4. Children's appraisals of their initial distress predict the development and maintenance of PTSD.
5. While interventions have a common target – the cognitive restructuring of maladaptive appraisals – they have to be matched to the child's developmental level.
6. Parents can be part of the solution to a child's PTSD, but equally they can be part of the problem, particularly if they themselves are also suffering from depression or PTSD.
7. The therapist has to ensure that each of the members of the triad (parent, child and therapist) is working collaboratively.

# Chapter Twelve

## WORKING WITH TRAUMATISED CLIENTS WITH A SEVERE MENTAL ILLNESS

*Historically, clients with a Severe Mental Illness (SMI) have been considered too fragile for psychological interventions and have, at best, been provided with support. But multiple traumas are the common currency of those suffering from a SMI. In the last decade there have been some encouraging studies of the efficacy of CBT for clients with a dual diagnosis of PTSD and SMI. Interventions have, however, to be delivered flexibly and the therapist may, for example, have to work around periods of hospitalisation when the client's psychosis is florid.*

Severe Mental Illness (SMI) is an umbrella term covering schizophrenia, bipolar disorder and treatment refractory depression. Clients with an SMI have often had exposure to 'multiple earthquakes' – a study by Subica et al. (2012) found sufferers were on average exposed to over four types of traumatic events and 41% met diagnostic criteria for PTSD. Further, in the Subica et al. (2012) study, PTSD was found to mediate the relationship between trauma, depression, substance abuse, mental health and physical health among SMI sufferers, leading the authors to conclude that it should be 'aggressively targeted'. However, PTSD is only documented in the records of clients with SMI in a fraction of cases. The under-diagnosis can be rectified by using a standardised structured assessment (see Chapter Three). PTSD may have a direct deleterious effect on SMI by making the client distance themselves from health and care providers and an indirect negative effect by increasing the chances that the person will abuse drugs or alcohol (Resnick et al. 2003).

Teaching SMI clients with PTSD coping skills may be a productive non-threatening intervention. There is a concern that treatments such as prolonged exposure may over-arouse SMI clients and the preference has been for cognitive restructuring interventions. To date, cognitive restructuring approaches to treating PTSD among SMI clients have produced positive but very modest results. For example, Lu et al. (2009) found that PTSD diagnosis fell from 100% at baseline to 69% at post-treatment, suggesting significant room for improvement. Mueser et al. (2008) compared the effects of CBT with treatment as usual in a sample of clients with a dual diagnosis of PTSD and SMI (85% had a major mood disorder and 15% schizophrenia or a schizoaffective disorder) and concluded that clients can benefit from CBT, despite severe symptoms, suicidal thinking, psychosis and vulnerability to hospitalisations. These conclusions are particularly good news as 25% of the sample in the Mueser et al. (2008) study also had a borderline personality disorder. The effects of CBT were strongest in clients with severe PTSD. Homework completion in CBT predicted a greater reduction in symptoms. Changes in trauma-related beliefs in CBT mediated improvements in PTSD.

For clients with PTSD and SMI the SIT programme described in Chapter Four can be used in conjunction with the mood management strategies described in Chapter Five. Callcott et al. (2004) have also provided useful illustrative case examples of treating clients with PTSD and schizophrenia, drawing on materials used to treat Axis I and Axis II (personality) disorders in *DSM IV TR* (American Psychiatric Association 2000). These authors make the important point that the timing and speed of treatment has to be adjusted to take into account the psychotic symptoms. Nevertheless, these clients can be treated psychologically rather than what has happened historically, when they have simply been contained.

The following case example illustrates a coping skills approach:

Siobhan, who had been diagnosed as suffering from schizophrenia, was assaulted and then suffered PTSD in relation to the assault. There was also a question mark over whether she also suffered from Obsessive Compulsive Disorder as she was obsessed with picking up litter. While doing this on one occasion, a group of youths ridiculed her, one of them head-butted her, and she was kicked while on the ground. She reported that her primary school years were normal, she was very close to her mother, and her father had a slight drink problem. Unfortunately, just as she went into secondary school her mother was diagnosed with cancer and died when she was aged 13. Siobhan coped with the loss by using cannabis and became somewhat obsessive about tidiness and symmetry. Her father became alcohol-dependent. By the time she was 18 Siobhan had become paranoid, she was convinced that people were watching her and would report her to some government department, and she wrote some strange notes to the Department of Social Security. It was thought that her psychosis arose from her years of cannabis consumption. After the assault, her Community Psychiatric Nurse (the CPN) became concerned that Siobhan was isolating herself more and more, was becoming more fearful than ever of going out, and was not looking after herself but was spending her day drawing incessantly. It was thought that Siobhan was probably too fragile for TFCBT in relation to the assault and might either disengage or decompensate if it was attempted. Rather, a coping skills approach would be adopted that tackled not only the better management of intrusions, but would also focus on interpersonal problems and emotional dysregulation. The CPN had wanted Siobhan to see the CBT therapist at a GP surgery two miles away, but Siobhan was too fearful, feeling that she wouldn't be able to stand 'all those people looking at me in the waiting room'. However, it was agreed that the CBT therapist would work through the CPN, sending her emails about lines of approach. As such, the CPN took on a limited parenting/treatment role and the CBT therapist acted as Consultant. From the CBT therapist's point of view the set up was far from ideal, but it illustrates the sort of compromises that may be necessary in dealing with a client with an SMI.

The first difficulty that confronted the CPN/CBT therapist was that of presenting the client with a convincing rationale for a new approach for her difficultie. It was decided that it would be useful to give Siobhan the PTSD Survival Manual, to explain the 'Pebble in the Water' Model of PTSD in relation to the assault. As the CPN was reading through this section with Siobhan, she realised that the same model could also be applied to her psychotic symptoms. The CPN thought that it could be plausibly argued that the 'trauma' with regard to the psychotic symptoms was Siobhan's protracted and intense use of cannabis, resulting in intrusions of people huddled together talking about her. Her avoidance was an attempt to give them 'nothing to report'. She postulated that Siobhan then became fed up that she could not have a normal life, go to art galleries, etc., and her concentration and sleep were poor. Finally, the CPN thought it plausible that Siobhan had then developed a negative view of herself (the final 'ripple') – that she was 'a waste of space, just like my Dad'. The CPN shared this formulation with the CBT therapist, who was taken aback but thought it had great potential. However, the CBT therapist cautioned that it might be most potent if the credibility of the model was first established by demonstrating its fruitfulness with the PTSD symptoms related to the assault, then moving on to the psychotic symptoms.

Both the CPN and the CBT therapist had concerns about the possible re-traumatisation of the client by directly focusing on traumatic material and decided on a coping skills/metacognitive approach, at least in the first instance. The essence of the metacognitive approach involved a redefinition of the problem: that it was not so much that the client had intrusions of the assault but that it was her extreme reaction to those intrusions that needed to be targeted. The CPN and CBT therapist considered what might need to be necessary stepping stones towards the client adopting an adaptive metacognitive approach. They were both mindful that the presentation of a credible rationale would mean drawing on Siobhan's experiences. It was decided that the CPN would focus on Siobhan's artwork. The CPN noted that they were all of landscapes; no people featured. At her next visit to Siobhan the CPN made a distinction between a 'picture' of a landscape and an actual landscape by touching a landscape picture that Siobhan had drawn. The following dialogue ensued:

*CPN*: This grass, is it wet?'

*Siobhan*: I don't know, it is not real.

*CPN*: In PTSD there is a mix-up between the picture of what happened and reality.

*(Continued)*

*(Continued)*

| | |
|---|---|
| *Siobhan:* | What happened to me is real! |
| *CPN:* | But does the picture you get in your head of the assault mean that you and I shouldn't walk down to the corner shop together to buy some tea bags and washing up liquid? |
| *Siobhan:* | Could you do with a cup of tea? |
| *CPN:* | Yes, but if I took your picture seriously, I wouldn't be risking going to the corner shop. |
| *Siobhan:* | My mum had the kettle on all the time, let's go. |

In the above exchange the meaning given to an intrusive image is implicitly challenged by the setting up of a behavioural experiment, but reaching this point with clients with SMI often involves more than the usual apparently off-task chat, and some limited re-parenting. After returning from the shop the exchange continued:

| | |
|---|---|
| *CPN:* | What you have just done is a 'dare'. You can get your confidence up by doing 'dares'. That is what the second section of the Survival Manual is about, going up one step at a time with dares. |
| *Siobhan:* | I was only safe because I was with you. |
| *CPN:* | Who did we see that might have done something? |
| *Siobhan:* | Nobody really. |
| *CPN:* | Sounds like you were going by the picture in your mind rather than what was there. |
| *Siobhan:* | My imagination runs away with me. I wanted to pick up some litter behind me but I knew you wanted to get to the shop. If I'd been by myself I would have stopped to pick it up but that's how I got beat up. |

The above exchange indicates that although the treatment focus is on coping skills, Socratic dialogue and cognitive restructuring are a necessary component of the approach. The CPN then addressed the third section of the Survival Manual (the advantage of the Manual is that an untrained therapist can utilise it under supervision), cognitive avoidance. It was suggested that the client might draw the 'Orangutan' as a way of remembering the futility of cognitive avoidance. However, the CPN felt out of her depth with the business of the client picking up the litter and had a discussion with the CBT therapist about it. The latter explained that in OCD a common problem is an excessive sense of responsibility, but it is often much less pressing for the person to perform the obsessive behaviour if they are accompanied because that responsibility is divided. At the CPN's next meeting with the client she suggested that it would be a dare not to pick something up and that another possible dare was that she would walk ahead of Siobhan to the local shop. It was explained further that 'dare' also stood for 'don't avoid a realistic experiment', and that they were testing out whether there are any negative consequences from these everyday behaviours. The following dialogue took place:

| | |
|---|---|
| *Siobhan:* | My mum would have wanted me doing everyday behaviours. She'd be pleased. |
| *CPN:* | Maybe when you are tempted to avoid a dare, perhaps you could do it out of respect for your mum. |
| *Siobhan:* | She never got a word in edgeways when I was little. |
| *CPN:* | Perhaps now is the time to listen to her and do what she would be saying. |
| *Siobhan:* | I like that. It's sort of in touch with her. |

The CPN was worried that she may have gone too far in introducing the client's mother into treatment and perhaps might trip a psychotic episode. She brought the matter up with the CBT therapist, who thought it very unlikely that there would be adverse consequences and that the results of this innovative experiment should simply be monitored. The CBT therapist commented that 'the mother' was, after all, a much more credible source of persuasion than anyone else. The focus at subsequent sessions moved on to a more adaptive management of intrusions. After discussion with the CBT therapist, the CPN decided to orient the client towards Self-Instruction Training, using her interest in art/drawing, as follows:

| | |
|---|---|
| *CPN:* | I came across a picture of 'The Scream' [*an agonised individual against a blood red sky*] by the Norwegian artist Edvard Munch. What do you think of it? |
| *Siobhan:* | It's like me, but frightening, that's why I draw landscapes. |
| *CPN:* | Maybe it's better to try and hold the beauty and the pain in the frame at the same time? |
| *Siobhan:* | I think what I got from drawing the Orangutan was that I became aware of the futility of blocking the horrors of Mum's dying and of the assault. |
| *CPN:* | Unfortunately you can't just forget the horrors. One way of looking at them is that each flashback is really a question, 'Does this mean anything about today?' |
| *Siobhan:* | How do you mean? |
| *CPN:* | Well, when you think of your mum dying, you could say for today this means I must let her get a word in about what to do. |

The above exchange is predicated on the assumption that when something is remembered, it is in a plastic state and can be updated. The therapist is encouraging the client to go with the grain of this updating process. The dialogue continues:

| | |
|---|---|
| *Siobhan*: | So that when I get a picture of the assault, I say to myself 'I'm just being asked, does this mean anything about today?' |
| *CPN*: | Yes, the first step in preparing for the flashbacks might be to say 'I'm just being asked a question. The picture doesn't speak for itself'. |
| *Siobhan*: | How do you mean? |
| *CPN*: | Well, looking at the picture of 'The Scream' you might say yes that tells me about how I feel today, but it doesn't tell me about how, say, you felt on holiday with your mum. |
| *Siobhan*: | I see. I could do drawings of some good times. |
| *CPN*: | Drawing or writing of a good time brings it alive. |
| *Siobhan*: | Good idea. |
| *CPN*: | So on this self-instruction form for flashbacks you might write on the second row, labelled 'Preparing for…', what? |
| *Siobhan*: | Flashbacks are an old movie, they are just asking me if they are relevant to today. |
| *CPN*: | The form also asks what you might say to yourself when they happen and when you are feeling overwhelmed by them. |
| *Siobhan*: | I think when they come on, I just need to tell myself it is today I'm at home, watering a plant, whatever. |
| *CPN*: | That's good. What about when you are feeling overwhelmed? |
| *Siobhan*: | Maybe I could text you. |
| *CPN*: | OK, we can see how that works out. We might need to tweak it a bit as we go along. |

At the next session the SIT was reviewed, using Appendix E, as follows:

| | |
|---|---|
| *CPN*: | I see under 'Looking back how I played it', you've written 'it helped but it is more difficult than I thought. It's so vivid'. Munch's blood red sky is very vivid but is it about today? |
| *Siobhan*: | No [*looking out*], it is a miserable November day. |
| *CPN*: | What you've just done is look at what the sky is actually like now, rather than get carried away by Munch's story. I think you might find it easier to go more by what is going on now than a story in your mind. |

*Siobhan*: I do that at night, in my dreams after the assault. I feel I've been placed in a body bag after the assault, and I can actually hear the sound of them zipping it up. I wake up in a terrible state.
*CPN*: So after the assault what happened?
*Siobhan*: The lads ran off.
*CPN*: What happened then?
*Siobhan*: An old guy came to my aid and a lady in a car stopped. Some nice people.
*CPN*: Maybe when you go out and do a dare you could count the number of people who look a bit like the old guy and the number a bit like the lady.
*Siobhan*: That's an idea, it would balance it up.

In the above exchange the therapist is tackling the client's tendency to view everything through a 'threat' template (technically called a schema) and to switch to processing the data of current experience, i.e. to move to predominantly bottom-up processing as opposed to top-down processing. Although the SIT is about the development of coping self-statements, the dialogue involves a great exchange of Socratic questioning and cognitive restructuring in its distillation. The homework assignment represents an application of the derived set of coping self-statements. In the above case, this was next applied to nightmares and daring to go out alone briefly. At the next session, the client volunteers that the coping strategies that she has found helpful for dealing with the PTSD symptoms might also be applied to her general paranoia, thus:

*Siobhan*: I'm calming myself quicker now when I wake from the nightmare, telling myself I do like to tell 'tales', 'bodybags'. My Mum used to say I was a 'drama queen'. Maybe I should think of my paranoia as just an 'awake dream'.
*CPN*: Could do. You might want to complete Appendix E for it and see how it goes.
*Siobhan*: OK.

This case illustrates how success in one area, such as managing PTSD symptoms, can give a client with an SMI confidence in trying to address other areas with the same non-threatening tools.

## SUMMARY

1. SIT can be used as an intervention for clients with a dual diagnosis of PTSD and SMI.
2. There appear to be no deleterious effects of intervening with CBT to treat PTSD among those with an SMI.
3. The SIT skills taught for the management of PTSD can also be used to manage psychotic symptoms and any additional comorbidities, such as substance abuse.
4. The therapist should budget that there will probably be interruptions to the intervention programme because of psychotic episodes, hospitalisations or periods of substance abuse and not regard the client as being back at 'square one'.

# Part Four

## SECONDARY TRAUMATISATION

# Chapter Thirteen

## THE CBT TREATMENT OF PAIN AND DISABILITY

*A naive CBT therapist may operate with a motto 'Think straight and all will be well' emblazoned across their forehead, to the chagrin of those with pain and disability following trauma. Yet appraisals, particularly catastrophising, can affect the perception of pain and the meaning attached to disability. As such, maladaptive appraisals are a fitting target for the CBT therapist but so too is behaviour, for example teaching clients to 'pace' themselves. Most Pain Management Programmes are geared to sufferers with back injuries which may or may not be trauma related, however there is rarely space within these programmes to cope with the needs of the PTSD client and the latter are often screened out. As pain and disability are common concomitants of PTSD, the former need to be addressed by therapists in the community. Clients presenting with pain as a result of disease (e.g. cancer) or as a result of a missing limb (phantom limb pain) present a particular challenge for the CBT therapist and in this chapter there are two case examples of interventions with PTSD clients whose pain and disability have arisen in different ways.*

The psychological effects of trauma are diverse, and so too are the physical effects, pain, disability, traumatic brain injury and disfigurement. Although CBT uses a computer metaphor to highlight the part played by information-processing biases in maintaining debility, this processing takes place via neurons rather than silicon chips and the distinction between the physical and the mental is more apparent than real – a convenient shorthand. It should be expected therefore that an individual's cognitions, behaviours and emotions will affect the management of pain, disability, head injury and disfigurement. If these 'physical' debilities are poorly managed, this in turn will have a deleterious effect on the client's

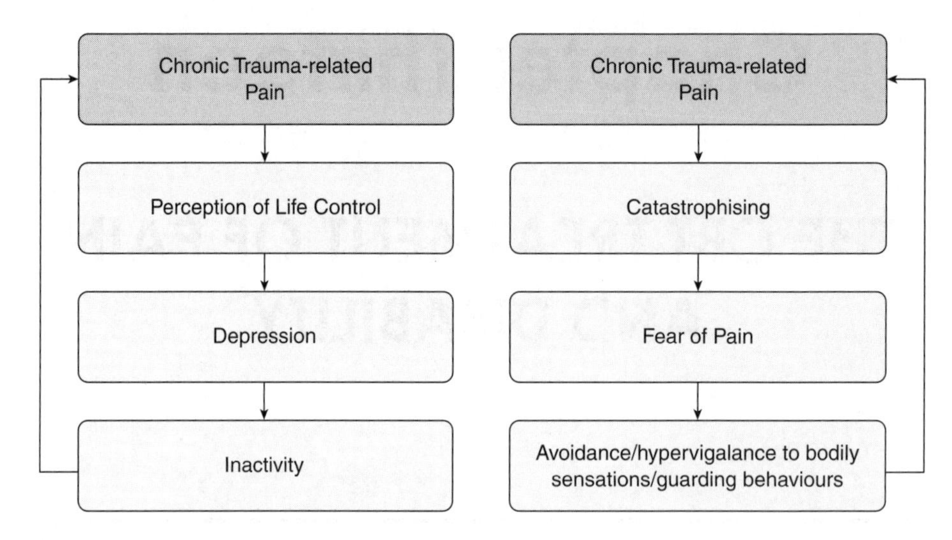


**Figure 13.1** Chronic Trauma-related Pain and Psychosocial Impairment

emotional well-being. This chapter focuses on moderating the impact of pain and disability by the development of adaptive coping strategies.

## PAIN AND DISABILITY

The relationship between chronic trauma-related pain, i.e. pain that persists for more than six months, and psychosocial impairment is summarised in Figure 13.1.

Chronic pain sufferers, who see their pain as overly threatening (i.e. they catastrophise about it, minimising their influence on it, magnifying its significance), have more severe outcomes (Jensen et al. 1999). The pain sufferer's beliefs about pain predict functioning. The right-hand column of Figure 13.1 shows that such beliefs lead to a fear of pain and avoidance of situations that might evoke pain. The CBT model of pain in Figure 13.1 is essentially a fear-avoidance model. The avoidance behaviour is associated with a constant scanning of the body for pain and guarding behaviour (e.g. looking at the pavement so as not to trip rather than looking ahead). The concepts of catastrophising and perception of life control are related but different constructs, and the left-hand column of Figure 13.1 suggests that the latter mediates the relationship between pain and depression. The more the pain sufferer believes that they are unable to organise life to meet their needs the more depressive symptoms they will have (Palyo and Beck 2005). Pain may also act as a reminder of the trauma, thus the inactivity of the depressed person (the left-hand column of Figure 13.1) is given added impetus as a means of avoidance of cued flashbacks. By being inactive/avoidant, the sufferer does not learn a tolerance of pain, an acceptance, the latter of which is very different from being resigned to pain. Acceptance of pain involves predominantly problem-focused

**Table 13.1** Treatment Targets and Strategies for Pain and Disability

| Treatment target | Treatment strategy |
|---|---|
| Catastrophising – rumination, magnification and helplessness | Cognitive restructuring and imagery |
| Perception of life control | Acceptance of pain but not resignation – empowering |
| Inactivity | Pacing |
| Hypervigilance | Attention training |
| Negative view of self | Reconstructing the view of self |
| Strained relationships | Communication and anger management |

coping as opposed to emotion-focused coping where the emphasis is on soothing. Inactivity/avoidance serves to perpetuate chronic pain (Figure 13.1). By contrast, graded *in vivo* exposure tends to mitigate pain (Vlaeyen et al. 2002).

Persistent pain almost inevitably results in role impairment, which in turn can result in low self-esteem and in some cases depression. The role impairment may result not only in self-criticism but also a perceived criticism from others, such as family or an employer. Attempts to function physically as prior to the trauma may result in irritability, straining relationships.

A pain management group programme is outlined by Thorn (2004) and Pincus and Sheikh (2009) have detailed the use of imagery for pain relief. The treatment targets and strategies for pain and disability are summarised in Table 13.1.

Pain may also occur in missing limbs – phantom limb pain. Sufferers can be reluctant to confide this, as it appears to be the antithesis of common sense, thus increasing a sense of isolation. The difficulties of the person who has lost a limb can be extensive and may include being unable to do the manual job they did before the traumatic amputation, concerns about attractiveness, impaired sexual relationships, and disturbing flashbacks/dreams of the trauma. Psychological treatment strategies for phantom limb pain are in their infancy but two strategies appear to make some difference in about half of cases (MacIver and Lloyd 2010): (a) the client views the mirror image of the remaining limb while moving the intact limb; and (b) following a relaxation exercise the client imagines comfortable and thorough movement and sensation in the missing limb. However, it is unclear which virtual reality technique is appropriate for which client. There is also a need to address the totality of such clients' difficulties but treatment takes place in a difficult terrain, including further operations and the search for and funding of a suitable prosthetic. Thus there needs to be a therapist commitment to providing comprehensive treatment, albeit when practicalities permit. In the interim, the therapist should provide periodic support with regard to current hassles and full re-assessment when there is a window of opportunity to provide treatment.

At the other extreme from a traumatic amputation a person may suffer from Chronic Regional Pain Syndrome (CRPS) from a minor injury, such as a fracture, usually to a hand or foot, from a minor incident, e.g. tripping over a raised flagstone. In CPRS, as time goes by the pain may migrate to other areas such as the spine or legs and the person may need crutches or a wheelchair. Thus there may be extreme debility arising from a comparatively trivial incident. However, there is no evidence that those suffering from CRPS are especially psychologically vulnerable (Marinus et al. 2011). Patients with CRPS are often treated with standard group CBT pain management programmes (such treatment also involves physical therapy tailored to the individual see: Lee et al. 2002) but they are sometimes too ill to attend.

## Case Examples

# 1. DEPRESSION AND PAIN

Syd was four feet up a ladder removing a product from a shelf in a supermarket store room when he missed his footing, tried to break his fall with his right arm and, in so doing, badly damaged his right elbow. He was off work afterwards for three months and when he returned he was placed on light duties for a couple of weeks doing administration. Syd knew the organisation was downsizing and there were considerable murmurings among staff about his doing administrative work and he began to feel low. He felt that he could not tell management the true extent of the pain in his right arm because he felt they would find some excuse to make him redundant, particularly as he was one of the oldest employees and he desperately needed the money. Syd had had to forego his hobby of golf since the incident, and his 20-year relationship with his partner broke up, he believed, because she now had to do the household tasks and because he was irritable. His pain reached a level of 8 out of 10 (where 10 is extreme pain) for about an hour a day most days. This intensity of pain was generated when he had used his right arm, for example moving cages about the store room. At other times he said his pain was 4 or 5 out of 10. Syd met diagnostic criteria for depression. Previously he had attended a Group Pain Management Programme which ran daily most weekdays for three weeks. However, he found he didn't like to discuss his problems with everyone and felt that hearing other people's problems did not help him resolve his own.

## First Interview

The first interview is used to establish the diagnostic status of the client (using the revised CBT Pocketbook (Scott 2011)), to review history, including treatment history, and to establish goals. The interview is complemented by the administration of psychometric tests. A wide selection is available free online from the IAPT website as a pdf file (www.iapt-data-handbook-appendices-). The Pain Catastrophising Scale (Sullivan et al. 1995) is particularly useful for clients with pain. It has three subscales (see Table 13.1) – rumination, magnification and helplessness – which can form the basis of treatment targets for intervention.

In Syd's case, he was found to be suffering from severe depression. He had a score of 24 out of 27 on the PHQ-9 (Kroenke et al. 2001), a measure of the severity of depression. At the first interview the following dialogue took place:

| | |
|---|---|
| *Therapist:* | Was your depression tackled in the Pain Management Group? |
| *Syd:* | They just talked about pacing yourself, so that if you have lots to do just go steadily with lots of breaks, not rushing. The relaxation CD they gave me was useful. |
| *Therapist:* | So it was helpful? |
| *Syd:* | Sort of, but you can't really pace yourself in work and I was still fed up. |
| *Therapist:* | Did they teach you how to check out that 'the photograph' you were taking of a situation that upsets you can often be taken from another angle that is less upsetting? |
| *Syd:* | No, I don't remember that. |
| *Therapist:* | Did they ask you to keep track of your mood between sessions and come up with better second thoughts than the first thoughts? |
| *Syd:* | No, they just asked us to keep a record of our activities and then we would discuss whether there was a better way of arranging them to make the pain better. I was annoyed when at lunch times people put their walking sticks to one side while they collected their lunch from the counter! |

In the above exchange the therapist has established that the client has not had full CBT for depression, although doubtless the Pain Management Programme organisers would see their programme as having been CBT-informed. The client's depression may have interfered with his taking on board what was actually being said in the programme, for example he appears to believe that the rationale for monitoring and reviewing activities was to take away pain rather than make it more manageable. Further, in a group context it is more difficult to check whether each member has understood what is being said. Thus despite the client's exposure to appropriate information on pain management in the group, his experience of pain is unchanged, and much of this is probably attributable to a failure to (a) tailor the programme to the client, (b) address reservations, and (c) address the depression. The case once again highlights the need to address comorbidity.

The therapist used the framework of the 4Ps (predisposing, precipitant, perpetuating and protective factors) (Weerasekera 1996) to distil a case formulation. Though the client had no psychiatric history, his sense of identity was

**Table 13.2** Treatment Targets and Strategies for Depression

| Treatment target | Treatment strategy |
|---|---|
| Low mood | MOOD thought record |
| Rumination | Worry postponement and thought record |
| Inactivity | Activity scheduling |
| Negative view of self, others and world | Revisiting the onset of negative views and updating them |

very bound up with being in paid work and a 'man' at home, and his depression was precipitated by the fall. The depression was perpetuated by his rumination about the effects of the incident and the pain served as an ongoing reminder. While the client perceived that since the incident he was not in control of his life, a protective factor was that prior to the incident he prided himself on being 'organised', arranging golfing holidays with friends. He also had the support of his son who worked renovating properties and renting them or selling them on.

For homework at the end of the first session, the client was asked to read *Moving on after Trauma* (Scott 2008) and to follow the story of a character who, like the client, also suffered from depression following a fall, and also to read the chapter on pain.

The treatment targets and strategies for depression are summarised in Table 13.2.

## Sessions 2–4

These sessions have a dual foci, pacing and depressive rumination, and thus from the outset the client's twin concerns of pain and depression are addressed. The second session began as follows:

*Therapist*: How did you get on reading the 'Pain' chapter in *Moving on after Trauma*?

*Syd*: Well, to be honest I didn't read it. I don't like to think about it all and my concentration is awful anyway.

*Therapist*: You could continue handling your pain and depression as you have being doing and, if you did, how would a typical day be in three months?

*Syd*: I'd probably be fed up and off work.

*Therapist*: How might it be in three months, if you read, in small doses, about different ways of playing the pain and depression?

*Syd*: Hmm, could be better. Sorry, I even hid the book under a magazine on the coffee table so it wouldn't remind me of my problems, but then my son visited. I went to make him coffee and when I come back into the living room there he is reading it! He asked me how come I had got this, but I was embarrassed, mumbled 'I just picked it up', and changed the subject.

*Therapist*: Sounds as though, in the Pain Management Group and with your son and with the book, you run away from talking and thinking about what bothers you.

*Syd*: I even did that with my partner after the fall. I think she left because I just went into myself and wouldn't talk to her about it. But I do spend all my time thinking about it.

*Therapist*: Thinking is problem solving, coming up with a new game plan. It sounds like what you have been doing is agonising, picking at it like a dog worrying a bone.

*Syd*: I bite my nails since the fall. Maybe I need to stop 'picking' as well.

*Therapist*: I think that one of the major things we need to address is your ruminating or picking, and there is strategy for dealing with this [*see Table 13.2, 'worry postponement and thought record'*] and there are other treatment targets and strategies. We would also need to look at your emotional avoidance, mentally running away when you experience any feelings associated with not being able to do what you did before. I suspect the book provoked such feelings and so you did a runner from it.

*Syd*: It's embarrassing, but you're right. It is only a book after all. I'll have a go again.

*Therapist*: But do it in small doses because of your concentration problem. Just read a few pages of Chapter 9, make a written note of what you have read to make it stick, and do this every couple of pages.

*Syd*: OK.

The above exchange highlights clients' oftentimes ambivalence to treatment. This was addressed using the motivational interviewing technique of helping the client elaborate and juxtapose different outcome scenarios and leaving him to decide which pathway he wished to follow. However, the therapist recognised that the client's depression may affect his ability to read and the reset homework was better tailored to meet this limitation. The discussion around the client's non-compliance with the homework assignment very naturally led on to one of the important treatment targets for clients with depression and pain – rumination. The topic of rumination could have been introduced by the therapist simply as an item that he/she believed it was important to address in the session, but it is preferable to introduce material when it has heightened relevance as a result of the topic under discussion. Thus there is a degree of flexibility about when the treatment targets and companion strategies (see Table 13.2) are addressed. The second session continued:

*Therapist*: Chapter 9 is very much about pacing yourself with pain.
*Syd*: Yes, I know about that. We did that in the Pain Management Group.
*Therapist*: So how did what you learnt in the Group about pacing make a difference at home and at work?
*Syd*: It didn't, I can't pace myself at work. The job has got to be done.
*Therapist*: But going at the pace you do in work is when the pain in your elbow can get to a level of 8 out of 10?
*Syd*: Yes, it is usually after pulling cages.
*Therapist*: An employer is legally obliged to make reasonable changes in the workplace to accommodate a disabled employee. Your Occupational Health Department might be able to look at what you do and either change what you have to do or alter it in some way.
*Syd*: I don't like talking about being disabled and you never know what they might do.
*Therapist*: Could they sack you?
*Syd*: Well no, I suppose not, but they might find an excuse.
*Therapist*: How would that look legally? You have had time off for a Pain Management Programme and if your conversation with Occupational Health is documented and they then failed to do anything they are in trouble, and if they have made changes it will look like discrimination and they are in trouble again.
*Syd*: I had not thought of it like that, but I don't like going to them saying 'I am disabled'.
*Therapist*: What does it mean to you to say you are disabled?
*Syd*: That I am a freak.

The above exchange illustrates the complexities of having clients apply the simple notion that if they have been injured they will need to perform activities at a slower pace. The obstacles in implementing pacing can be both structural and intra-psychic (a wish not to acknowledge disability). The session continued:

*Therapist*: What about pacing yourself at home?
*Syd*: I don't do anything there.
*Therapist*: Why is that?
*Syd*: I think it is because I can't be bothered, some days I get up with good intentions but I just put it off.
*Therapist*: What makes you do that?
*Syd*: I might think of hoovering, but then I'm right handed and I might set off the pain.
*Therapist*: But in work you do use your right hand, don't you?

| | |
|---|---|
| *Syd:* | Yes, usually just aches a bit working on the checkout. |
| *Therapist:* | What is to stop you doing things to the point of your right arm 'aching a little bit' at home? |
| *Syd:* | I should really do like I do in work except for really heavy things. |

The above exchange illustrates a common phenomenon when clients have to deal with pain, a lack of generalisation of corrective experience. Although the client had found he could do many physical tasks when he returned to work, this was not translated into doing similar tasks at home. This client is also over-generalising a negative experience: having had a negative experience with his arm in work he expects the same at home. In the exchange he was also using other information-processing biases, including selective abstraction, assuming that because he had difficulty with his arm in work he would lose his job and jumping to conclusions that his employer would have a plan to dismiss him. But the client's difficulties are not confined to information-processing biases, there are also problems with cognitive content in relation to the client's negative view of himself (Table 13.2). So both content and process need addressing. The second session continued:

| | |
|---|---|
| *Therapist:* | So how do you spend your time at home? |
| *Syd:* | I just go over how stupid it was that I was up the ladder. If my colleague hadn't been off sick I wouldn't have been doing his job. Then I think how my life has changed and about what is going to happen. |
| *Therapist:* | Does that help, going over it all day? |
| *Syd:* | Well, no. |
| *Therapist:* | What do you do it for? |
| *Syd:* | I just do. |
| *Therapist:* | It has had a big effect on your life so you probably can't help but think of it a bit, but we could look at training your mind so that there is a time and a place for going on about it, a worry time at a special time, when you might sort out on paper what you might do and stop yourself picking at it all at other times. This would give you space in the day at home to get on and do things. What we are doing is stopping depressive rumination [*see Table 13.2*]. |
| *Syd:* | I do need to move on. I'll give it a try. |

At the third and fourth session the client's successes in using pacing and worry time are reviewed and the MOOD thought record (see Table 5.1) is introduced. The MOOD chart is introduced not only to address low mood (see Table 13.2), but also as a way of analysing thought patterns when there is an increase in pain. Thought processes that lead to maladaptive coping in response to pain include rumination (e.g. 'I am in pain and must make it my sole pre-occupation'), magnification (e.g. 'I am in pain and I can't stand it') and helplessness (e.g. 'There is nothing I can do that will make any difference'). The final column of the MOOD chart is an antidote to depressive rumination, in that once the client has arrived at more objective second thoughts about their pain and/or depressive thoughts, they are invited to switch their attention to a behaviour and its completion, such as massaging the affected area or playing their favourite music. The actions decided on in the final column may involve imagery in relation to pain (e.g. imagining the pain filling different coloured balloons and floating away in a field where there is the smell of freshly cut grass and a light breeze). Clients can be invited to practise such imagery and given a CD that is a meditation on such imagery.

Clients should be asked routinely whether they experience an image when they have pain. In the authors' experience only a minority do so, but having them reconstruct that image can be helpful. For example, one client had an image that a snake was squeezing his spine when he was in pain and the coping imagery involved 'seeing' the snake uncoil and slither away. A further advantage of using the MOOD chart (Table 5.1) for pain and emotional distress is that it stresses that there is a reciprocal interaction between the two. Use of the MOOD record obviates the need to make the dualistic distinction between mind and body and the implication that the pain is 'in your mind', which so alienates clients troubled by pain and depression – the neurobiological reality is that neural pathways for pain and emotion appear to be wrapped around each other, resulting in reciprocal interactions.

In order for clients to refine their pain management strategies it is important for them to keep a daily record of pain, activities and practised coping strategies. Pain can be recorded on a scale of 0–10, where 10 is the worst pain imaginable, and the severity can be recorded at least in the morning, afternoon and evening. The pain record can provide data that contradict a client's belief that they are always in intense pain, so that they can learn that their recall has a depressive bias.

## Sessions 5–8

The new focus in these sessions is on the client's negative view of themselves, others and their personal world, but these sessions are also devoted to refining pain management coping strategies. The following dialogue took place at the fifth session:

*Therapist:* I notice from the MOOD record that you were upset after visiting a property your son was refurbishing.

*Syd:* Yes, I lifted a pile of plasterboards with him from the van, but then when I had done this I couldn't even lift the wheelbarrow. I felt stupid. His father-in-law was there getting stuck in.

*Therapist*: In the first column you have written down the situation that made you upset, but not about the thinking that led to the upset.

*Syd*: How do you mean?

*Therapist*: Well, if a couple of years ago you were giving a neighbour a hand, say with some fencing in his garden, and he had to stop part way because of back trouble, and he got upset about it, what would you have said to him?

*Syd*: I'd tell him it's no trouble. I'd just have got on with it.

*Therapist*: Would you have thought any less of him?

*Syd*: No.

*Therapist*: But it sounds like you have thought less of yourself in a similar situation.

*Syd*: Hmm, one law for me and another for others.

*Therapist*: Looks that way.

*Syd*: I think it was embarrassment with his father-in-law being there.

*Therapist*: Would he have thought less of you?

*Syd*: No, it's just me and I was in agony for about an hour after.

*Therapist*: It goes back to pacing and being up front about what you can do and not do.

*Syd*: I don't want to give in to what I can't do.

*Therapist*: But if your son tried to drive further than the amount of petrol he had in the tank, what would you think?

*Syd*: When you put it like that I can see what you mean.

*Therapist*: Sure, use up what 'petrol' is in the tank, but don't pretend it is a full tank.

*Syd*: I go from acting as if there is no petrol in the tank, and laze around all day at home, to pretending there is a full tank and hurting myself.

*Therapist*: When you don't use the 'petrol' you have got, you are likely to feel depressed and when you try and operate as if there is a full tank you get pain and probably become irritable.

*Syd*: I was like a bear with a sore head after I tried to help my son.

*Therapist*: Pacing is about carefully calculating what you can do, so you are not out of the game for ages after.

*Syd*: I think if I had helped with just a few plaster boards I would have been OK.

*Therapist*: When you go from 'blitzing' to doing 'nothing' you put yourself on an emotional rollercoaster. Pacing stops this and you do more in the end.

*Syd*: It should mean I will stop biting people's heads off.

*Therapist*: You can use irritability as a first sign you are doing too much, the warning light on the dashboard.

The above dialogue indicates the complexity of clients applying the notion of 'pacing' to their everyday situation. Very careful tailoring is needed to help a client take the concept beyond an intuitively appealing idea to achievable goals before the next session. Further pacing can be 'sabotaged' by a client's negative believes about themselves and others. The MOOD thought record provides a framework for the distillation of more adaptive believes about self and others, as the following exchange illustrates:

| | |
|---|---|
| *Therapist:* | I remember at an earlier session you referred to yourself as a 'freak'. I guess if this comes on stream, it immobilises you. |
| *Syd:* | Yes, I didn't like to say but after the incident my libido became almost non-existent, and I couldn't sustain an erection, so I just avoided my partner. She thought it was something to do with her. I told her it wasn't, but I never explained. |
| *Therapist:* | Did she say she didn't fancy you? |
| *Syd:* | No, it just added to my feelings of being a 'freak'. |
| *Therapist:* | Maybe you just 'freak out' in certain situations rather than that you are a 'freak'? Then others freak out because you freak out. |
| *Syd:* | I need to Stop and Think in those situations. |
| *Therapist:* | Yes it is a question of coming up with a gameplan for each situation. You can use the framework of Table 4.2 and you could write the script for, say, pacing yourself, or if you had known of this framework after the incident you might have applied it to sexual encounters with your partner. To illustrate how to use these coping self-statements we could use the example of having to move cages in work. What could you tell yourself about moving cages before you go into work? |
| *Syd:* | Maybe tell the boss I will move them but only when they are already on a pallet on a trolley and I can just use my left hand to pull the trolley. |
| *Therapist:* | The third row of Table 4.2 is what you might tell yourself when you get into work. |
| *Syd:* | I think I've got to tell myself to relax, maybe do the relaxation exercise they taught on the Pain Management Course, take a deep breath, breathe out slowly and say re-lax, then tighten my toes for five seconds, relax for ten seconds and do the same with each muscle group except my right arm. |
| *Therapist:* | Sounds OK. What about when you are feeling overwhelmed? |
| *Syd:* | That would be if I found the cage not on a pallet and trolley, I'll feel angry. |
| *Therapist:* | You could just be assertive using the broken record technique, just repeat over and over again the same one-liner: 'I'll move it when it is made safe for me'. |
| *Syd:* | The boss might 'flip' at this. |
| *Therapist:* | But what could he do if, say, you had cleared it with Occupational Health? |
| *Syd:* | Nothing really. |
| *Therapist:* | What could you say to yourself after being assertive, the fourth row on Table 4.2? |
| *Syd:* | I'm managing it all better. |
| *Therapist:* | Do 'freaks' manage it better? |
| *Syd:* | No, I suppose not. |

The above dialogue shows that both SIT and cognitive restructuring can be used to better manage stressful situations and the latter can also be utilised to challenge excessively negative views of self and others. At succeeding sessions the effectiveness of the self-statements are reviewed and refined.

## Sessions 9–12

The final sessions are devoted to recapping the taught material and the client is asked to review the homeworks and underline those aspects that they found most salient. It is useful to space these sessions so that the client has more opportunity to apply what has been taught *in vivo* and there is correspondingly an increase in the possibilities of refining strategies. In these sessions the therapist should be particularly alert for any problems in implementing the taught material. On occasion, the saboteur of a real-world application is cultural rather than intra-psychic. For example, if the client comes from a collectivist culture, it can be very difficult for them to explain to family members that they need time and space to go at their own pace. Culturally, a dichotomy may operate that either the family member is well and joins in all communal activities or they are ill and in bed. If the therapist is from an individualistic culture it may not occur to them that the client is operating in a very different milieu. In such circumstances the client might be advised to invite the most receptive family member to read the Pain chapter in *Moving on after Trauma* (an Arabic translation is also available: Scott 2010) and may therefore be empowered to better liaise with other family members.

# 2. PHANTOM LIMB PAIN, PTSD AND DEPRESSION

Stefan was cleaning a machine at work when it was inadvertently switched on. Three fingers of his right hand were severed and the thumb and index finger crushed. He was having nightmares and flashbacks of seeing a colleague picking up one of his fingers. Some of his nightmares were of himself deliberately cutting off his fingers. Stefan couldn't bear to look at his hand. He would wear a mitt over it and hide it from view. Fortunately, Stefan was left-handed and while his work might not be impossible with one hand, he was very fearful of returning to the scene of the incident. He reported that he was in constant pain from the missing limb and that the pain was at 7 out of 10, where 10 was the worst pain imaginable. His missing right hand felt clenched and burning, 'as if someone was standing on it'. But he noticed that if he was wholly distracted the pain would reduce to a 5 out of 10. Stefan was avoiding contact with friends that he played and watched football with. He attended the initial assessment with his wife.

## First Interview

For clients with traumatic amputations it is especially important to involve their partner. Such is the effect of the amputation on the client's self-image that intimacy often becomes a major problem, though it is rarely voiced because of a focus on debilitating pain, the difficulties in getting a suitable prosthetic, and sleep disturbed by nightmares. The following dialogue illustrates this:

| | |
|---|---|
| *Stefan*: | The nightmares are so bad that we sleep in separate rooms [*looking at his wife, Cora*] because she has got to go to work the next day. |
| *Cora*: | You don't even give me a hug. |
| *Stefan*: | I do the baby. |
| *Cora*: | But not Christine, our eldest daughter. |
| *Stefan*: | Well, no. |
| *Therapist*: | Whose idea was it to sleep in separate beds? |
| *Stefan*: | Mine. |
| *Cora*: | I sort of went along with it. |
| *Therapist*: | Are you saying that there is no sexual relationship between you? |
| *Stefan*: | Hardly any. |
| *Therapist*: | What gets in the way? |
| *Stefan*: | It is the state of my right hand, it doesn't belong there. |
| *Therapist*: | Where? |
| *Stefan*: | In the bedroom. |
| *Cora*: | [*Exasperated*] I've told him I'm not bothered about it! |
| *Stefan*: | But I am. |

In the above dialogue the client's view of himself has been clarified as well as his interaction with significant others. In the absence of the client's partner it would have been much more difficult to access this information. At this interview not only is the severity and nature of phantom limb pain determined, but also those situations that intensify and reduce the pain. The session continued:

| | |
|---|---|
| *Therapist*: | What makes the pain worst? |
| *Stefan*: | The cold. |
| *Therapist*: | Anything else? |
| *Stefan*: | Well, it's weird, when I'm with a group, say, in a pub, it tightens, burns more, and pulls into me. |
| *Therapist*: | There can be lots of unusual sensations with phantom limb pain. It seems that the mind carries a map of the body, but this map is dated before the incident. It is the only one available and assumes that there is 'traffic'(electric signals) along all 'roads' (limbs), and then the 'traffic control centre' in the brain becomes 'confused' about the 'feedback' it is getting from the missing limb. This 'confusion' finds expression in the phantom limb pain. |

*Stefan:* So I am not going mad?
*Therapist:* No, it is just a problem with your 'traffic control system'. Most people who lose a limb experience phantom limb pain.

In the above exchange the therapist is concerned to give the client a coherent rationale for symptoms that make no 'common sense', normalising their symptoms. The process of normalising symptoms is also extended to the client's symptoms of PTSD. Using the PTSD Survival Manual (see Appendix G), the therapist introduces this in the first interview and uses Figure G.2 in Appendix G to illustrate that many of the symptoms are attributable quite simply to a 'dodgy alarm' (a hypersensitive amygdala). By the end of the first interview the client should feel that they have a credible rationale for all their symptoms.

## Sessions 2–4

The intended therapeutic focus of these sessions is on coping strategies for managing the pain, PTSD and depression, but with clients who have suffered traumatic amputations of recent origin, roughly in the past one to three years, they will often have other more pressing problems that need to be addressed before these obvious therapeutic targets, as this exchange shows:

*Therapist:* I was planning to look at better ways of handling the pain, PTSD and depression, but is there anything else that you want to put on the agenda?
*Stefan:* I think I would be better off having my right hand cut off at the wrist and getting a proper hand, but they say it will not change the pain. I hate looking at my right hand. The thumb and index finger are no use, I can just about put them together but can't even lift a cup with them. I'd like them to cut both finger and thumb off but the surgeon and Cora aren't keen.
*Therapist:* What would a typical day be like in say six months if you had the thumb and finger removed?
*Stefan:* I could maybe get a sensible prosthetic.
*Therapist:* What, you think it would look more normal?
*Stefan:* People wouldn't stare as much.
*Therapist:* That gets to you, does it?
*Stefan:* I always thought that I would handle something like this. Before the accident if people didn't like me, I'd think 'tough' it's their problem. Now I hide it away. Coming here on the train I kept it in my pocket. Even at

*(Continued)*

*(Continued)*

| | |
|---|---|
| | home when relatives come or the children have their friends visit I make sure I have my mitt on. |
| *Therapist*: | Even when your mum visits? |
| *Stefan*: | Yes, she saw it once and she cringed. |
| *Therapist*: | Does she think any the less of you? |
| *Stefan*: | No, she's lovely [*wiping a tear away*]. |

The above exchange illustrates that a major issue for many amputees is trying to pass as normal, but there are limits to the extent that they will pass as 'normal', even with the best prosthetic, and learning to tolerate some embarrassment is necessary. The level of embarrassment to be tolerated is that generated by normal social interaction, such as social gatherings. Therapeutically, the goal is to help the amputee balance social interaction and embarrassment. They can be thought of as operating at either end of a see-saw, as the following exchange indicates:

| | |
|---|---|
| *Stefan*: | I can go swimming on holiday with just the kids in the pool but not if anyone else was around. |
| *Therapist*: | Would you like to swim with other people around? |
| *Stefan*: | Yes, but I would be too embarrassed. |
| *Therapist*: | Could you train yourself to be less embarrassed by gradually daring yourself to go to your local pool at increasingly busy times? |
| *Stefan*: | I could see myself doing it when it is fairly empty, kids at school, but not at normal times. |
| *Therapist*: | That would be a start, just see how far you can go. |
| *Stefan*: | I need to get back to running as well. I'venot done anything since the incident. |
| *Therapist*: | Regular exercise is a great antidote to depression. |

In the above exchange the therapist has addressed the client's pressing concerns. Not to have done this would have impaired the development of a therapeutic alliance, without which it would not be possible to address the PTSD. However, the disruptions to the therapeutic programme can be protracted, either because of further surgery or because a prosthetic device doesn't fit, causes pain or is unsightly, and it is easy to lose sight of the target difficulties: pain, PTSD and depression. Indeed, the client's depression is often linked to these difficulties. By about the fourth session the client's phantom limb pain can be addressed, as the following exchange illustrates:

*Therapist*: One way of addressing phantom limb pain is by viewing movement of the unaffected limb in a mirror. This can trick the confused traffic control centre in the brain into thinking that movement is occurring and reduce pain. Would you be prepared to give this a try?

*Stefan*: OK.

*Therapist*: How is the pain at the moment on a scale of 0 to 10, where 10 is the worst pain?

*Stefan*: A 7, it feels tight and burning.

*Therapist*: Rest your left arm on the table and just look into the mirror, start with your fingers clenched and then very gradually opening them out and we can see how this goes over five minutes.

*Stefan*: OK.

*Therapist*: [*after about 5 minutes*] How does the pain feel now?

*Stefan*: Much the same, a 7.

*Therapist*: And the burning sensation?

*Stefan*: The same.

*Therapist*: OK, we can try it without the mirror. Close your eyes and focus on your right fist, see yourself slowly moving your thumb, now your index finger, now the middle finger, now your second finger, now your little finger. Imagine these fingers resting gently on piano keys and making tiny movements of each key in turn. Hear the sound, now imagine the fingers gently opening, moving from touching your palm. Let's try the piano again, first your thumb and then each of the other fingers, now the fingers moving out from the palm. How was that?

*Stefan*: It felt like the fingers were straightening out just a little.

*Therapist*: How is the pain?

*Stefan*: It's down a little to about a 5, not burning as much.

*Therapist*: I think, in view of this, that it might be worth trying this imagery exercise for a couple of minutes about three times a day.

*Stefan*: Just making some difference, even if it is short-lived, is something.

The above dialogue illustrates the need for flexibility in the imagery strategy used, as invariably no strategy will work solely by itself (MacIver et al. 2008). Although imagery is thought to be the active ingredient in change, the developers of the approach have preceded it with relaxation exercises and therapists may wish to incorporate these into the exercise. By the end of the fourth session the client should also be set the task of writing a page a day about their trauma.

## Sessions 5–9

These sessions are devoted to strategies to teach the client to interact more adaptively with the traumatic memory, reconstruct the negative view of self, and refine pain management strategies. But they often take place against a changing background in relation to surgery and prostheses, requiring a flexible scheduling of appointments and a preparedness on the part of the therapist to address current concerns, as follows:

*Stefan*: Finally got an NHS myoelectric hand but it is huge, I would be too embarrassed to use it. They have also given me a purely cosmetic hand but it looks so unnatural.

*Therapist*: You must be pretty fed up with it.

*Stefan*: I am fed up, there are delays over whose catchment area you are in for funding, then what is offered doesn't fit and you need to go back for further fittings.

*Therapist*: I thought that the insurers would pay for it privately?

*Stefan*: I've got as far as an agreement that they will fund a cosmetic hand, and the one I have seen privately looks really good, with hairs and blemishes. I've seen private myolectric hands on the internet with individual finger movement but the insurers have said they would only pay for an assessment and three-month trial.

*Therapist*: So your hopes of getting a private myolectric were raised but then dashed?

*Stefan*: Yes, I'll go ahead with it but it's not right.

The above exchange illustrates that there is often a necessary support element in conducting CBT with amputees. However, the therapist has also to remain conscious of the importance of addressing the therapeutic targets, where possible using current concerns as a gateway to address them, as shown in the following dialogue at the ninth session:

*Therapist*: How is the pain when you are using the new private myoelectric hand?

*Stefan*: Well, you are not supposed to wear it all the time, but sometimes I'm just sitting there, now almost without thinking, playing at moving individual fingers with signals that come from me in the top of my forearm, and after a few minutes of doing this the phantom limb pain is less – about a 5 out of 10. It sort of feels like I am moving my own fingers.

*Therapist*: It might be an idea to do this three times a day with the new device on but also do this in your imagination three times a day without any device on.

*Stefan*: OK.

*Therapist*: How are the nightmares now?

*Stefan*: I don't get the nightmares of cutting my hand off now, but I still wake from the nightmare of my colleague picking up my fingers. But I am getting back to sleep more quickly.

This exchange illustrates the importance of a flexible approach to the management of phantom limb pain and echoes the need for clients to develop a flexible experimental mindset for the management of pain (Wicksell et al. 2010). Pain acts as a reminder of the trauma. Arguably, the less intense the pain, the less vivid the intrusions. A diminution in the intensity of pain may itself depend on a lessening of the sense of helplessness via experimentation with differing coping strategies. However, the intrusions also have to be addressed using the strategies for flashbacks outlined in Chapters Four and Five.

## Sessions 10–12

Sessions 10 and 11 involve a review of materials already taught. The client is asked to make their own written notes about what they have found most useful and instructions to themselves for managing deteriorations in mood and exacerbations of pain. The client's Survival Manual is individualised, for example some clients find using guided imagery/meditation/relaxation/massage very useful while others do not. The particular strategies are less important than whether the client has distilled a range of coping strategies they can apply and can readily access these.

The final session should be held some months after the penultimate session to allow the client sufficient time to test out the viability of the pain management coping strategies. This session should also include a full diagnostic workup and should not be confined to just re-assessing the disorders with which a client originally presented. While a client may have been identified as having recovered from say PTSD and depression and is managing their pain, if the therapist considers that this is a case of 'job done', the client may be re-referred by their GP, ostensibly because that client still considers they are suffering from PTSD. In such circumstances, at re-examination the therapist will likely discover that although there are sub-syndromal levels of some PTSD symptoms, some other disorder, such as generalised anxiety disorder, has in fact developed and needs addressing. It is better to pick up this new disorder at the final session than a client suffering the demoralisation that is involved in the process of re-referral.

## SUMMARY

1. Pain and disability are common concomitants of a trauma response and may make the treatment of any associated disorder, such as PTSD and/or depression, more difficult. Attempts to treat merely the pain or just the disorders are often unsuccessful.
2. The amount of pain experienced is not proportional to the amount of tissue damage. The absence of an identifiable source of the pain does

not mean that it can be assumed that it is 'all in the mind'. Pain can occur without an obvious stimulus, such as in phantom limb pain.

3. The perception of controlling one's life mediates the relationship between pain and depression. Catastrophising is another mediating variable between the latter two. Treatment involves cognitive restructuring focused upon perception of life control and catastrophising.
4. SIT and the MOOD chart can both be used for the management of pain, and the latter can also be used to tackle low self-esteem.
5. TFCBT can be used for PTSD in pain clients but initially the emphasis should be on coping skills. Should the latter prove insufficient, the client can be stepped up to the more intense intervention.
6. For phantom limb pain there are two main treatment approaches: (a) viewing the intact limb in a mirror and moving it; and (b) having the client close their eyes and imagine movement in the missing limb.

# Chapter Fourteen

# THE CBT TREATMENT OF HEAD INJURY

*Nine out of ten victims of head injury suffer a mild traumatic brain injury (MTBI) and only a small minority of these suffer from persistent postconcussion syndrome (PPCS). Victims' appraisals of their initial postconcussion symptoms play a pivotal role in the development of PPCS. In this chapter a CBT model of PPCS is described together with an example of an intervention using the model. However, the effects of head injury can be devastating, resulting in significant long-term cognitive impairment. Despite this, CBT can help the victim and those close to them to adapt. The specifics of helping a client with moderate/severe head injury are illustrated by a further case example.*

Traumatic brain injury (TBI) is the most common type of physical injury sustained by combatants in Afghanistan and Iraq (Stein and McAllister 2009). In the UK there are at least 1 million attendees a year at hospital emergency departments with a head injury, 90% of whom have a mild-traumatic brain injury (MTBI) (Kay and Teasdale 2001). The American Congress of Rehabilitation Medicine (ACoRM) (1993) has defined MTBI as involving: a loss of consciousness of not more than 15 minutes; an initial Glasgow Coma Scale (GCS) score of 13–15 (the GCS measures a person's ability to generate an eye opening response (0–4), a verbal response (0–5) and a motor response (0–6); see Teasdale and Jennett 1974); and post-traumatic amnesia of not more than 60 minutes. Loss of consciousness is not a necessary requirement for MTBI. There may simply be an alteration in mental state at the time of the accident (e.g. feeling dazed, disoriented or confused). MTBI is, however, excluded if there is a focal neurological deficit. It has been suggested that damage to the medial prefrontal cortex may compromise the neural networks implicated in emotion regulation and this may contribute to increased psychiatric

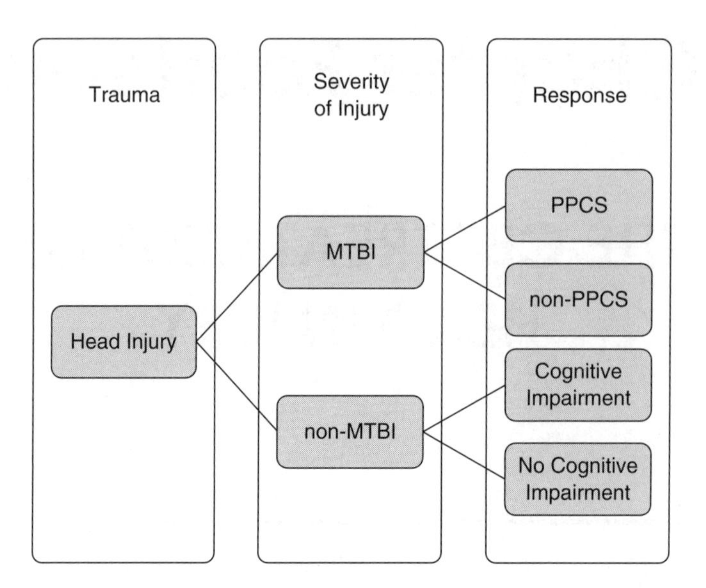


**Figure 14.1** Head Injury Pathways

morbidity following MTBI (Bryant 2008). Thus MTBI is commonplace, but only a significant minority (15–30%) go on to develop postconcussional syndrome (PCS), which, according to ICD-10 (World Health Organisation 1992), requires at least three symptoms from: headaches, dizziness, fatigue, irritability, impaired concentration, insomnia, memory problems, and problems tolerating stress/emotion/alcohol. The majority of PCS sufferers recover within days or weeks, but a very small minority, 15% at most (see McCrea 2008) have symptoms persisting beyond six months – known as persistent postconcussion syndrome (PPCS). However, 10% of head injury victims follow the lower pathway shown in Figure 14.1.

Those suffering a moderate/severe head injury may suffer cognitive impairments. This is not to say that those with PCS may not also suffer cognitive impairments but they are much less readily identifiable via neuropsychological testing or a scan. PCS is best explained by stress reactions following injury rather than neurological insult (Meares et al. 2008).

This chapter begins with a guide to assessing PCS – a cognitive behavioural model of PCS – and a description of the treatment of a client with persistent PCS. The latter half of the chapter goes beyond MTBI to the CBT treatment of those with more severe head injuries.

## SYMPTOMS OF PCS AND FUNCTIONING

A client's functioning with regard to PCS may be gauged by enquiring about each symptom (see Table 14.1) and determining whether it is absent (1), present but

**Table 14.1** PCS Assessment Framework

| | Symptoms | Functioning |
|---|---|---|
| 1. | Headaches | |
| 2. | Dizziness/light-headed | |
| 3. | Nausea/feeling sick | |
| 4. | Fatigue | |
| 5. | Extra sensitive to noise | |
| 6. | Irritable | |
| 7. | Feeling sad | |
| 8. | Nervous or tense | |
| 9. | Temper problems | |
| 10. | Poor concentration | |
| 11. | Memory problems | |
| 12. | Difficulty reading | |
| 13. | Poor sleep | |

not significantly interfering with functioning (2), significantly interfering with functioning (3), or insufficient information available (0) over the past two weeks

Those PCS items rated a '3' can be specifically targeted in treatment. However, there is considerable overlap between the symptoms of PCS and those of depression and chronic pain (Iverson 2006) and it is likely to be unreliable to diagnose PCS in the presence of either of these conditions. Persistent symptoms may be associated with both neurological and non-neurological variables (Prigatano and Gale 2011).

PCS is defined differently in ICD-10 (World Health Organisation 1992) and *DSM IV TR* (American Psychiatric Association 2000), and the latter additionally includes apathy, personality change, and changes in affect, and insists that it should only be diagnosed following neuropsychological testing. In practice when PCS is diagnosed it rarely involves neuropsychological testing. The symptoms of PCS covered in Table 14.1 are those featured in the British Columbia Postconcussion Symptom Inventory (Iverson 2006). The BC-PSI assesses the frequency and intensity of each of these symptoms, but for routine clinical use in Table 14.1 an overall measure of functional impairment with regard to each symptom is, in the authors' view, more practical.

# A COGNITIVE BEHAVIOURAL MODEL OF POSTCONCUSSIONAL SYNDROME

The common-sense model of the self-regulation of illness behaviour (see Cameron and Moss-Morris 2010) specifies that individuals hold beliefs about the cause, timeline, and cure/controllability of their condition, as well as emotional

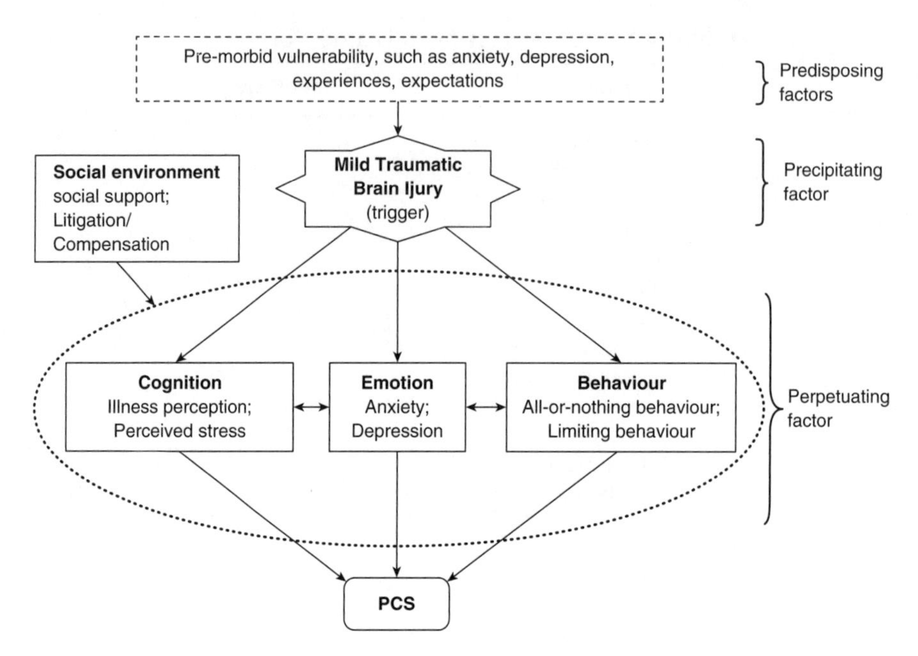


**Figure 14.2** CBT Model of PCS (reproduced by permission)

responses which influence whether they seek help or adhere to treatment recommendations. In a study of clients who had just experienced a mild traumatic brain injury, 22% went on to develop postconcussional syndrome (PCS) (Hou et al. 2012). The strongest predictor of the development of PCS six months post-injury was the client's negative perceptions of their acute mild head injury (e.g. 'I have got a physical condition outside my control'). Their all or nothing behaviour (overdoing things when they believe symptoms are abating and then spending prolonged periods recovering when symptoms reappear) was the key predictor for the onset of PCS at three months. This suggests that targeting salient cognitions/behaviours may prevent/ameliorate PCS. Hou et al. (2012) have proposed a cognitive model of PCS (see Figure 14.2).

Although Hou et al. (2012) included social support and litigation/compensation in their model, they did so on the basis of other studies. Their own study did not show these variables to have predictive value. Figure 14.1 also suggests that some PCS sufferers may attribute their non-specific pre-existing complaints to the injury, misinterpreting these as negative consequences of the brain injury. It is useful to make a distinction between postconcussion syndrome (PCS) and persistent postconcussion syndrome (PPCS). PCS can be regarded as an initial expression of debility following trauma (rather in the way a person may have some PTSD symptoms within the first couple of weeks). But whether PPCS develops depends on the person's appraisals of their symptoms (in much the same way that PTSD only develops if maladaptive appraisals follow initial symptoms). Therapeutically, the target is therefore PPCS rather than PCS.

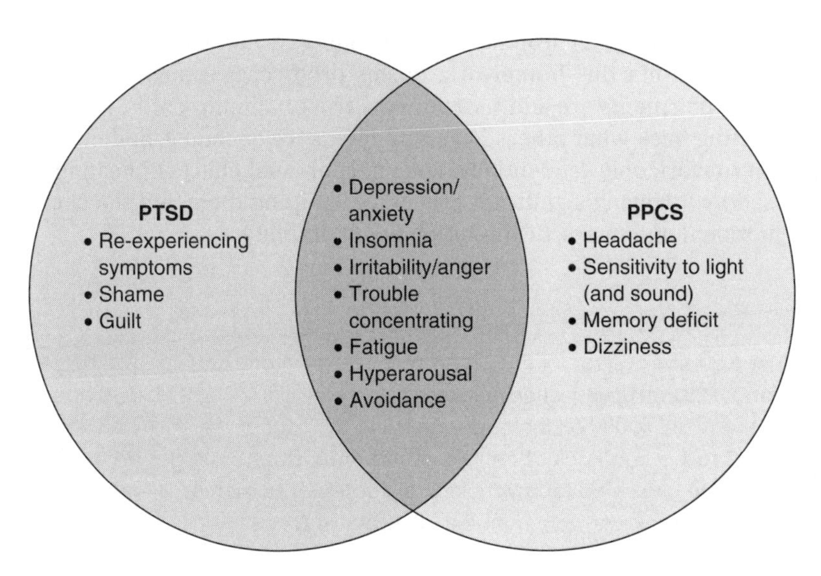


**Figure 14.3** Interface of PTSD and Persistent Postconcussive Symptoms Following Mild TBI that Involves Biomechanical Force to the Brain with a Loss of Consciousness, Amnesia and/or an Altered Mental State (from Stein and McAllister 2009)

# OVERLAP OF MTBI AND PTSD

There is a considerable overlap between the symptoms of MTBI and PTSD/ depression (see Figure 14.3, from Stein and McAllister 2009) and this has led to some questioning of the validity of the distinction, but in the present state of knowledge it appears most appropriate to treat both disorders. (See Stein and McAllister 2009 for a discussion.)

The PTSD and depression may also be associated with other psychological problems, such as substance abuse (Graham and Cardon 2008) and suicidal behaviour, which would also need addressing.

# PERSISTENT PCS (PPCS)

Symptoms rated a '3' in Table 14.1 should be therapeutic targets. In addition, clients should be asked about metacognitions, beliefs and behaviours, specifically (a) how much they ruminate (dwell) on these symptoms and (b) what they take the above symptoms as signifying, e.g. 'irreversible brain damage'. Maladaptive metacognitions and behaviours should also become a therapeutic target.

The model of PCS in Figure 14.2 suggests that treatment might profitably target the difficulties subsumed under the headings 'cognitions', 'emotions', 'behaviour' and 'social environment'. There follow two illustrative case examples of treatment within this framework. In this protocol it is suggested that mild cognitive impairments are addressed by the use of: memory aids, paraphrasing and reflecting back what others have said to ensure encoding, and encouraging the client to work only sequentially. The interpersonal effects of head injury are addressed by involving significant others and helping them and the client cope with emotional numbness, disinhibition and irritability.

Terry was an outside contractor at a prison, servicing the metal gratings over the windows. He was about 20 feet up in a cherry-picker when the grating he was holding above head height slipped, hitting him on the head. He fell to the floor of the cherry-picker and was he believed to be unconscious for two or three minutes. Colleagues at ground level rescued him. He presented for psychological treatment 18 months later with his partner, Siobhan. Their complaints are summarised in Table 14.2.

**Table 14.2** Complaints of PPCS client and his Partner

1. Difficulties planning organising
2. Effected by bright lights
3. Headaches front top of head
4. Unable to concentrate
5. Argumentative over minor things
6. Dropped most friends
7. Gazes into space
8. Can't do things spontaneously
9. Seeks reassurance
10. Not depressed, can't be bothered going fishing or taking children to the park
11. Partner says he says inappropriate things – disinhibited
12. Feels a need to blame someone
13. Has to check if his handwriting is correct

From Table 14.2 it is clear that this client has most of the symptoms of PCS detailed in Table 14.1. However, some of the complaints – difficulty planning/organising, gazing into space, inability to do things spontaneously, motivational problems without depression, disinhibition, difficulties with handwriting – are suggestive of possible cognitive impairment and also need to be addressed. A comprehensive list of symptoms and levels of functional impairment is more likely to be determined by the inclusion of the client's partner or family member who may be more aware of symptoms such as disinhibition than the client themselves.

Figure 14.2 indicates the elements that compose a case formulation: predisposing factors, precipitant (head injury) and the perpetuating factors. In the case of the above client there was no obvious predisposing factor except that twenty years previously he had been briefly suicidal when a relationship with a girlfriend had broken up. His current partner felt that there had been a personality change since the head injury. The perpetuating factors in his PPCS included all or nothing functioning (in that unless he was operating as he did before the head injury he thought he may as well do nothing) and a belief that he was permanently damaged. The PPCS client may show considerable irritation and ambivalence, and treatment may be best regarded as having three phases: engagement, treatment and relapse prevention.

## Engagement

At the first interview the following exchange took place:

*Therapist*: Are you bothered by heights now?
*Terry*: Wouldn't fancy being up in a cherry-picker.
*Siobhan*: We had roofers repairing the roof a few weeks ago after heavy winds. They told us that the gutters are all blocked up and you [*looking at her partner*] said you would sort it out but you didn't.
*Terry*: That's because you kept nagging me about doing it.
*Therapist*: Were you afraid to go up a ladder?
*Terry*: No, I just can't be bothered with the headaches.
*Siobhan*: He doesn't do anything – go fishing, take the kids the park – then when I ask him it's 'nagging'! He just sits there and stares into space.
*Terry*: I don't need this, I'm off!
*Therapist*: You could go, but if I was a betting person I would bet you will be in the same position in six months' time. Or we could look at different ways of handling the symptoms you have had since the head injury... the choice is yours.
*Terry*: I should be over this by now. It was only a bang on the head.
*Therapist*: Who said you should be over it?
*Terry*: I do.
*Therapist*: I'm sure that if it was just a matter of willpower you would have done it, but with the type of postconcussion symptoms you have got, like headaches, they have to be 'played' special ways.

The above exchange illustrates the ambivalence of many PPCS clients to treatment and shows that this can be addressed by juxtaposing the possible different courses of action and placing responsibility on the client for the direction they take. Further, the dialogue shows how the client's maladaptive metacognitive beliefs about their symptoms serve to perpetuate their difficulties. Care has been taken to first elucidate explicitly the client's cognitions/emotions behind a behaviour before deciding on a therapeutic target. In this example it could have been easily assumed from the input from the client and his partner that he had developed a height phobia when the behaviour relates more to apathy. At the second interview the maladaptive cognitive beliefs were again in evidence:

*Terry*: There is something really wrong with me but the CT scan was normal. I don't understand it.
*Therapist*: We are not too sure of what is going on physically in PPCS, but we know that if the symptoms are handled in particular ways, gradually, you can function much as before the head injury.
*Terry*: So, it is not permanent?
*Therapist*: No, that's the good news; the bad news is that it takes a couple of months of treatment to make a real difference and it is a question of two steps forward and one back during treatment, as you get the hang of the strategies.
*Terry*: How do you mean?
*Therapist*: Well, say if we were looking at a person's temper problems, we might teach them to count to ten before they open their mouth and, to begin with, they will be often have difficulty in doing this, but gradually they will be more able to do it.
*Terry*: I've tried counting to ten, it doesn't work.
*Therapist*: As you are counting to ten we get you to think what is the likely consequence in 30 minutes' time if you 'shoot from the hip'.
*Terry*: When I 'shoot' them, they just desert me!
*Siobhan*: What do you expect us to do, sit there and take all this ****?
*Terry*: OK, I will give it a try.

The above exchange illustrates that there is often something of an empathy deficit in clients with PPCS in that they may not anticipate the emotional consequences of their actions on others and this could lead not only to expressions of irritability but also to insensitive comments, as the following dialogue at the third interview shows:

*Siobhan*: He made a show of me last week. We were at my niece's christening and he told my sister off for eating something and becoming a 'fat ***'.
*Terry*: I was joking!
*Siobhan*: She didn't think it was very funny. She has been struggling to lose weight since the baby was born!
*Terry*: I'm like a five year old since the head injury. I just say what comes into my mind.

| | |
|---|---|
| *Therapist*: | You could try counting to ten when you are going to make a personal comment. |
| *Terry*: | It has helped for the anger. It might help me to become at least an eight year old. |
| *Therapist*: | I think half the battle is realising that you have been doing the five-year-old thing, where adults just wish you had a battery which they could take out. |

The above exchange highlights the client's problems with disinhibition and their impact on those around them. The first step in having clients address this problem is getting them to acknowledge that this is indeed a problem. The treatment strategies used mirror those for the management of anger. But these empathy difficulties can be manifested during sessions, as the following exchange at the fourth treatment session indicates:

| | |
|---|---|
| *Therapist*: | When I collected you from the waiting room just then, it seemed like you had had an argument with the receptionist. |
| *Terry*: | Stuck up ***. |
| *Therapist*: | What went wrong? |
| *Terry*: | She was asking me who I was waiting to see and I said to her 'what is it to you?' |
| *Therapist*: | Would you have said that if Siobhan had been with you? |
| *Terry*: | I don't think so. |
| *Therapist*: | Why not? |
| *Terry*: | It's just being like a stupid kid, isn't it? |
| *Therapist*: | It's not what I think that matters, it's what you think. |
| *Terry*: | Trouble is I didn't plug my brain in and think before speaking. |

The above dialogue illustrates that difficulties in engaging the client with PPCS can often be used to make valuable teaching points that have an experiential rather than a didactic quality and thereby also have a 'felt' relevance. Further, the therapist has gone with the client's own metaphor, 'the five year old', to better enter his assumptive world rather than import a general analogy. In some instances, however, there are no metaphors used by the client that have obvious therapeutic potential and the therapist's input into creating a suitable 'story' for managing the PPCS symptoms is greater. The therapist has to some degree to be an opportunist with regard to metaphor. This highlights the fact that treatment is as much an 'art' as a 'science'.

## Treatment

The engagement and treatment phases both follow the standard CBT format of setting an agenda for a session and the setting and review of homework, but in the latter phase client ambivalence is not an issue. If it raises its head again in the course of treatment then the focus shifts again to 'engagement' and the use of motivational techniques. Thus there can be an ebb and flow between 'engagement' and 'treatment', though typically just five or six treatment sessions are necessary.

A major feature in the treatment of PPCS is activity scheduling, but it differs from the same procedure with depressed clients in that it often simply does not occur to the head injury victim that there is a need to be active. However, the PPCS client has similar difficulties to the depressed client in being unable to persist with a task, complete it in a timely manner, and deal with interruptions. The following dialogue illustrates some of the difficulties and ways forward:

| | |
|---|---|
| *Terry:* | I can sit there at home all day, then I panic when I hear Siobhan's key in the door and the dishes are in the sink and I haven't hoovered. |
| *Therapist:* | When people have a head injury there is often a difficulty in tracking what you do and ensuring that what you do is climbing a rung of a ladder toward a goal. |
| *Terry:* | I just doodle at the bottom of the ladder. |
| *Therapist:* | Then get told off for doodling instead of working? |
| *Terry:* | Yes, it's back to the five year old. |
| *Therapist:* | You've been doing the eight year old in some areas, like managing your anger, so maybe you could do it in some other areas, like hoovering? |
| *Terry:* | I should be able to but it doesn't seem to happen. |
| *Therapist:* | You can do them if Siobhan is there as a reminder, so maybe you need other reminders, such as working to a timetable? |
| *Terry:* | Yes, I worked to a timetable when I was at work. I could do with one at home. |

In this dialogue the therapist has introduced the client to the notion of a 'ladder' as a metaphor to enable him to counter deficits in means–ends problem-solving. Though the client has derived some benefit from the analogy, he has chosen his own favourite analogy of 'the five year old' and the therapist has followed the grain of the client's story rather than push his own metaphor. For many PPCS sufferers their working memory is limited and they are likely to be very stressed by attempts to work on tasks simultaneously. The following exchange illustrates a coping strategy using the notion of a turnstile:

*Terry*: When I think of how I used to be able to juggle things at work. I would get a call about another job elsewhere in the middle of a job and I would have to keep both sets of customers happy and the boss. I could never do that now – it would 'freak' me out.

*Therapist*: Well there is an alternative to having an open door to all problems and that is to use a turnstile. If you have an 'open door' now it's like having an open gate at a football game – you will get 'crushed' – but if you have a turnstile you will get through in one piece. You can make a list, which is the order that 'people' are in, outside the turnstile and let them in one at a time, have a break, then let the next one in, and so on.

*Terry*: At home I suppose I could start with the hoovering as soon as Siobhan has gone to work, then have a cup of tea and then do the dishes.

*Therapist*: Right, that's great, but sometimes there are interruptions, such as you are part way through the dishes when there is a phone call from school to pick up one of the kids who has been sick.

*Terry*: That's when I would go ballistic!

*Therapist*: What you could do there is place the doing of the dishes on the other side of the turnstile and place the collecting of the kids this side of the turnstile. There are always interruptions but so as long as you are chipping away through the queue it doesn't really matter.

*Terry*: It is like when I was at work, no matter how hard I worked there was always too much to do. But I feel bad when Siobhan has gone to work and I am at home.

*Therapist*: We can look at some special ways to manage your mood using a MOOD chart.

In the above dialogue the therapist has successfully marketed a coping strategy to counter some of the deficits found in many PPCS clients but in so doing problems in mood management have been flagged up that need to be addressed. The use of the MOOD chart with PPCS clients is identical to its usage with depressed clients, discussed earlier in this volume.

## Relapse Prevention

The final two sessions are devoted to recapping what has already been taught. At the penultimate session the client is asked to review their notes for homework and underline aspects that they think are important. If possible there should be a gap of at least a month between these sessions to allow the client adequate time to practise their skills. The final session is devoted to troubleshooting difficulties encountered and emphasising the relevance of coping strategies already taught. Clients are also re-assessed in these sessions using Table 14.1.

## MODERATE/SEVERE HEAD INJURY

A CT (computed tomography) scan or magnetic resonance imaging (MRI) scan may reveal brain injury such as a subdural haematoma. A subdural haematoma occurs when a blood vessel in the space between the skull and the brain (the subdural space) is ruptured. Blood escapes from the ruptured blood vessel, leading to the formation of a blood clot (haematoma), which places pressure on the brain and may cause brain damage. However, there is no inevitability about a scan confirming brain injury. For example, in a study by Chard et al. (2011) of 29 clients treated for PTSD and a traumatic brain injury (TBI), with a modification of cognitive processing therapy, only a third (nine clients) had abnormal scans.

Those with moderate/severe brain injury often show variations in levels of consciousness in the days/weeks after the injury. The level of pre-trauma and post-trauma amnesia is an indicator of the severity of head injury. For example, those with pre- and post-trauma amnesia of a week or two are likely to be judged as having a severe head injury. Usually cases of moderate/severe head injury are picked up within a month or two by an Acute Brain Injury Rehabilitation Team and, typically, fortnightly contacts are made alongside provision of physiotherapy and occupational therapy, but brain-injured clients may present to the CBT therapist two years or more down the line via a GP referral or as part of a litigation process. By this time a neuropsychological assessment has probably already been conducted, including, for example, the Wechsler Adult Intelligence Scale. Such a test might reveal that the client has no intellectual loss but shows evidence of a reduction in processing speed. Other tests might reveal deficits in planning and organising, cognitive inflexibility, and difficulties with word finding and naming. The client's relatives may report a personality change, inappropriate behaviour, irritability, mood swings, egocentricity and detachment. At present there is no standardised evidence-based approach to the treatment of moderate/severe head injury, however it is possible to call on a variety of CBT strategies that will address most of the problems that such clients manifest. In this connection, Chard et al. (2011) used a modification of cognitive processing therapy in their study of war veterans with PTSD and TBI. They omitted the element of writing/reading trauma accounts with the veterans and this appeared effective, albeit that there was no control group in their study. Table 14.3 shows a Sat Nav that may be used to help address the sequelae of moderate/severe head injury, although its applicability depends on the severity of cognitive impairment. It is suggested that rather than attempt to pre-judge the applicability of Table 14.3, the treatment strategies should be put to the test and refined or abandoned in light of the results. However, it is recommended that, as in the Chard et al. (2011) study, clients should not as a general rule be asked to read aloud or write about their trauma, and the coping skills approach elaborated in Chapter Four for PTSD symptoms is likely to be more appropriate than the trauma-focused approach of Chapter Five.

**Table 14.3** Sat Nav for the Sequelae of Moderate/Severe Head Injury

| Therapeutic targets | Treatment strategies |
|---|---|
| 1. Beliefs about head injury | Normalisation of symptoms – utilisation of Moving on After Trauma |
| 2. Impulsivity/inappropriate behaviours comments | Brief relaxation exercise/empathy |
| 3. Concentration | Graded exposure utilising encoding strategies |
| 4. Productivity and cognitive control | Tracking activity – working to a timetable, breaking tasks down to manageable sub-tasks, working sequentially using a 'turnstile', buying time |
| 5. Blitzing and inactivity | Pacing |
| 6. Exaggeratedly negative view of performance, self and others | Cognitive restructuring – use of MOOD chart |
| 7. Worry about forgetting and long-term functioning | Challenging maladaptive metacognitive beliefs about worry |
| 8. Emotional numbness/lack of spontaneity | Connecting with significant others |

**Table 14.4** Role Performance Questionnaire

This questionnaire is designed to help assess any changes in your ability to carry out everyday roles (e.g. as a mother) since the incident. Please indicate using a scale 0–10 (where 10 would be performing a role superbly, 0 would be carrying out the role very badly, and 5 would be performing the role 'so-so') how well you were doing before and now. For example, a score of 7 would mean you were playing a particular role pretty well, while a score of 3 would mean you were carrying out a role pretty badly. Just complete the questionnaire for the roles that apply to you and leave blank those that do not apply. If there is a role that is not included in the list but is important to you (e.g. grandfather, student) add this on to the list and rate your performance before the incident and now.

| As: | Before the incident | Now |
|---|---|---|
| Mother | | |
| Father | | |
| Daughter | | |
| Son | | |
| Wife | | |
| Husband | | |
| Partner | | |
| Employee | | |
| Employer | | |
| Friend | | |
| | | |
| | | |

Clients with moderate/severe head injury often perceive impairments in various roles. These perceptions may or may not accord with those of significant others and might affect the client's mood and relationships. The client's role performance can be distilled by having the client complete Table 14.4.

The following case example illustrates the application of the moderate/severe head injury Sat Nav.

Don ran his own ground maintenance company, employing eight staff. His wife did the administration and he enjoyed solving difficult practical tasks. He was a keen keep-fit enthusiast. He was told by others that he was cycling one day when a car pulled out of a side road and hit him, but Don had no memory of the preceding week or the week after the incident. In hospital in the days after the incident, his level of consciousness fluctuated from 9 to 13 on the Glasgow Coma Scale (GCS) and a CT scan revealed a subdural haematoma. He was referred to a CBT therapist two years after the accident because his marriage was under strain and he had difficulty motivating himself.

## Engagement

Clients with moderate/severe head injury often have a different perception of their performance in various roles from those around them. For this reason initial interviews should include a partner or significant other for all or part of the appointment. Completion of Table 14.4 by the client and partner will make any discrepancies in perception of performance apparent. It is sometimes the case that a partner or family member perceives poor performance in one role as in need of change while the client does not see it as an area in which they need to change. The following exchange illustrates these difficulties:

*Therapist*: I notice, Don, that you felt you performed your job at 9 out of 10 before the bicycle accident and now you put it at 7 out of 10.

*Don*: Yes, with these headaches I have to have a sleep in the afternoon, so I can't do as much.

*Therapist*: And Diana [*Don's wife*], you also gave Don a 9 out of 10 for before the incident and now a 5 out of 10, which is a bit lower than Don's 7 out of 10?

*Diana*: I don't just do the administration now, I have to keep the peace between the men. We've got five of them now, when we used to have eight.

*Don*: It's just the recession, Local Councils cancelling ground maintenance contracts.

*Diana*: We probably would have let two go because of losing contracts, but Bob went because you kept taking off on him when he wanted advice on what to do.

| | |
|---|---|
| *Don*: | He should have known things after all the years he had been with us. |
| *Therapist*: | How did you get on with Bob before the accident? |
| *Don*: | Fine, I'd often have to sort out things for him, like when a motor mower wasn't working, but I didn't mind. |
| *Therapist*: | So are you more impatient with work colleagues now? |
| *Don*: | It's not just that, it's more difficult for me to sort things out now, so I don't like it when people give me problems, I just get angry. |
| *Therapist*: | That seems like two areas that might be worth working on – how to best problem solve now and how to manage impatience. |
| *Don*: | Yes, I'm not getting things sorted out these days. |
| *Therapist*: | Diane and yourself might find it useful to have a read about Tessa in *Moving on after Trauma* (Scott 2008). Tessa had similar problems and learnt to manage them better. It could make you feel less isolated with the problems and that there are ways forward, and you could discuss some of them. |
| *Don*: | OK. |
| *Therapist*: | Yes, I noticed on the Performance Questionnaire you felt that you performed 9 out of 10 as a father before, but now it's a 6 out of 10. |
| *Don*: | I know my daughter is wary of me because I'm like a bear with a sore head. I've let her down. |

The above dialogue illustrates how much easier it is to highlight the deficits in performance of clients with moderate/severe head injuries when a significant other is present. Such deficits then become therapeutic targets, but only if the client has first acknowledged that these deficits have caused problems and will continue to cause problems unless addressed.

## Treatment

Treatment begins with psychoeducation. In this connection the client can be asked to read about a character with a brain injury in *Moving on after Trauma* (Scott 2008) and the steps they have taken to manage their impairment. This can then be a focus of discussion in the session. At the second session the following dialogue took place:

| | |
|---|---|
| *Therapist*: | How did you get on Don, reading about Tessa in *Moving on after Trauma*? |
| *Don*: | I didn't feel I was up to reading ... never was much of a reader. |
| *Diana*: | I read about Tessa. It was really interesting. She wasn't performing in her job anything like she was before, but she got round it by doing just one thing at a time and taking her time. You [*looking at her husband*] could do that. |

*(Continued)*

*(Continued)*

| | |
|---|---|
| *Don:* | Like a turnstile, but it feels like everyone is trying to crowd in and get into a rugby match just before kick off. |
| *Therapist:* | Just as a turnstile gives control over the crowd going into a match, cognitive or thought control means concentrating on the task in hand and not getting hooked by other things that are going on, such as a couple of people wanting everything done immediately. |
| *Don:* | A bit like putting blinkers on a horse in a race. |
| *Therapist:* | I had not thought about it like that, but I suppose so. |
| *Don:* | Perhaps I should pretend I am Red Rum. |
| *Diana:* | He's dead! |
| *Don:* | Well you know, like a stallion! |
| *Diana:* | Stallion isn't what comes to mind of late. |
| *Therapist:* | [*laughing*] Ah I think we might be going into a different area now but the idea of keeping focused, even being Red Rum, sounds good. |

The above dialogue highlights the need to focus on increasing the client's sense of cognitive control (see Table 14.3). However, for those with moderate/severe head injuries, dealing in abstractions is likely to be problematic. Fortunately the client has themselves furnished a concrete metaphor to facilitate cognitive control. The inclusion of another family member in a treatment session has led to the highlighting of psychosocial stressors that the client might not volunteer, giving the therapist permission to venture into that area. At the third treatment session the following exchange took place:

| | |
|---|---|
| *Therapist:* | I noticed on the Performance Questionnaire, Don, you gave yourself an 8 out of 10 as a husband before the incident and now you give yourself a 6 out of 10. Diana you also gave Don an 8 out of 10 for before but now give him a 4 out of 10. What do you think the difference in the present score is about? |
| *Diana:* | If I wait for him to take the initiative physically, I'll wait forever; when I do, I almost feel like I'm abusing him. |
| *Don:* | I'm just not bothered about sex these days. I can't believe it. |
| *Therapist:* | I think if something is a problem for one of you, it is a problem for both and you need a gameplan. One of you could just choose to ignore a problem but it is likely to build up to a tsunami. |
| *Diana:* | How long do I have to go on just waiting? |
| *Therapist:* | It is a difficult question to answer. Often with serious head injury there is an emotional numbness. When, if at all, that will resolve itself is almost impossible to answer. All we can do is a series of mini-experiments and see what effect they have in reconnecting you. |

In the above exchange the focus has shifted to another of the treatment targets for clients with moderate/severe head injury, emotional numbness (see Table 14.3). The therapist has avoided giving unrealistic reassurance but suggests progress may be made by a series of mini-experiments. The dialogue continued:

*Therapist*: What type of situations could you create that might increase the chances of intimacy?
*Diana*: We used to go away for weekends in North Wales.
*Therapist*: Would that be possible now?
*Diana*: I suppose we could [*looking at her husband*].
*Therapist*: [*after a long silence*] You seem very quiet Don.
*Don*: We haven't got that much money with the way work has been going.
*Therapist*: You have to choose what to invest in. If you don't invest in intimacy, there is no return. It is up to you.
*Don*: Like not investing in new machinery.
*Diana*: [*laughing*] So now I'm like a lawn mower!
*Don*: Well, only a bit!
*Diana*: [*with a hint of sarcasm*] That makes me feel a whole lot better!
*Therapist*: With any investment you do what is necessary for the long term, how you feel at the moment you put to one side. Are there any investments you could both see yourself doing in the next week?
*Don*: We used to go to the Nature Reserve, take the binoculars and do some bird watching.
*Diana*: That would be a start.

In this dialogue the therapist has sought to elicit specific mutually agreed first steps towards the couple's intimacy. However the therapist has not rushed to conclude a contract. Having noted the client's ambivalence in this matter, the therapist has let the client experience the cognitive dissonance of knowing that affirmative action will probably mean short-term pain but long-term gain, leaving it to the client to resolve the dissonance. At the fifth session the homework was reviewed:

*Therapist*: Did you go to the Nature Reserve?
*Don*: Yes, it was good, met an old guy there who had not been there before and showed him some of the spots.
*Diana*: Yes it was good to both get out, but that night the kids were doing a stopover at their friends, perfect opportunity, and he just sat glued to the football on the TV.

*(Continued)*

*(Continued)*

| | |
|---|---|
| *Don*: | Well you never said. |
| *Diana*: | It is not something you spell out! |
| *Therapist*: | I think one of the difficulties when people have a moderate/severe head injury is that they don't catch on to the story that is going on with other people and this means, at least to begin with, that the friend/relative has to really spell it out. |
| *Diana*: | It is like coming home from visiting my mother and finding the dishes haven't been done, the carpet hasn't been hoovered, the washing has not been cleared. |
| *Don*: | When she says this I wonder what I've been doing – just staring into space. |

The above exchange illustrates the motivational and emotional deficits of clients with moderate/severe head injuries. Encouraging clients to timetable in activities in manageable doses (Table 14.3), and to ask themselves regularly what the current 'story' of those close to them is, can help counter the emotional/motivational deficits. At the eighth treatment session the following dialogue took place:

| | |
|---|---|
| *Don*: | I went the park with my son, so he could go for a run as part of his training for his football team, but after half a mile running with him I had to give up. I just went over to the exercise machines there. I was annoyed. Before the accident he would have struggled to keep up with me for the three mile run around the park. I let him down. |
| *Therapist*: | Did he say or do anything to show that you had let him down? |
| *Don*: | No, but I did. |
| *Therapist*: | I don't understand that he didn't do or say anything but you let him down? |
| *Diana*: | Actually, what my son said to me is 'Dad's getting an old codger'. |
| *Therapist*: | Don, can you think back to thinking your Dad was getting 'an old codger'? |
| *Don*: | Yes. |
| *Therapist*: | Did you think he had let you down when you began to think of him as an 'old codger'? |
| *Don*: | No. |
| *Therapist*: | So is the story with your son that he thinks less of you? |

In this dialogue the therapist has questioned the client using bemusement/befuddlement in the style of the TV detective Columbo, and has then used

Socratic dialogue to help the client appreciate the 'story' of others. The focus in this exchange has been on increasing the client's sense of empathy, as clients with moderate/severe head injury tend to be egocentric. In their encounters with others, such clients can be trained to use a *Stop and Think*! strategy. The thinking refers to constructing a story about the functioning of the other before a verbal/behavioural response. In cases of moderate brain injury it is also possible for clients to utilise the MOOD chart (see Chapter Four).

## Relapse Prevention

The final two to three sessions of the programme are devoted to relapse prevention. This involves: (a) a review of the skills already taught; (b) a greater opportunity to apply those skills because of a longer time interval between the final sessions; and (c) a review of the application of skills, refinement of strategy and distillation of support network. Although the functioning of clients with moderate/severe cognitive impairment can be improved by teaching the skills elaborated in Table 14.3, they (and their carer) may require two or three support sessions a year indefinitely. The transcript below is of a final treatment session, and illustrates the types of difficulty encountered, the treatment response, and the difficulties in securing ongoing support:

*Therapist*: It is two months since we last met, how are things going Don?

*Don*: Well I'm still struggling with these headaches. The neurologist started me on new medication but I think it makes them worse if anything. Then I read that a side-effect of the antidepressants I take can be a loss of libido.

*Diana*: He did try leaving off the antidepressants for a week but he was terrible – irritable and shaking.

*Therapist*: Don, are you saying you just suddenly stopped the antidepressants?

*Don*: Yes, I don't want to be dependent on all these medications.

*Therapist*: But you can get awful withdrawal symptoms from stopping the antidepressants suddenly. Usually there is no problem if you do it over a period of weeks. So it might be that you can manage without the antidepressants but it needs to be done slowly. But is it the right time to try it while your neurologist is trying to sort out your headaches?

*Diana*: I told him not to, he's rushing everything, to get the business going. He's just having an hour's sleep in the afternoon, but he needs a couple of hours.

*Therapist*: One of the first things we looked at in the programme [Table 14.3] is 'pacing' yourself. You are running a marathon, it's not your fault that you have not got the petrol in the tank you had previously. You mustn't pretend that it's not half empty, otherwise you damage the engine and are likely to become irritable.

*(Continued)*

*(Continued)*

*Don*: That is what has been happening with just an hour's sleep in the afternoon.

*Therapist*: Don, you can only go at your new optimum cruising speed; if you go at your old speed you will be in trouble.

*Don*: I've got to push myself, no use in sitting back.

*Therapist*: You are right to a point, but the pushing has to be very gentle. Look at the results and if they are not better for pushing, stop. No brute force, just play it skilfully. You wouldn't use brute force fixing parts of equipment. You would use skill lining up appropriate parts before pushing.

*Don*: You mean don't do it the way kids would do it?

*Therapist*: Exactly. Diana can be something of a referee about whether you are keeping to the rules but she can be dismissed because she is 'Diana'. Perhaps ideally we should arrange a chat a couple of times a year just to keep your skills up to date and make sure that they are being put into practice. But I don't quite know whether funding could be made available for this long term. You might need to approach your solicitor. I could probably provide the odd telephone chat in an emergency free of charge.

This exchange illustrates the need to recap material taught early on in the programme. While some of the techniques, such as 'pacing', seem very simple, their application is fraught with difficulties that need to be addressed. Further, clients with moderate/severe cognitive impairments need lifelong support, but there can be problems not only with the quantity of that support but also with the quality of it.

## SUMMARY

1. While the majority of those suffering a head injury have no long-term impairment, a minority will suffer from persistent postconcussion syndrome or moderate/severe head injury. Both sub-populations require CBT, but will follow different protocols.
2. There is a considerable overlap between PPCS and the symptoms of PTSD and depression but they are sufficiently distinct as to make different interventions appropriate.
3. Maladaptive appraisals appear to mediate between PCS and PPCS.
4. There is no evidence-based CBT protocol for moderate/severe head injury but it is possible to draw on existing interventions for many of the symptoms.

# Chapter Fifteen

# THE CBT TREATMENT OF DISFIGUREMENT

*Trauma may result in disfigurement of varying degrees. At its most extreme clients can become virtual hermits, venturing out only wearing a mask, and at the other extreme clients can become preoccupied with a minor physical anomaly, restricting their interactions and lowering their self-esteem. The disfigurement can also act as a reminder of the trauma, perpetuating a trauma response. It is suggested that clients with mild disfigurement may be suffering from trauma-induced body dysmorphic disorder and in this chapter a CBT model for this is described, with reference to a case example. This chapter begins with a consideration of the impact of severe disfigurement and the delineation of appropriate CBT treatment strategies.*

## SEVERE DISFIGUREMENT

Simon Weston, a soldier in the Welsh Guards, suffered severe facial injuries and 46% burns when his ship the *Sir Galahad* came under attack during the Falklands War. In his autobiography, *Walking Tall* (Weston 1989), he describes nightmares, depression and alcohol abuse, which gradually resolved, and he was then left to cope with his disfigurement. The social and personal difficulties of those with very visible disfigurement are illustrated by the following extract from his autobiography:

> I was desperately trying to live like a normal human being, but I had to look at life in a different way because people looked at me differently. Inside I was normal but outside I was scarred. I wanted to go places and do things, but everywhere people stopped and stared. The fact was, most people felt revulsion when they saw me ... One night outside

> a disco in Cardiff, a pair of teenage girls stared, pointed and laughed at me. If only they could have known how much more that hurt me than any other kind of pain I had had to endure ... Sometimes on a train people would keep on and on staring, and when they looked too long I felt like jumping up and poking them in the eye. I knew very well that if I had been them, I'd have stared too, because it's human nature. But I got fed up with being looked upon as a freak. (Weston 1989: 198, 199)

Clients with disfigurement or disability encountering the above situations face a stark choice: whether to retreat into a land of avoidance or venture forth into a land of approach. Newell and Marks (2000) have suggested that avoidance is prompted by fear and the anticipation of a negative outcome and leads to the individual engaging in an increasingly restricted range of activities, with ever more innocuous situations determined as threatening. Newell and Marks (2000) found that the phobic scores of their sample with facial disfigurements were similar to a sample suffering from social phobia, suggesting that the core problem may be a phobic anxiety rather than a generalised anxiety. The CBT treatment of disfigurement (Newell and Marks 2000) has therefore been a mirror of the treatment of social phobia, emphasising the importance of exposure. However, from the relatively few studies that have been conducted it is unclear which aspects of the CBT treatment programmes have been most effective, whether it has been the opportunity to meet those with similar impairments or the specific CBT components such as exposure and social skills training.

A person's subjective perception of how noticeable their difference is from others is a better predictor of psychological and body image disturbance than is the assessment of a dispassionate observer or clinician (Harris 1997). However, the visibility of a difference can be an additional stressor. If large areas of the face are affected, the disfigurement is likely to be immediately obvious in most social encounters. However, disfigurements can arise from traumas such as electrocution, where the body parts affected may not be on public view but may affect intimacy, self-esteem, and the sorts of clothes worn.

## DISFIGUREMENT AND THE 'OBSERVER' PERSPECTIVE

A key feature of the CBT model of social phobia (Wells 1997) is that the sufferer sees others as reacting to a particular model of themselves which is composed of their supposed defects (e.g. blushing, stammering), rather than to the whole of them. For ease of reference, the model is reproduced from Scott (2011) and applied to the social anxieties of the person who has an acquired disfigurement (see Figure 15.1).

The model in Figure 15.1 can usefully be applied to the difficulties of sufferers with disfigurement. In anticipation of a social situation, the person with a disfigurement may imagine a 'social meltdown'. For example, if they have a facial

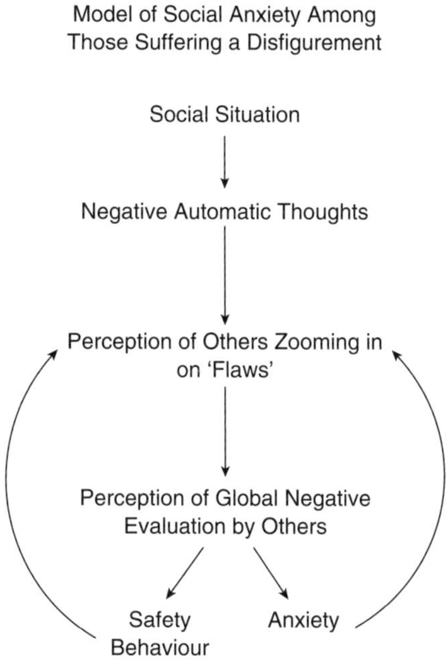

Model of Social Anxiety Among
Those Suffering a Disfigurement

Social Situation

Negative Automatic Thoughts

Perception of Others Zooming in on 'Flaws'

Perception of Global Negative Evaluation by Others

Safety Behaviour

Anxiety

**Figure 15.1** Model of Social Anxiety Among Those Suffering a Disfigurement

disfigurement which has damaged muscles around the mouth, they may drool when they eat or drink, and would thus view it as catastrophic if they do this in public. The person may imagine others focusing on this and negatively evaluating them as a 'freak', and become highly anxious about attending a social gathering. They may then engage in a safety behaviour such as not going to the gathering or avoiding eating/drinking if they do go. Such safety behaviours mean the person continues to focus on their 'deficits', perpetuating their social anxiety and thus causing the vicious circle shown in Figure 15.1.

# A CBT TREATMENT FOR DISFIGUREMENT

Clients are unlikely to be referred directly for help with adjusting to their disfigurement. Rather, these difficulties will present in the context of a referral for co-existing problems, such as pain or PTSD, where the latter may be addressed using the materials in the earlier chapters of this volume. The CBT treatment for disfigurement seeks to break the vicious circle in Figure 15.1 that maintains social anxiety, and interventions may take place at any point in the model.

Clients with a disfigurement are often very ambivalent about social engagement and motivational interviewing can be used to help them resolve this ambivalence. It is important that the therapist does not minimise the cost for the client of socialising, but simply juxtaposes the consequences with the alternative of social retreat and perhaps, in the long term, depression. Further, the commitment to

**Table 15.1** CBT Treatment Programme for Clients with a Disfigurement

| |
|---|
| Session One: Remembered humiliations and anticipated interactions |
| Session Two: Safety, social death, and daring to come out |
| Session Three: Who do you think you are? |
| Session Four: Losing battles, winning the war |
| Sessions Five and Six: Difficult situations, problem solving, and relapse prevention |

engagement should not be seen as a 'once and for all' event, but as something that they may well struggle to renew when there are setbacks.

Clients with disfigurements/disabilities wish to pass as normal, and to this end the use of skin camouflage (provided via Changing Faces, www.changingfaces.org.uk) or a prosthetic that does not look out of place may be important stepping stones to their engagement in the social world. However, the view that a client takes of their camouflage/prosthetic is likely to be very idiosyncratic and may be open to adaptive revision in treatment. Historically, those with a disfigurement/disability have at best been offered 'support', but many may better benefit from a more focused six-session CBT intervention in the year after the often numerous operations have been completed. A suggested programme is outlined in Table 15.1.

Dilip was at home one evening with his wife and daughters when they were subjected to an armed robbery. He struggled with the intruders and they poured a kettle of boiling water over his head when he insisted that he didn't know where the keys to his car where. His pain was excruciating and they prevented him from applying cold water to his head and face until they had searched and ransacked the house ten minutes later. He was very fearful that his wife and daughters would be attacked but they were not. Dilip was referred 18 months later by his GP with suspected PTSD. At interview, the scarring on the right-hand side of Dilip's face and the top of his scalp was very noticeable and the female therapist noted that he sat slightly at an angle so that the left-hand side of his face was more visible to her. As part of the evaluation Dilip completed the Severity of Psychosocial Stressors form (see Appendix H) and it was noted that he had severe problems fitting in with others and with finances and working. A diagnostic interview revealed a sub-syndromal level of PTSD and the focus of his intrusions was not so much on what had happened to him but on what could have happened – that his 'wife and daughters could have been violated'. At the first treatment session the following dialogue ensued:

*Therapist:* I noticed on the Severity of Psychosocial Stressors form you indicated severe problems fitting in. Can you tell me a bit more about those?

| | |
|---|---|
| *Dilip*: | I don't like going to my clothes shop now, sometimes 'yobs' come in and they call me 'scar face'. Then I don't go in and lose money. I don't know how much longer I can keep the business going. |
| *Therapist*: | Those types of problems are quite common when you have been through the type of experience you have been through. |
| *Dilip*: | I think the final straw was when a 'yob' said in the shop 'We will do the other side of your face next time'. It was as if he knew something. |
| *Therapist*: | So you probably go over and over that hurt? |
| *Dilip*: | I do, particularly on days when trade is very bad with the recession and I'm spending time re-arranging stock instead of serving customers. |
| *Therapist*: | [*Showing the client Table 15.1*] This is an outline of a programme we use for people with an acquired injury. The first thing we look at is the way in which we all do a 'mental time travel', going back to past events to anticipate the future. For example, let's say you were visiting an old friend, you might remember that they avidly support a particular football team and remind yourself to mention some recent game they lost badly! You anticipate the banter as you say this and you look forward to the visit. So one of the main purposes of memory is to help us anticipate the future and hopefully motivate us. But if you have suffered a minor traumatisation, whenever there is the possibility of meeting people socially, automatically you do 'time travel' back to the details of your humiliation and can then bring this forward in time to today, anticipating something approaching social meltdown. Faced with this, a person can want to retreat into their own bubble and may seek to minimise contacts. |
| *Dilip*: | That is exactly what I have done. The business has suffered enough from my absence because of the operations, but now that they are past I should be making up for lost income and not making excuses like closing on Mondays because customers are always fewer then. I think I hardly admit to myself what I am doing. I've felt too ashamed to tell my wife the real reason behind the Monday closure. With the recession, I have had to let colleagues go, so it is all down to me. |
| *Therapist*: | What I would like to work on in this session is recognising the automatic 'time travel' you are doing with regards to the 'worst humiliations', but then telling yourself to travel back to occasions recently when you have had banter with old customers. Recall those occasions in graphic detail and travel forward with them and this may motivate you to go into work more. |
| *Dilip*: | I think I try to just block out the memory of the humiliations by busying myself. |
| *Therapist*: | The more you block a memory the more it comes to the front, and that applies as much to humiliations as the extreme trauma that happened to you. |
| *Dilip*: | Yes, I have just got to face them but put them into context with other memories. |
| *Therapist*: | That is it. |

The above exchange illustrates that it is as important to circumvent cognitive avoidance in the remembering of humiliations as it is in the handling of traumatic memories. In the first session, the way in which the client engages in mental 'time travel' (Schacter 2007) is first normalised before suggesting a switch of attention to more appropriate content, which would more likely increase motivation.

The second session begins with a review of the client's efforts at properly anticipating social events. The following dialogue ensued:

*Dilip*: I felt better remembering the good as well as the bad, and I decided to tell my wife the real reason behind the Monday closure.
*Therapist*: What did she say?
*Dilip*: Stupid ***** and then gave me a hug. It was such a relief.
*Therapist*: Good, what I wanted to look at [*showing Table 15.1*] in this session is the consequences of playing it safe, hiding in your bubble.
*Dilip*: That is easy, loss of money, might have to close the business.
*Therapist*: And the other part of this session is daring to come out.
*Dilip*: I suppose opening Mondays would be a start. I did discuss this with my wife.
*Therapist*: Is there anything else you might start to do?
*Dilip*: When I do go in I've been taking sandwiches instead of going to Ali's café nearby. I could start going again.
*Therapist*: Why did you stop?
*Dilip*: I didn't want to be looked at and for people to see me drooling.
*Therapist*: Would that actually happen?
*Dilip*: Ali is as short of customers as me so it is probably not that bad. I can give it a go.

The third session begins with a review of the previous one and focuses on what the person takes their appearance to mean about themselves. At this third session the following exchange took place:

*Therapist*: How did you get on daring to come out?
*Dilip*: Well I opened on Monday and I have been to the café most days.
*Therapist*: Most days?
*Dilip*: I didn't go yesterday.
*Therapist*: Why was that?
*Dilip*: The day before when I went a young child knocked his plate and drink off a table. Without thinking I got up to help the mum clear up and the child pointed at my face and said 'Eeee'. I was so embarrassed I left without paying.

*Therapist*: What do you think the mum thought of you?
*Dilip*: Probably grateful that I got up to help her and mortified at her son saying 'Eeee'.
*Therapist*: What about Ali?
*Dilip*: Probably wondering why I rushed out and without paying.
*Therapist*: Would he think less of you?
*Dilip*: No, I've known him all the years I've been in the town centre and he's got the same business problems. He's a nice guy.
*Therapist*: What you think of yourself can make a big difference, whether you hide away or not.
*Dilip*: I don't know whether I would employ me working in a shop; for people who don't know you it could put them off.
*Therapist*: If a person with your injury applied to work in your shop you might not employ them, but would you think badly of them?
*Dilip*: No, they might be fine on the inside and I would probably give them a chance. I'm not sure, though.
*Therapist*: How can you communicate to others that you are fine on the inside if you run away from people?
*Dilip*: You can't, can you?
*Therapist*: What could you plan to do?
*Dilip*: Pay Ali.
*Therapist*: Anything else?
*Dilip*: Customers in my shop sometimes just stare and I just turn away.
*Therapist*: Does that work?
*Dilip*: No, I just feel angry that they are being ignorant but I suppose, to be honest, in the same position as them I would look twice.
*Therapist*: Before the incident if you saw a customer stare in your direction what would you have done?
*Dilip*: I would have gone over to them and said 'Hi, can I help?'
*Therapist*: What is there to stop you doing that now?
*Dilip*: Nothing really, just embarrassment.
*Therapist*: Embarrassment could win or you could win.
*Dilip*: I should do that at least with a young child in the shop who stares. It would make the parent that is with them less embarrassed.
*Therapist*: Maybe you could try this in the shop and then, when you are comfortable trying it there, you could try it in other social situations?
*Dilip*: Yes, I need to take the initiative instead of expecting others to be 'nice'.

In the above dialogue the therapist has helped the client challenge a perception of a global negative evaluation by others (see Figure 15.1) based on his appearance. This has then been used as a springboard to ensure that the client continues to engage in the social world despite inevitable setbacks. But it has also been necessary to equip him with a new social skill, going out of his way to greet others, to facilitate engagement. At the fourth session the focus is on a 'coping' rather than a 'mastery' model of adjusting to disfigurement: 'Losing the battle, winning the war'. As with the previous session it begins with a review of homework:

*Dilip*: I've been going out more, even went to a local Traders' Association meeting.

*Therapist*: That's great, but I noticed when you sit, even with me, you do so a bit side-on so I can do so just see your left-hand side.

*Dilip*: Yes, I can do, it's embarrassment.

*Therapist*: Sitting side-on is a 'safety behaviour' [*showing the client Figure 15.1*], but it feeds the idea that you only avoided humiliation by putting your best side forward and were others to see your right-hand side they would be very negative towards you. In the long term you can reduce social anxiety by giving up safety behaviours, breaking the cycle in Figure 15.1.

*Dilip*: It is daft that I sit this way with you.

*Therapist*: Are there any other safety behaviours you use?

*Dilip*: I noticed at the Traders' Association meeting I didn't have tea or coffee because I thought I would drool and I was really thirsty.

*Therapist*: Maybe a dare would to be take a drink and see whether there is any difference in people's reactions when you do from when you don't. Dare also stands for don't avoid a realistic experiment and you are testing out whether your fear (a negative evaluation by others, which is the centre of Figure 15.1) is really borne out.

*Dilip*: The real enemy might be my imagination again.

*Therapist*: Could be.

In the final sessions anticipated difficult situations are addressed within the problem-solving framework of Table 15.2. Problem solving is advocated as a tool to prevent relapse.

**Table 15.2** Steps in Problem Solving

1. Defining the problem
2. Brainstorming solutions
3. Choosing and implementing a solution
4. Reviewing the solution in light of experience
5. Choosing another solution if other strategy is either unsuccessful or only partially successful

At the fifth session the following exchange took place:

| | |
|---|---|
| *Dilip:* | I mentioned at the last Traders' Association meeting that I had been setting up a website to get some sales over the internet and I've been asked to give them a talk on how I have gone about it at the next meeting. It fills me with dread. |
| *Therapist:* | Would it have bothered you before the incident? |
| *Dilip:* | A little, but I wouldn't have been that bothered. |
| *Therapist:* | What is it that bothers you now? |
| *Dilip:* | I think it is if any new people are there. |
| *Therapist:* | What we have just done is sort out exactly what it is that is bothering you about the next Traders' meeting, which is Step 1 in Table 15.2, spelling out exactly what is concerning you. If you leave it vague (e.g. 'I just hate meeting people') then you can't solve it. The next stage is to look at the menu of options. I suppose one option is not to go to the meeting. The other one is obviously to go but you could attend and choose to carry different stories about newcomers: 'They will just notice my scarring and won't hear anything else and think "who does he think he is, standing up there?"' Or the story you carry to the meeting might be: 'They are as desperate as me to keep their business going so anything that might help has their total attention'. So, there at least three options on the menu. Which one would you choose? |
| *Dilip:* | I think I should go with the story that the other Traders are interested in survival and not in my appearance. |
| *Therapist:* | Using Table 15.2 you would see how your chosen solution works out. In general, if a solution doesn't work out, you will try something else. It is rather like you are already trying another solution to falling sales by using the internet. It seems that problem solving is what you do ordinarily with your business without realising it, it is just doing the same type of thing for the 'hot potato' issue of your appearance. |

In the above dialogue the therapist has enhanced the client's self-efficacy with regard to problem solving by suggesting that he has already used it successfully but without realising it. Further, the problem solving has been marketed as something that is as applicable to personal matters as impersonal matters. As such, it is applicable to other situations where the client might put their disfigurement centre stage. The person with a social phobia constructs an image of what others see on the basis of their own idiosyncrasies. Successful treatment involves a focus instead on the story of the observer. In a similar fashion, in the above exchange the egocentricity of the person with an acquired disfigurement is circumvented by a switch of attention to the story of the observer.

## TRAUMA-INDUCED BODY DYSMORPHIC DISORDER

Clients can suffer significant functional impairment as a result of minor or imagined trauma-induced marks or scars. In a study of women who had experienced intimate partner violence (Weaver et al. 2007), for those with an appearance-related residual injury (marks or scars left after an acute injury has healed) there was a moderate to large correlation between body image distress and severity of PTSD, whereas for those without marks or scars there was only a small correlation between body image distress and PTSD severity. The differences between the two correlations were significant. Weaver et al. (2007) noted that the appearance-related residual injuries were small and unremarkable, and the victims were more displeased than two objective observers. The authors further observed that this highlighted the subjectivity of the client's interpretation. However, some care is needed in relying on this study in that only a self-report measure of PTSD was used – there was no diagnostic assessment. Interestingly, however, these authors used the Body Dysmorphic Disorder Examination (BDDE) (Rosen and Reiter 1996) to assess body image distress and this raises the interesting question of whether clients with appearance-related residual injuries may not merit a diagnosis of *DSM IV TR*-defined body dysmorphic disorder (BDD) as part of a more comprehensive description of their difficulties. *DSM IV TR* (American Psychiatric Association 2000) defines BDD as an exaggerated concern over an imagined or minor physical anomaly but makes no reference to the aetiology of the disorder, which has been traditionally understood as a somatic one. Clients with a trauma-induced BDD differ from clients traditionally given this diagnosis in that the latter's difficulties usually begin in adolescence (Phillips et al. 2005). Further, the focus of the traditionally diagnosed BDD cases is on numerous body areas (Phillips et al. 2005), while the preoccupation of the trauma-induced BDD client is with a more circumscribed area. However, trauma does appear to feature in the aetiology of traditionally defined BDD in that a study by Buhlmann, Marques and Wilhelm (2012) found that a BDD group reported more retrospective experiences of physical and sexual abuse in childhood or adolescence than mentally healthy controls. Surprisingly, there were no significant group differences in reports of emotional abuse in early life.

In a single case study, Roskes (1999) reported a man as having suffered from BDD for six years following the witnessing of a shooting, the consequential loss of his right eye, and a preoccupation with the replacement prosthetic eye. The records made no reference to a diagnosis of BDD but indicated diagnoses of PTSD and depression a year after the shooting. The depression took a variable course and was absent when the man's business was doing well, and the PTSD had resolved by the time of Roskes' assessment (six years after the shooting). Roskes reported that after his injury the man began to view himself as 'ugly', 'half a man', 'I can't even stand to look at myself'. He became convinced that people around him could easily identify his prosthetic eye and began wearing glasses to hide it, but Roskes was unable to discern which eye was the prosthetic until the man tapped it with his fingernail. This case is particularly interesting as the man's distress and preoccupation with the prosthesis persisted even at those times when the PTSD and depression were not present, i.e. these concerns were not just a depressive preoccupation. This study and the Weaver et al. (2007) study suggest that perceived disfigurement may be an appropriate therapeutic target and that some cases may fall under the rubric of BDD. Clearly, however, there are other cases of disfigurement involving burns and amputations where a BDD diagnosis would not be an appropriate diagnosis.

## THE CBT TREATMENT OF BDD

There are only two randomised controlled trials of the efficacy of the CBT treatment of BDD (Rosen et al. 1995; Veale et al. 1996). In the Rosen et al. study, 54 women with various appearance complaints (weight or body shape, facial features, breast size, skin blemishes, head hair, body hair, and teeth) were recruited. Clients were treated in groups for eight sessions. Therapy involved a modification of intrusive thoughts of body dissatisfaction and overvalued beliefs about physical appearance, exposure to avoided body image situations, and the elimination of body checking. By the end of treatment, 81.5% of those undergoing CBT were clinically significantly improved using the BDDE (Rosen and Reiter 1996) as an outcome measure. In the Veale et al. study (1996), 19 clients were randomly allocated to twelve sessions of CBT or a waiting list. Seven of the nine clients in the CBT group no longer met the diagnostic criteria for BDD at the end of the trial, but the control clients all remained in the clinical range for BDD. The seven clients in the BDD group scored lower than the control clients on key BDD and depression measures. However, it cannot be assumed that the encouraging findings of these two trials would generalise to clients with a trauma-induced BDD or indeed to males.

The CBT sessions in the above trials focused on cognitive restructuring, exposure to social situations, and reduction of rituals such as mirror checking and seeking reassurance. More recently, perceptual retraining (Wilhelm et al. 2010) has been added to the armamentarium of treatment strategies. The rationale for these interventions derived from a cognitive-behavioural model of BDD, as well as from theories of and research on social phobia and OCD. Such interventions are potential candidates for use with clients suffering from trauma-induced BDD but, more appropriately, the targets and strategies should derive from a specific CBT model of trauma-induced BDD.

## A CBT MODEL OF TRAUMA-INDUCED BDD

An extreme trauma may lead not only to primary traumatisation (a direct response to a trauma), i.e. disorders such as PTSD and depression (see Figure 15.2), but also to secondary traumatisation (a response to a consequence of the trauma), such as a perception of a defect in appearance and/or pain. It is suggested that if the perceived defect is catastrophically misinterpreted, this leads to avoidance/ safety behaviour and the client's beliefs about the significance of the 'defect' are

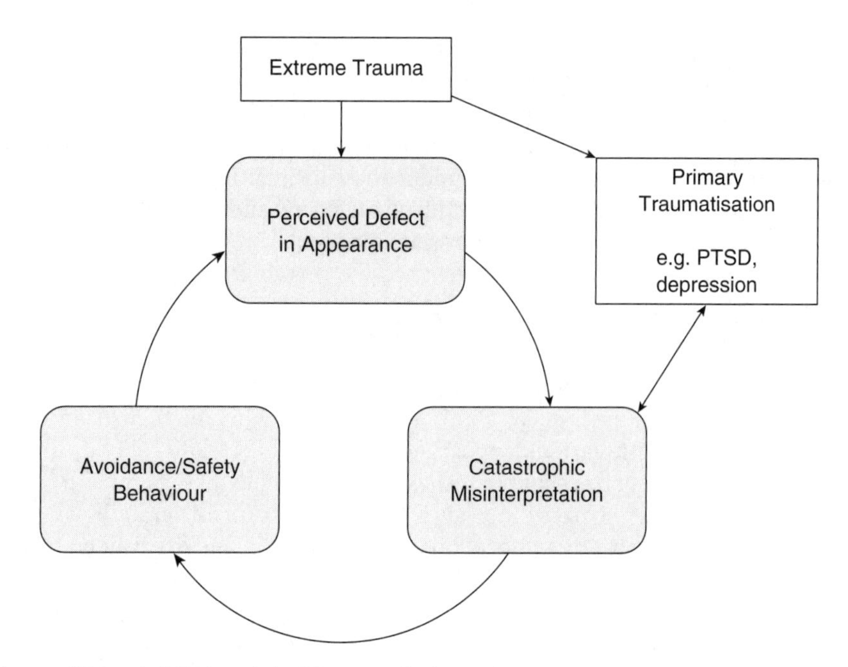


**Figure 15.2** A CBT Model of Trauma-induced BDD

not open to disconfirmation. The client thus becomes stuck in a vicious circle leading to the maintenance of the trauma-induced BDD.

The presence of a primary traumatisation disorder increases the likelihood that the 'defect' will be interpreted in a catastrophic manner and in turn this serves to maintain dysphoria. The catastrophic misinterpretations have two foci: (a) self – a perception of the magnitude of the gap between their appearance before and post-trauma; and (b) others – a perception that others view them and their appearance much more negatively than pre-trauma and, further, others' views of them are largely determined by their appearance. The sufferer's reaction to being 'flawed' may be to engage in avoidance behaviour (e.g. to avoid public scrutiny or intimacy and to engage in safety behaviours such as covering a facial scar with a hand or checking on its visibility). Such behaviours give short-term relief but offer no opportunity for the BDD sufferer's prejudices against themselves to be disconfirmed. The prejudice against self is maintained by information-processing biases which include an overestimation of the attractiveness of others' faces, threatening interpretations for non-threatening scenarios, and a bias towards detailed information processing rather than a focus on global, organisational features (Wilhelm et al. 2010).

## THE ASSESSMENT OF TRAUMA-INDUCED BDD

A *DSM IV TR* (American Psychiatric Association 2000) diagnosis of BDD requires that two criteria are met: *Criterion A* is a preoccupation with an imagined defect in appearance. If a slight physical anomaly is present, the person's concern is markedly excessive. *Criterion B* is that the preoccupation causes clinically significant distress or impairment in social, occupational or other important areas of functioning.

At assessment the therapist should note whether any defect is not observable, minimal or marked. If the latter is the case this would exclude the possibility of a BDD diagnosis. In forming a judgement about whether the client's concerns are 'markedly excessive', the therapist may also seek the views of colleagues (e.g. reception staff) about whether they noticed anything in particular about X. The assessment interview should then proceed to examine rumination. Unless a client is preoccupied with a deleterious change in their appearance since the trauma, they would not meet criterion A for BDD. Further, this preoccupation would need to be upsetting and/or to interfere with tasks. In order to determine whether a client would meet Criterion B for trauma-induced BDD, the therapist should enquire about any changes in socialising since the trauma(s). If the frequency of socialising, intimacy or being in public situations has reduced since the incident(s) because of a fear of a global negative evaluation by others arising from a focus on the defect, then criterion B would be met. Similarly, avoidance of or upset at looking in a mirror post-trauma (when it was not present before) would be evidence of meeting Criterion B. Phillips et al. (2008) have suggested asking the questions listed in Table 15.3 to aid the diagnosis of BDD.

**Table 15.3** Questions to Aid in Diagnosing Body Dysmorphic Disorder (Phillips et al. 2008)

1. Ask 'Are you very worried about your appearance in any way?' Or: 'Are you unhappy with how you look?'
2. Invite the client to describe their concern by asking 'What don't you like about how you look?' Or: 'Can you tell me about your concern?'
3. Ask if there are other disliked body areas – for example, 'Are you unhappy with any other aspects of your appearance, such as your face, skin, hair, nose, or the shape or size of any other body area?'
4. Ascertain that the client is preoccupied with these perceived flaws by asking 'How much time would you estimate that you spend each day thinking about your appearance, if you add up all the time you spend?' Or: 'Do these concerns preoccupy you?'
5. Ask 'How much distress do these concerns cause you?' Ask specifically about the resulting anxiety, social anxiety, depression, feelings of panic, and suicidal thinking.
6. Ask about any effects of the appearance preoccupations on the client's life – for example, 'Do these concerns interfere with your life or cause problems for you in any way?' Ask specifically about effects on work, school, other aspects of role functioning (e.g. caring for children), relationships, intimacy, family and social activities, household tasks, and other types of interference.
7. While compulsive behaviours are not required for the diagnosis, most clients will perform at least one of them (usually many). Ask about the most common ones: camouflaging, comparing, mirror checking, excessive grooming, reassurance seeking, touching the disliked body areas, clothes changing, skin picking, tanning, dieting, excessive exercise and excessive weight lifting.

Carmen was at work as a laboratory assistant, adding two chemicals together, when she was distracted by a colleague (who had accidentally knocked some equipment on to the floor). She added too much of one chemical, causing the agents to spurt out of the flask, and she was splashed on the forehead. She immediately rinsed her forehead in cold water but the burning sensation continued and she was hospitalised. In the months after the incident she had a number of skin grafts and became depressed. Initially she was fearful of returning to work but these feelings waned after she was back at work a few months. Despite assurances from her mother and female friends that the scarring was 'hardly noticeable', Carmen was depressed and had become a social recluse. Her relationship with her boyfriend of six months broke up three months after the chemical burn because he 'no longer found me physically attractive'.

**Table 15.4** BT Treatment Programme for Trauma-induced BDD

| | |
|---|---|
| Session One: | Socialisation to the CBT model (see Figure 15.2), prescription of reading material from *Moving on after Trauma* (Scott 2008), identifying how self-image was constructed and consideration of alternative structure |
| Session Two: | Cognitive restructuring, MOOD chart, information-processing biases |
| Sessions Three and Four: | Behavioural experiments – closing the gap between expectation and experience |
| Sessions Five to Eight: | Safety behaviours |
| Sessions Nine and Ten: | Review and development of coping strategies for potential dangers, problem solving |

A treatment programme for clients with trauma-induced BDD is outlined in Table 15.4.

Treatment of a client's BDD begins with psychoeducation. The client can be invited to read about 'Tessa', who has trauma-induced BDD, in *Moving on after Trauma* (Scott 2008), as well as about any other character that reflects any additional disorder from which they may be suffering. The following dialogue took place at the start of the second treatment session with the above client:

*Carmen:* Reading about 'Tessa' was like reading about myself. She messed up her relationship after her fall but fortunately my concentration problems haven't been as bad as hers. I could also identify with 'Joan' and her depression. Her husband was full of 'put downs', just like my boyfriend, and it was interesting to read about getting gradually more active and using the MOOD chart for managing my mood.

*Therapist:* Yes, the idea of the book is to find characters that match closest to yourself and then you can follow in their footsteps.

*Carmen:* It makes me feel it is not just me and there are ways out.

*Therapist:* Good. I was interested that you said you messed up your relationship but then said your boyfriend was full of 'put downs'. I'm a bit confused as to who was responsible for the break up.

*Carmen:* So am I. When my mood is better I think it was him and I feel angry, but then when I'm low I think it was me.

*Therapist:* Sounds like you do black and white thinking. It is described on page 99 of *Moving on after Trauma* as 'Dichotomous thinking' – either it was him or me. I wonder, do you do that with your appearance? Before the incident, what did you think of your appearance?

*Carmen:* I was happy enough with it, could have done with losing a few pounds but basically OK.

*Therapist:* And now?

*Carmen:* Crap, I feel like Cyclops with an extra eye in my forehead. It goes more pink in the cold.

*Therapist:* Has anyone called you Cyclops?

*Carmen:* My boyfriend, when he got annoyed that I wouldn't go to his friend's 21st birthday celebration. I thought 'So that is what he really thinks of me'.

*Therapist:* Had you used the term 'Cyclops' before?

*Carmen:* Yes, I used to joke to begin with, before my operations, Cyclops is not coming out because I will scare everyone.

*Therapist:* I wonder whether you are using 'Jumping to Conclusions', which is another of the biases in information processing on page 99 – assuming that your boyfriend found you unattractive when perhaps he was using the term 'Cyclops' simply because it would annoy you and he was annoyed with you for not going out.

*Carmen:* I think I have got into the habit of assuming the worst.

*Therapist:* Perhaps for homework read Chapter 8 in *Moving on after Trauma* and try to identify situations in which you are using one or more of the biases listed on page 99.

*Carmen:* OK.

*Therapist:* I'd like to show you a model [*Figure 15.2*] of how I think trauma-induced BDD comes about. At the top of the diagram there is a traumatic incident, in your case the chemical burn, which led on both to depression and your concern about your appearance, but soon afterwards (going clockwise around the figure) you saw yourself as Cyclops and this image of yourself has stuck and at least currently represents a catastrophic misinterpretation of a slight defect. Unsurprisingly, being 'Cyclops' you avoid the social world, but this avoidance makes you think of the defect more.

*Carmen:* I know what you mean. I read about the 'safety behaviours' 'Tessa' uses, covering her forehead with a fringe, panicking if it is windy, all this just keeps my attention on it.

*Therapist:* As in the diagram you just go round in a vicious circle.

*Carmen:* Yes, I've got to start with another take on it all.

In the above dialogue over the first two sessions the therapist has socialised the client to the CBT model of trauma-induced BDD and explained the basics of cognitive restructuring, including the part played by information-processing biases. However, the approach has been bottom-up rather than top-down, taking the data from the client's experience to illuminate the theoretical points. The therapist has, by careful questioning, been able to elicit how the client has constructed what she believes others 'see' and has raised the possibility that there may be alternative perspectives. In the third session, after a review of the homework, the focus shifts to behavioural experiments, as follows:

*Therapist*: At the last session you mentioned that since the incident you assume the worst, well, I would like you to create a laboratory for these assumptions and your job is to test them out [*laughing*], just don't mix chemicals in this lab!. To help you conduct these experiments I would like to introduce you to my 'telegraph pole' (see Figure 15.3).

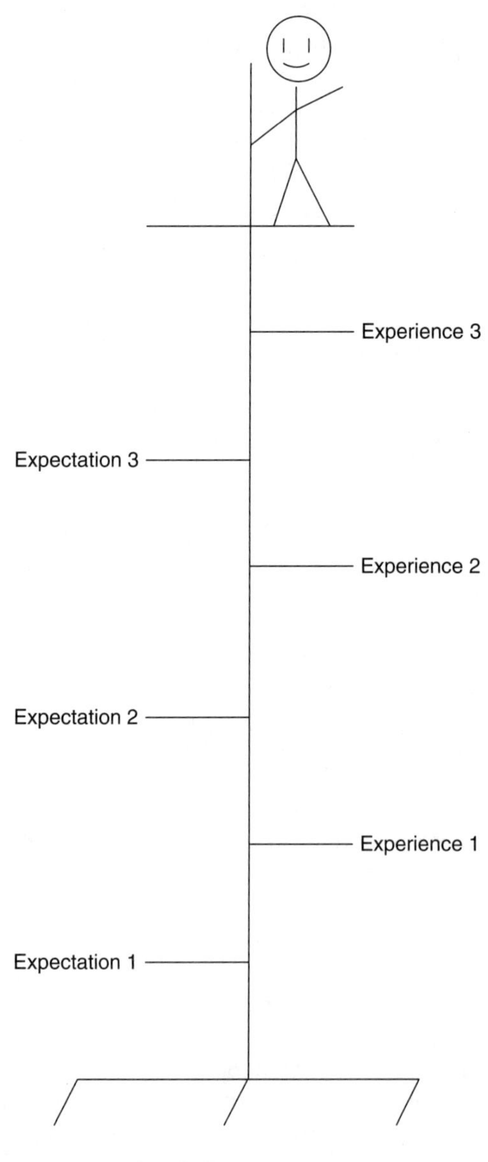


**Figure 15.3** Climbing out of Embarrassment

You can see how you climb this 'telegraph pole' with regard to fear by, say, considering learning to swim when you were little. Expectation 1 might be that you would drown if you jumped off the steps of the pool into your mum's arms. You did it and your Experience 1 was that you did not drown and got lots of praise from Mum. But then Mum suggests you jump in now off the side. Expectation 2 is that you really will drown but you try it anyway and your Experience 2 might be that although you did not actually drown, you did get a mouthful of water and weren't too happy about this. So you practised jumping off the side a couple of times with Mum catching you before contemplating anything more dangerous. Then Mum suggests you jump in without being caught, but she will be there. Expectation 3 is that you will definitely drown so you stand for a long time at the side of the pool getting your courage up and then you jump. Experience 3 is fine and you are very pleased with yourself ,and you have climbed out of fear to the top of the telegraph pole. In the same way you can overcome embarrassment by 'baby step' dares. In the lab you are testing out each negative prediction (expectation) rather than assuming each is true. How might you climb the first rungs of the telegraph pole?

*Carmen*: I think I am afraid of vertigo at the top!

*Therapist*: The person at the top in Figure 15.3 looks happy.

*Carmen*: I have got to make a start.

*Therapist*: You can always rest a while at any point, it is up to you – you are in control, not me.

Sessions 5–8 of treatment are devoted to behavioural experiments and the relinquishing of safety behaviours. In the fifth session the following dialogue took place:

*Therapist*: Isn't it a bit warm wearing the woolly hat today?

*Carmen*: I can pull it down so it keeps my fringe in place.

*Therapist*: Do you have your hat on in work?

*Carmen*: No, because I am with people I know.

*Therapist*: What if you go to a vending machine or the hospital café, do you put it on then?

*Carmen*: No.

*Therapist*: In work, have you noticed anyone looking at you that you don't know?

*Carmen*: No.

*Therapist*: You could wear your hat to the hospital café and then count the number of strangers who look at you and the next day don't wear the hat to the café and see how many strangers look at you.

*Carmen*: It could be that my hat wearing in fact attracts attention. I spend ages looking in the mirror checking it is properly in place before I go out.

*(Continued)*

*(Continued)*

| | |
|---|---|
| *Therapist:* | The mirror checking and hat wearing are safety behaviours in Figure 15.2. Using Figure 15.3, a first expectation is that something terrible will happen if you don't adjust your hat before going out. You could try not adjusting it and see what the first experience is. You could then climb further up the telegraph pole by looking at your second expectation – 'If I don't wear the hat something terrible will happen' – by not wearing it and seeing what happens (Experience). |
| *Carmen:* | I can try at least getting part way up the pole. |

The above exchange illustrates how work on behavioural experiments and safety behaviours can be integrated. Further, many of the strategies that have been successfully employed with clients suffering from a social phobia, such as comparing the effects of a day performing an activity with a day of non-performance, are equally applicable to clients suffering trauma-induced BDD.

Sessions 9 and 10 are devoted to any outstanding issues, and at the ninth session the following dialogue took place:

| | |
|---|---|
| *Therapist:* | Is there anything we have not looked at that you think might need addressing? |
| *Carmen:* | I don't want to come home to an empty flat for ever and a day, but the thought of dating freaks me out. |
| *Therapist:* | Why is that? |
| *Carmen:* | I couldn't bear to go to a club. I always thought they were a bit like cattle markets, but now I just couldn't stand them. |
| *Therapist:* | For problems that come up try the problem-solving framework in Table 15.2. You have already defined the problem – the difficulty in meeting someone with a view to a long-term commitment – and you have gone on to step 2, brainstorming solutions, and you came up with going to a club. Are there any other options you can think of? |
| *Carmen:* | I suppose there is internet dating, but then I would have all the hassle of fussing over the picture of me that I would send. |
| *Therapist:* | Any other options? |
| *Carmen:* | I've always fancied learning Latin American dancing. |
| *Therapist:* | OK, that is three options so far. The third stage in problem solving is to choose a solution. Sometimes there isn't a good solution and you just go for the least worst. The fourth stage is seeing how the chosen solution works out, and if it doesn't, you try something else. |

*Carmen*: It sounds so simple but if anything goes wrong I will think it is me and my scar.

*Therapist*: That takes us back to Personalisation, one of the information-processing biases (see page 99 of *Moving on after Trauma*). This appears to be your Achilles heel and to help prevent a relapse you will have to watch that you mentally correct yourself when you do this almost instinctive personalisation. It might also be worth reading about prejudice against yourself on page 102 of *Moving on after Trauma*, as this prejudice can sabotage your endeavours.

*Carmen*: At least now I've got a gameplan, I've just got to tweak it as I go along.

The above exchange illustrates how the final sessions include a revision of previously taught material but it is done in such a way as to make the material germane to current concerns, thereby increasing the likelihood of application. Further, the client is taught a general problem-solving strategy to help cope with the unexpected, but is cautioned that a prejudice against the self can sabotage such efforts if it is not identified and stepped around.

## SUMMARY

1. Post trauma, clients will rarely present asking directly for help to manage their trauma-induced disfigurement, although the impact of the latter can be gauged by the client's completion of the Severity of Psychosocial Stressor Questionnaire (see Appendix H). In particular, question 2 asks: 'How have you felt you have been fitting in with people in general?'
2. Social anxieties following disfigurement can be addressed by utilising a CBT model for social phobia. The treatment of severe disfigurement also has to address clients' memories of humiliations.
3. Traumatised clients can become preoccupied with a focus on an acquired minor physical anomaly (trauma-induced body dysmorphic disorder). Catastrophic misinterpretations of 'defects' lead to the maintenance of their distress. Cognitive restructuring and behavioural experiments should be conducted to challenge this 'catastrophising'.
4. Clients can be helped to climb out of embarrassment/fear by noting the gaps between 'expectations' and 'experience' in gradually more challenging situations.

# Appendix A

# DIAGNOSTIC QUESTIONS FOR *DSM V* PTSD (PROPOSED CRITERIA) AND SAT NAV

## A. TRAUMA

1. Have you been in a situation in which you thought you were going to die as a result of what happened?
2. Have you been in a situation in which you thought others were going to die as a result of what happened?
3. Have you been in a situation in which you thought yourself or others were going to have a serious injury as a result of what happened?
4. Have you been in a situation in which you were or thought that you were going to be sexually violated?

A positive response to at least one of the above is required

## B. INTRUSIONS

1. Do memories of a traumatic incident play on your mind? Do you get upset by them?
2. Do you have distressing dreams of the traumatic incident?
3. Do you lose awareness of your surroundings when you get pictures/ thoughts of the traumatic incident coming into your mind?
4. When something reminds you of the traumatic incident, do you get distressed?
5. Do you get any particularly strong bodily reactions when you come across reminders of the traumatic incident?

A positive response to at least one of the above is required

# C. AVOIDANCE

1. Do you block out thoughts or pictures of the incident(s) that pop into your mind?
2. Do you avoid conversations, people or places that bring back memories of the incident(s)?

A positive response to at least one of the above is required

# D. EMOTIONAL NUMBING/DYSPHORIA

1. Is there an important gap in your memory of the incident?
2. Since the incident(s) do you feel very negative about yourself, others or the world, or more negative than you used to?
3. Do you blame yourself or others about the incident(s) more than you really need to?
4. Since the incident(s) do you feel negative emotions such as fear, anger, horror, guilt or shame most of the time?
5. Since the incident(s) have you stopped doing activities that used to be important to you or lost interest in them?
6. Since the incident(s) do you feel cut off from others?
7. Since the incident(s) are you almost always unable to feel good?

A positive response to at least three of the above is required

# E. HYPERAROUSAL

1. Since the incident(s) are you more snappy or having more outbursts of anger?
2. Since the incident(s) do you do dangerous or destructive things?
3. Since the incident(s) are you on guard, checking things?
4. Since the incident(s) do you jump at unexpected noises or sudden movements?
5. Since the incident(s) have you had problems with concentration?
6. Since the incident(s) do you have problems either getting to sleep or staying asleep?

A positive response to at least three of the above is required

**Appendix Table A.1** Revised PTSD Sat Nav

| Therapeutic targets | Treatment strategies |
|---|---|
| 1. Beliefs about PTSD | Normalisation of symptoms – utilisation of *Moving On After Trauma* |
| 2. Cognitive and behavioural avoidance | Advantages and disadvantages of short- and long-term avoidance |
| 3. 'No one can understand what I've been through' | Realistic portrayal of discomfort to be expected, underlining the similarities of trauma and responses |
| 4. Managing reminders | The menu of options for handling reminders |
| 5. Behavioural avoidance<br>Fear of anxiety | Beginning the journey of a return to normality by gradual 'dares' |
| 6. Processing a traumatic memory | Written or verbal account of the trauma and its effects – elaboration of the memory. Prolonged imaginal exposure. |
| 7. Motivation | Motivational interviewing |
| 8. Rumination<br>Cognitive avoidance<br>Disturbed sleep/nightmares | Addressing the traumatic memory at a specific time and place |
| 9. Discrimination of triggers | Using similarities and differences |
| 10. Irritability, emotional avoidance – 'control freak' | Traffic light routine. Managing 'seething' over the trauma and its effects, coping strategies |
| 11. Persistent and exaggerated negative expectations of oneself, others or the world and persistent distorted blame of self about the cause or consequence of the traumatic event – Core Maladaptive Schemas in PTSD | Use of MOOD chart to modify observed thinking and underlying assumptions<br>Use of magnifying glass analogy to illustrate exaggeratedly negative view of self, others and world |
| 12. Cognitive avoidance<br>Behavioural avoidance<br>Hypervigilance for danger | Attention control and detached mindfulness<br>Continuing to 'dare' |
| 13. Impaired relationships | Beginning to invest in people |
| 14. Low mood, pain/disability<br>View of self, world and future | Mood management strategies cognitive restructuring, the importance of a broad investment portfolio. |
| 15. Relapse prevention | Budgeting for unpleasant reminders and distilling a protocol<br>Constructing a PTSD Survival Manual |

# Appendix B

## THE 7-MINUTE INTERVIEW – REVISED

This screen is an interview format for The First Step Questionnaire – Revised (Appendix C) and provides guidance on interpreting the latter. It covers the common mental disorders and positive findings can be investigated further using the CBT Pocketbook (freely available online at www.routledgementalhealth.com/simply-effective-group-cognitive-behaviour-therapy) which provides diagnostic questions for each disorder (for *DSM V* PTSD, Appendix A in this volume provides the diagnostic questions). If the focus is on auditing the effects of an intervention, the timeframe for questions can be altered, e.g. for the last two weeks.

**Table B.1**

| 1. Depression | Yes | No | Don't know |
|---|---|---|---|
| During the past month have you often been bothered by feeling depressed or hopeless? | | | |
| During the past month have you often been bothered by little interest or pleasure in doing things? | | | |
| Is this something with which you would like help? | | | |

A positive response to at least one symptom question and the help question suggests that a detailed enquiry should be made using the CBT Pocketbook (Scott 2011).

**Table B.2**

| 2. Panic Disorder and Agoraphobia | Yes | No | Don't know |
|---|---|---|---|
| Do you have unexpected panic attacks, a sudden rush of intense fear or anxiety? | | | |
| Do you avoid situations in which the panic attacks might occur? | | | |
| Is this something with which you would like help? | | | |

A positive response to at least one symptom question and the help question suggests that a detailed enquiry should be made using the CBT Pocketbook.

**Table B.3**

| 3. Post-traumatic Stress Disorder<br>In your life, have you ever had any experience that was so frightening, horrible or upsetting that, in the past month, you | Yes | No | Don't know |
|---|---|---|---|
| i. Have had nightmares about it or thought about it when you did not want to? | | | |
| ii. Tried hard not to think about it or went out of your way to avoid situations that reminded you of it? | | | |
| iii. Were constantly on guard, watchful, or easily startled? | | | |
| iv. Felt numb or detached from others, activities, or your surroundings? | | | |
| Is this something with which you would like help? | | | |

A positive response to at least three symptom questions and the help question suggests that a detailed enquiry should be made using Appendix A in this volume.

**Table B.4**

| 4. Generalised Anxiety Disorder | Yes | No | Don't know |
|---|---|---|---|
| Are you a worrier? | | | |
| Do you worry about everything? | | | |
| Has the worrying been excessive (more days than not) or uncontrollable in the last six months (a timeframe of the last two weeks can be used if the intent is to audit an intervention rather than screen)? | | | |
| Is this something with which you would like help? | | | |

A positive response to at least two symptom questions and the help question suggests that a detailed enquiry be should made using the CBT Pocketbook.

**Table B.5**

| 5. Social Phobia | Yes | No | Don't know |
|---|---|---|---|
| When you are or might be in the spotlight, say in a group of people or eating/writing in front of others, do you immediately get anxious or nervous? | | | |
| Do you avoid social situations out of a fear of embarrassing or humiliating yourself? | | | |
| Is this something with which you would like help? | | | |

A positive response to at least one symptom question and the help question suggests that a detailed enquiry should be made using the CBT Pocketbook.

**Table B.6**

| 6. Obsessive Compulsive Disorder | Yes | No | Don't know |
|---|---|---|---|
| Do you wash or clean a lot? | | | |
| Do you check things a lot? | | | |
| Is there any thought that keeps bothering you that you would like to get rid of but can't? | | | |
| Do your daily activities take a long time to finish? | | | |
| Are you concerned about orderliness or symmetry? | | | |
| Is this something with which you would like help? | | | |

A positive response to one or more symptom questions and the help question suggests that a detailed enquiry should be made using the CBT Pocketbook.

**Table B.7**

| 7. Bulimia | Yes | No | Don't know |
|---|---|---|---|
| Do you go on binges were you eat very large amounts of food in a short period? | | | |
| Do you do anything special, such as vomiting, or go on a strict diet to prevent gaining weight from the binge? | | | |
| Is this something with which you would like help? | | | |

A positive response to the symptom questions and the help question suggests that a detailed enquiry should be made.

**Table B.8**

| 8. Substance Abuse/Dependence | Yes | No | Don't know |
|---|---|---|---|
| Have you felt you should cut down on your alcohol use/ drug taking? | | | |
| Have people got annoyed with you about your drinking/ drug taking? | | | |
| Have you felt guilty about your drinking/drug use? | | | |
| Do you drink/use drugs before midday? | | | |
| Is this something with which you would like help? | | | |

A positive response to at least two of the symptom questions and the help question suggests that a detailed enquiry should be made.

**Table B.9**

| 9. Psychosis | Yes | No | Don't know |
|---|---|---|---|
| Do you ever hear things other people don't hear, or see things they don't see? | | | |
| Do you ever feel like someone is spying on you or plotting to hurt you? | | | |
| Do you have any ideas that you don't like to talk about because you are afraid other people will think you are crazy? | | | |
| Is this something with which you would like help? | | | |

A positive response to at least one of the symptom questions and the help question suggests that a detailed enquiry should be made.

**Table B.10**

| 10. Mania/Hypomania | Yes | No | Don't know |
|---|---|---|---|
| Have there been times, lasting at least a few days, when you were unusually high, talking a lot, sleeping little? | | | |
| Did others notice that there was something different about you?<br>If you answered 'yes', what did they say? | | | |
| Is this something with which you would like help? | | | |

A positive response to at least one of the symptom questions and the help question suggests that a detailed enquiry should be made.

IMPORTANT NOTE: If, when you inspect the 7-Minute Mental Health Screen or the First Step Questionnaire – Revised, the person screened positive for either items 1 (depression), 8 (substance abuse/dependence), 9 (psychosis) or 10 (mania) ask:

Have you been hurting or making plans for hurting yourself?

# Appendix C

## THE FIRST STEP QUESTIONNAIRE – REVISED

This questionnaire is a first step in identifying what you might be suffering from and pointing you in the right direction. In answering each question just make your best guess. Don't think about your response too much, there are no right or wrong answers.

**Table C.1**

| 1. | Yes | No | Don't know |
|---|---|---|---|
| During the past month have you often been bothered by feeling depressed or hopeless? | | | |
| During the past month have you often been bothered by little interest or pleasure in doing things? | | | |
| Is this something with which you would like help? | | | |

**Table C.2**

| 2. | Yes | No | Don't know |
|---|---|---|---|
| Do you have unexpected panic attacks, a sudden rush of intense fear or anxiety? | | | |
| Do you avoid situations in which the panic attacks might occur? | | | |
| Is this something with which you would like help? | | | |

**Table C.3**

| **3.** | | | |
|---|---|---|---|
| **In your life, have you ever had any experience that was so frightening, horrible or upsetting that, in the past month, you** | | | |
| | **Yes** | **No** | **Don't know** |
| i. Have had nightmares about it or thought about it when you did not want to? | | | |
| ii. Tried hard not to think about it or went out of your way to avoid situations that reminded you of it? | | | |
| iii. Were constantly on guard, watchful, or easily startled? | | | |
| iv. Felt numb or detached from others, activities, or your surroundings? | | | |
| Is this something with which you would like help? | | | |

**Table C.4**

| **4.** | **Yes** | **No** | **Don't know** |
|---|---|---|---|
| Are you a worrier? | | | |
| Do you worry about everything? | | | |
| Has the worrying been excessive (more days than not) or uncontrollable in the last six months? | | | |
| Is this something with which you would like help? | | | |

**Table C.5**

| **5.** | **Yes** | **No** | **Don't know** |
|---|---|---|---|
| When you are or might be in the spotlight, say in a group of people or eating/writing in front of others, do you immediately get anxious or nervous? | | | |
| Do you avoid social situations out of a fear of embarrassing or humiliating yourself? | | | |
| Is this something with which you would like help? | | | |

**Table C.6**

| 6. | Yes | No | Don't know |
|---|---|---|---|
| Do you wash or clean a lot? | | | |
| Do you check things a lot? | | | |
| Is there any thought that keeps bothering you that you would like to get rid of but can't? | | | |
| Do your daily activities take a long time to finish? | | | |
| Are you concerned about orderliness or symmetry? | | | |
| Is this something with which you would like help? | | | |

**Table C.7**

| 7. | Yes | No | Don't know |
|---|---|---|---|
| Do you go on binges were you eat very large amounts of food in a short period? | | | |
| Do you do anything special, such as vomiting, or go on a strict diet to prevent gaining weight from the binge? | | | |
| Is this something with which you would like help? | | | |

**Table C.8**

| 8. | Yes | No | Don't know |
|---|---|---|---|
| Have you felt you should cut down on your alcohol use/ drug taking? | | | |
| Have people got annoyed with you about your drinking/ drug taking? | | | |
| Have you felt guilty about your drinking/drug use? | | | |
| Do you drink/use drugs before midday? | | | |
| Is this something with which you would like help? | | | |

**Table C.9**

| 9. | Yes | No | Don't know |
|---|---|---|---|
| Do you ever hear things other people don't hear, or see things they don't see? | | | |
| Do you ever feel like someone is spying on you or plotting to hurt you? | | | |
| Do you have any ideas that you don't like to talk about because you are afraid other people will think you are crazy? | | | |
| Is this something with which you would like help? | | | |

**Table C.10**

| 10. | Yes | No | Don't know |
|---|---|---|---|
| Have there been times, lasting at least a few days, when you were unusually high, talking a lot, sleeping little? | | | |
| Did others notice that there was something different about you?<br>If you answered 'yes', what did they say? | | | |
| Is this something with which you would like help? | | | |

# Appendix D

# GUIDED SELF-HELP POST TRAUMA

Following screening (Appendix C) and a semi-structured face-to-face diagnostic interview (Appendix A), treatment can be tailored using the diagnoses to select which of the 20 characters in *Moving on after Trauma* (Scott 2008) the client is asked to read about. If, as is often the case, the client is suffering from more than one disorder, then they are encouraged to read about a character for each disorder. Some of the characters reflect additional difficulties, such as pain and head injury. One or more of these characters can be specified for recommended reading if necessary. Reading about how a person just like them has overcome their difficulties socialises the client for treatment and gives them a roadmap.

After the initial face-to-face meeting, guided self-help can be provided by a weekly 15-minute telephone call or email contact to direct and troubleshoot the reading. Depending on the complexity of the client's difficulties and their ability to utilise the material, six to ten weekly contacts are likely to be necessary. Social support is the biggest predictor of how people manage post-traumatic stress symptoms. Try the following weekly brief chats.

## Chat 1: 'What's happening to me?' (Scott 2008: Chapter One)

1. How did you get on reading Chapter 1? Did it make you feel understood?
2. Did you complete the Trauma Screening Questionnaire (TSQ) on page 10?
3. How many 'yes's did you put (more than six is probable PTSD)?
4. Did you tell the brief story of what happened by completing the thumbnail sketch on page 21?

## Chat 2: 'Making sense of my reaction' (Scott 2008: Chapter 2)

1. Does it sound right thinking of yourself as having developed an oversensitive alarm that keeps overreacting?

2. Does it sound right thinking of yourself as now living in a bubble?
3. Does it sound right thinking of yourself as like a lemonade bottle without the top on, with no fizz?
4. Did you find that one or more characters in the book sounded like you?
5. How do you feel about trying to follow in their footsteps to recovery?

## Chat 3: 'Resetting the alarm' (Scott 2008: Chapter 5)

1. Did the idea of gradually daring yourself to do things make sense?
2. Did you come up with any little 'dares'?
3. Have you done any dares yet?
4. How will you reset your alarm without beginning to do some dares?
5. Have you read any more about the characters in the book who seemed like you?

## Chat 4: 'Better ways of handling the memory' (Scott 2008: Chapter 6)

1. What did you think of the idea that blocking the memory doesn't actually work?
2. How did you feel about the idea of creating space for the normal things in life by pigeon-holing the memory to be sorted out in a special way at a special time?
3. Which way did you think you might try for sorting out the memory in the day so that it doesn't disturb your sleep at night?
4. Did you try any special ways of dealing with the memory?
5. You have already made a start confronting the memory of the incident, which is like a 'bully', by doing the Thumbnail Sketch. There seem to be different ways of getting the 'bully' to back down, such as writing a page a day about the incident and its effects for 2–3 weeks, after which time you will become bored with it instead of re-experiencing it. Could you have a go at that? [If the answer is 'no'...] What about writing about it just once and reading it over out loud three times a day? [If the answer is still 'no'...] Has your way of handling the memory up to now worked? [If the answer is 'no'...] Can you be absolutely sure that trying a different way might not work?

## Chat 5: 'Resetting the alarm' (Scott 2008: Chapter 5) and 'Better ways of handling the memory' (Scott 2008: Chapter 6)

1. Are there still things you avoid that you did before?
2. Which would be the easiest of the avoided things to have a go at?

3. What could you say to yourself to make it easier to cope with the dares (e.g. play music, sing)? When you tried what you have been avoiding did you spell out the similarities and differences to the incident?
4. How have you gone on in your special time confronting the bully? Keeping on confronting him/her means he/she backs down. Did it make sense that in writing or talking about it you are coming up with an updated version of it that the mind can work on rather than the old version (which is often a fantasy of something worse happening even though it didn't actually happen)?
5. Have you read any more about the characters who seemed like you?

    1. Chat 6: 'Restoring relationships' (Scott 2008: Chapters 5–7 and 'Managing mood' (Scott 2008: Chapter 8)How are the dares going?
    2. Are there further dares you could try?
    3. How is it going at the special time confronting the bully?
    4. Could you invest a little more in relationships?
    5. Could you invest in small doses in doing some things to give you a sense of achievement or pleasure?
    6. How did you go at trying to come up with more objective second thoughts when your mood dips?
    7. Did you use the MOOD thought record on page 95?
    8. After you had come up with the more objective second thoughts did you get on and do things instead of agonise?

It is also possible to have slightly longer chats (of about 20 minutes a week) and cover the material in four sessions of guided self-help.

# Appendix E

## SELF-INSTRUCTION FOR PTSD

**Table E.1**

| | Self Instruction for PTSD |
|---|---|
| Preparing for | |
| Encountering | |
| Coping with feeling overwhelmed | |
| Looking back at how I played it | |
| Gameplan | |

| | Flashbacks |
|---|---|
| Preparing for | |
| Encountering | |
| Coping with feeling overwhelmed | |
| Looking back at how I played it | |
| Gameplan | |

*(Continued)*

*(Continued)*

| | Nightmares |
|---|---|
| Preparing for | |
| Encountering | |
| Coping with feeling overwhelmed | |
| Looking back at how I played it | |
| Gameplan | |

| | Dissociative flashbacks |
|---|---|
| Preparing for | |
| Encountering | |
| Coping with feeling overwhelmed | |
| Looking back at how I played it | |
| Gameplan | |

*(Continued)*

*(Continued)*

| | Reminders |
|---|---|
| Preparing for | |
| Encountering | |
| Coping with feeling overwhelmed | |
| Looking back at how I played it | |
| Gameplan | |

| | Reminders that cause alarming physical symptoms |
|---|---|
| Preparing for | |
| Encountering | |
| Coping with feeling overwhelmed | |
| Looking back at how I played it | |
| Gameplan | |

*(Continued)*

*(Continued)*

| | Daring to do an activity that reminds me of the incident |
|---|---|
| Preparing for | |
| Encountering | |
| Coping with feeling overwhelmed | |
| Looking back at how I played it | |
| Gameplan | |

| | Difficulty in sleeping |
|---|---|
| Preparing for | |
| Encountering | |
| Coping with feeling overwhelmed | |
| Looking back at how I played it | |
| Gameplan | |

*(Continued)*

*(Continued)*

| | Short fuse situations |
|---|---|
| Preparing for | |
| Encountering | |
| Coping with feeling overwhelmed | |
| Looking back at how I played it | |
| Gameplan | |

| | Difficulties in concentrating |
|---|---|
| Preparing for | |
| Encountering | |
| Coping with feeling overwhelmed | |
| Looking back at how I played it | |
| Gameplan | |

*(Continued)*

*(Continued)*

| | Giving up sentry duty |
|---|---|
| Preparing for | |
| Encountering | |
| Coping with feeling overwhelmed | |
| Looking back at how I played it | |
| Gameplan | |

| | Being jumpy |
|---|---|
| Preparing for | |
| Encountering | |
| Coping with feeling overwhelmed | |
| Looking back at how I played it | |
| Gameplan | |

*(Continued)*

*(Continued)*

| | Investing |
|---|---|
| Preparing for | |
| Encountering | |
| Coping with feeling overwhelmed | |
| Looking back at how I played it | |
| Gameplan | |

| | Connecting |
|---|---|
| Preparing for | |
| Encountering | |
| Coping with feeling overwhelmed | |
| Looking back at how I played it | |
| Gameplan | |

*(Continued)*

*(Continued)*

| | Gaps in memory |
|---|---|
| Preparing for | |
| Encountering | |
| Coping with feeling overwhelmed | |
| Looking back at how I played it | |
| Gameplan | |

| | Numbness |
|---|---|
| Preparing for | |
| Encountering | |
| Coping with feeling overwhelmed | |
| Looking back at how I played it | |
| Gameplan | |

# Appendix F

# CORE CASE FORMULATIONS FOR PTSD AND SUB-SYNDROMAL PTSD

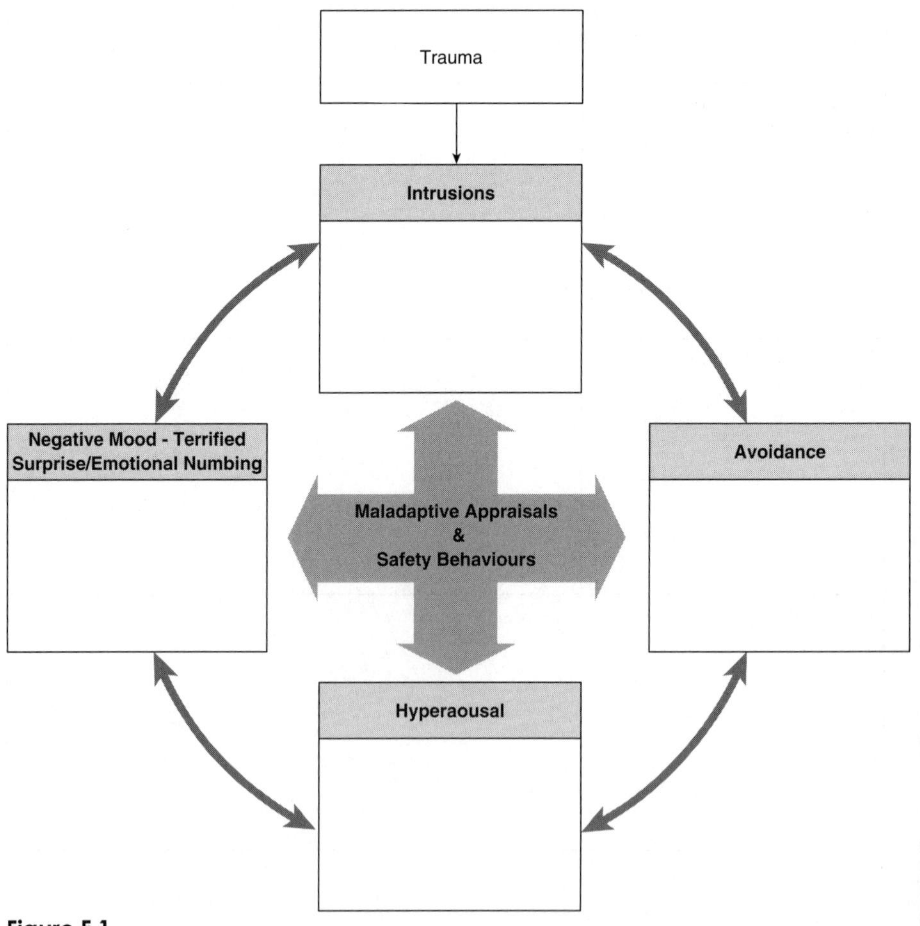


**Figure F.1**

Adapted from the Balanced Scorecard by Robert S. Kaplan and Dave P. Norton. Harvard Business School Press, 1996.

# Appendix G

## PTSD SURVIVAL MANUAL – REVISED

Serious road traffic accidents, assaults and explosions are the types of event that can give rise to post-traumatic stress disorder. Such events can act like a 'Pebble in the Water' (Figure G.1) spreading out in their effects.

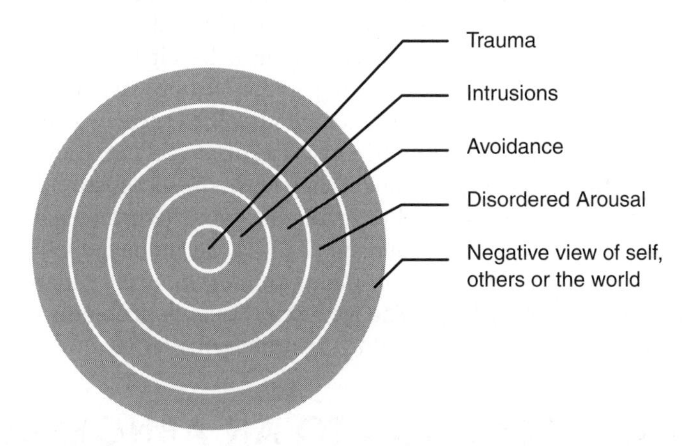


**Figure G.1** 'Pebble in the Water' Effect of Trauma

After an extreme trauma you might experience pictures of the incident coming into your mind, sometimes for no reason. At other times the memories are brought on by reminders. The memories are like unwelcome guests (Intrusions in Figure G.1) and may be joined by other intruders – nightmares of what did or could have happened. The intrusions are horrible and you probably try to make sure that they are not triggered by, for example, avoiding conversations about the incident or by staying away from the scene of the incident. Thus avoidance (see Figure G.1) is the second major ripple effect of the trauma. If you are preoccupied

**Table G.1** Disordered Arousal

| |
|---|
| ➢ disturbed sleep |
| ➢ increased irritability |
| ➢ poor concentration |
| ➢ hypervigilance (on 'sentry duty') |
| ➢ easily startled |

by memories of the incident and are avoiding anything connected with it, this is likely to cause a major disruption of your life, resulting in disordered arousal (Table G.1).

The collective name for the above symptoms is disordered arousal, which is the third ripple in Figure G.1. As the wave of PTSD spreads out through intrusions, avoidance and disordered arousal it extends as far as a fourth and final ripple in Figure G.1 – a negative view of yourself, others or the world (e.g. 'I am bad', 'No one can be trusted', 'My whole nervous system is permanently ruined', and 'The world is completely dangerous'). There is a common-sense connection between an extreme trauma and flashbacks/nightmares and avoidance, but few victims anticipate how negative they have become about almost everything.

You are not alone with these reactions. You might find that reading this brief Survival Manual is a stepping stone to reading the self-help book, *Moving on after Trauma* (available from amazon.co.uk or your bookshop), where you can read about the steps taken by someone just like yourself to recover from PTSD. The book is also a guide for relatives and friends, who often feel that they are 'walking on egg shells' with the trauma victim – if they leave the victim alone the latter is inactive and accuses those close to them of abandoning them; alternatively, if they encourage the victim to be more active, they are accused of nagging. Many trauma victims try to cope with their sleep problems and fearfulness by increasing their alcohol intake or by taking drugs. The latter can become problems in their own right, distracting attention from tackling the underlying PTSD.

## 1. NORMAL REACTION TO AN ABNORMAL SITUATION

Intrusions, avoidance, disordered arousal and disturbed relationships are normal reactions to an abnormal situation. The good news is that the majority of people recover from PTSD and for those who do not, 7 out of 10 recover by the end of cognitive behaviour therapy.

The trouble is that your reactions may not feel at all normal. You can feel a sense of danger/threat even though you know there is no danger. You can say all the sensible things to yourself but as soon as you are in a situation remotely like what happened to you all logic seems to go out of the window. Well, you are not going crazy, it just feels like it! The key problem is a 'dodgy alarm' (Figure G.2).

The brain has its own alarm called the amygdala. It is as if, ordinarily, the alarm is over to the left, in the 10 o'clock position, but should something 'alarming' happen, e.g. a person approaches you with a weapon, the alarm rings, you pump oxygen to your muscles ready to take flight or maybe even to fight. However, for some people, when the alarm rings it becomes stuck in a 'war zone' position, the 2 o'clock position to the right. In this position there is a sense of threat even though objectively there is little or no danger.

The amygdala is also the seat of emotional memory, and it works on matching

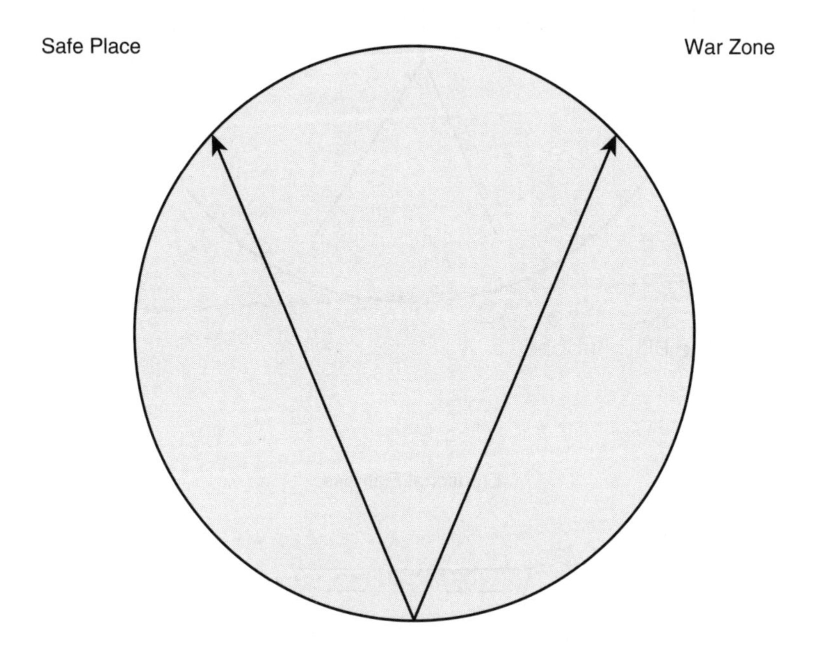


**Figure G.2** Dodgy Alarm – Amygdala

rather than logic, so that whenever you come across anything even vaguely like the incident, it goes off. When it does go off, you may feel a surge that appears to go from the top of your stomach into your chest. It is as if you are in a war zone but others are in a safe place, and this leads to a sense that you are in your own world (Figure G.3), disconnected from those around you.

This sense of isolation can lead to feelings of numbness or emptiness, a flat feeling (Figure G.4), as if somebody has left a fizzy drink standing around for a long time.

**Figure G.3** The PTSD Bubble

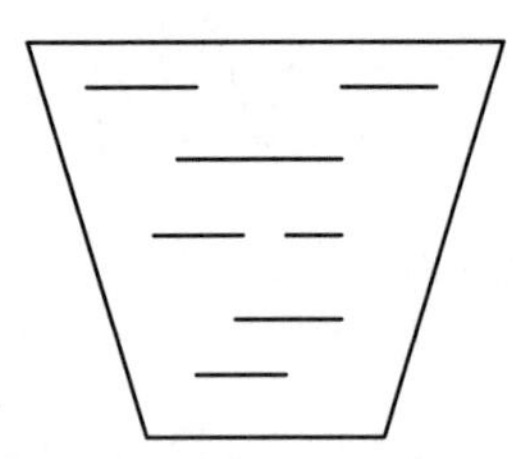

**Figure G.4** Emotional Flatness

Such emotional flatness can lead to guilty feelings, such as not feeling warm towards your partner, and a deterioration of relationships, such as no enthusiasm for returning a friend's phone call.

Recovery involves:

- resetting the alarm (Figure G.2) by moving it gradually anti-clockwise from the war zone position to the vertical 12 o'clock position (an area of less conflict) and finally back to the 10 o'clock position, a safe place.

- stretching the bubble (Figure G.3) by gradually reconnecting with people.
- getting the 'fizz' back (Figure G.4) by beginning to invest again in life.
- learning not to take the alarm's ringing seriously by putting its activation into context.

## 2. RESETTING THE ALARM

Over-reacting in every possible way is one of the hallmarks of PTSD. Knowing that you over-react will lead you to avoid situations that might trigger these extreme responses. Without fully realising it, you have spotted that you have developed an over-sensitive alarm and you have dedicated your life to not tripping it. Unfortunately, just as exercise is usually necessary for back trouble despite an increase in discomfort, so to it is necessary to trip the alarm in order to reset it. Although you may know with your head, in your better moments, that certain situations are not really dangerous, your 'guts' do not. Such 'gut' reactions change most powerfully when a person dares themselves to do what they have been avoiding and discovers that nothing bad happens. The alarm can be coaxed back to a 'safe place' by gradual dares. The situation is rather like teaching a toddler to swim: the first dare might be to have them jump in and you catch them, then when they are comfortable doing that they might jump in next to you without you catching them, etc. Thus, for example, a person with PTSD following a road traffic accident might, week by week, take the steps in Figure G.5.

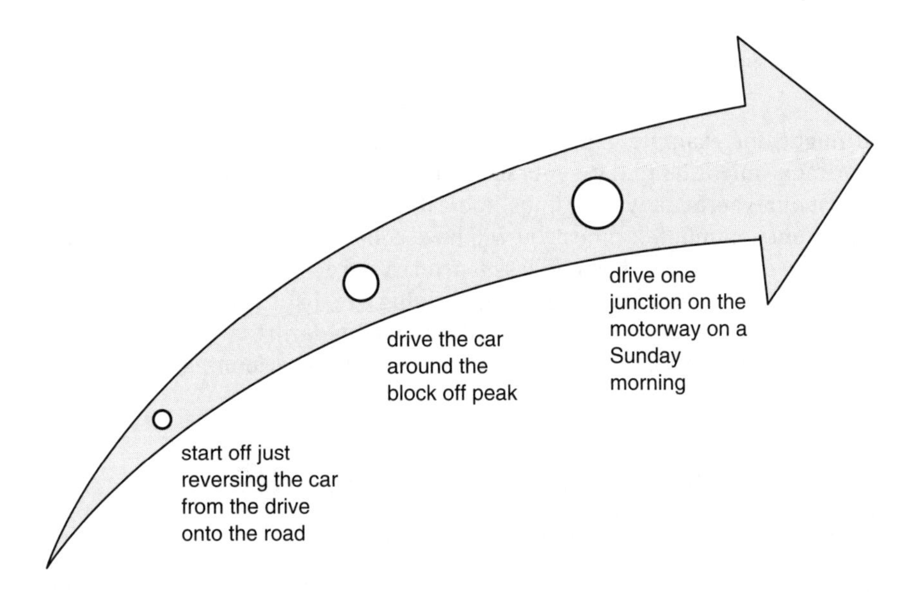


**Figure G.5** Resetting the Alarm by Daring Small Steps

When each dare or step trips the alarm it will feel awful at the time, but afterwards the alarm moves anti-clockwise a notch. What 'dares' could you have a go at? Just jot them down below:

1. ..........................................................................................
2. ..........................................................................................
3. ..........................................................................................

Start off with the easiest of the dares. In this way, you can gradually build your confidence. The idea is not to become a 'dare devil' but to gradually, simply, dare to do what you would have done before the trauma. The more you can get back to doing what you did before, the better you are likely to feel.

Unfortunately, learning anything is never smooth. It is often the case that after making significant progress the person comes across an all too vivid reminder of their trauma. It is very tempting at this point to abandon the training programme. But while the alarm may have moved slightly clockwise, continued dares will soon repair the situation and the alarm will be reset in a safe place. It is necessary to understand that training will be a matter of two step forwards and one step back, and not become demoralised.

Dares can show that what you feared is not as dangerous as you thought. In fact, dares can be thought of as experiments to test out whether your gut reactions have much to do with everyday reality now. The letters of the word dare also stand for:

- **D**on't
- **A**void a
- **R**ealistic
- **E**xperiment

You might, for example, have a fear of a busy shopping centre, so a realistic experiment might be to dare yourself to go into such a centre for just one item and test out whether anything unbearable does actually happen. If you repeat the experiment a number of times you will have collected a great deal of evidence of no danger and you will become less fearful. A dare is a two-sided coin. On one side it is about changing your thinking by doing a realistic experiment and on the other side it is about changing your behaviour by daring to do something you have been avoiding. Dares are a gesture of defiance, proclaiming that no horror has the last word.

## 3. BETTER WAYS OF HANDLING THE TRAUMATIC MEMORY

You have probably tried to blank out the memory, distracting yourself by doing something or talking to someone. The trouble is that doing so works only briefly. Here is why. If I say to you:

**'Do not think about the Orangutan'**

**Figure G.6** The Orangutan

what did you think about? As you continue to read, you are probably still thinking about the orangutan (perhaps you think he looks like somebody you know!). The more you try to deliberately not think of something, the more you think about it.

Sufferers from PTSD fear that if they don't try to block the memory it will dominate and spoil their life. But if you try to do so, it is certain that it will be constantly on your 'mental TV'. Realistically, though, you cannot help but think about the incident sometimes as it has had such a big impact on your life.

The secret of handling this traumatic memory is attention control. At times you need to let the memory just float in and out of your mind without getting involved or rising to the bait, while having a special time when you address your concerns about the incident and its effects. It is rather like children pestering you to do something when you are busy doing a task. If you just say 'Go away, I'm busy', two minutes later they are back. But if you say 'I'm busy right now but I'll fix your bike at about 11 am', provided you do turn up at 11 am they may leave you alone. There are a number of ways of dealing with the memory at a special time (see Table G.2).

**Table G.2** Better Ways of Handling the Memory

- Write a page a day about the incident and its effects
- Dictate the story of the trauma and ask someone to write it down
- Dictate the incident into a recording device, e.g. a mobile phone

Your first reaction to the alternative ways of handling the memory may well be 'no way'. Perhaps you feel that you will be 'overwhelmed by the memory or become uncontrollable'. But if you approach such tasks as if they are dares, a small step at a time, even though it is uncomfortable, it is manageable. Perhaps when you first begin to write/dictate you might leave out the most painful part or only write a few lines. That's fine. Day by day you just gradually dare yourself to do a bit more. Usually, after about two or three weeks of this, you just become bored with what you are writing/dictating. When you are bored by something you no longer have nightmares about it, nor are you distressed in the day by the memory of it. The goal is to become as 'bored' as the orangutan looks. This usually takes about 20 minutes a day of writing/re-reading or dictating/reading/listening for about two to three weeks.

## 4. SAFETY FIRST?

Since your trauma you probably do many things for safety that you didn't do before. Just take a moment and jot a few of these down:

1. ..........................................................................................
2. ..........................................................................................
3. ..........................................................................................

Your safety behaviours might include repeatedly checking the front door is locked, or checking that the children are still breathing when they are asleep, or perhaps insisting that you are in the front passenger seat rather than the rear one, or only driving to places you know.

**To what extent do you try to persuade others close to you to do what you now do?**

Here is a space for your answer ............................................................................

**If not doing what you do now is really dangerous, what stops you making more efforts to persuade others to behave just like you?**

Here is a space for your answer ............................................................................

**If there is a clear and present danger to those close to you from their not behaving just like you, would you not insist and check on them even when they are out of sight and might laugh at you if you rang or left a text message?**

Here is a space for your answer ............................................................................

**Do you do these 'safety behaviours' as a way of trying to avoid discomfort rather than because you believe that not doing them is dangerous?**

Here is a space for your answer ............................................................................

**Is it embarrassment that stops you trying to persuade people in your local area (say, via local radio) to behave exactly as you do? Surely, as a caring person you would do more?**

Here is a space for your answer ............................................................................

**Are you truly putting safety first or are these new behaviours simply a way of trying to calm the stormy seas that you feel you are sailing through?**

Here is a space for your answer ............................................................................

One possibility is that the new 'safety behaviours' are more about wanting to feel in control because you may have felt so out of control in the incident. Young children often engage in magical thinking, such as not stepping on the cracks on the pavement as they go to school so that teacher does not shout at them. Can you be sure that your new 'safety behaviours' are not magical thinking? Consider dropping the new 'safety behaviours' by engaging in gradual dares.

## 5. PHOTOGRAPHING THE TRAUMA AND ITS CONSEQUENCES FROM DIFFERENT ANGLES

The mind is rather like a camera, and how you take a photograph of the trauma makes a big difference. For example, you might be leaving your camera on what could have happened and end up regularly watching a 'horror video' of family members at your funeral. Not surprisingly, using the camera in this way is upsetting. You could instead focus on the reality. For example, there was a nasty accident that caused some injuries, but even though it was unpleasant, the 'reality video' is much less upsetting than the 'horror video'. Are you addicted to watching horror videos of what happened? If you are, what about practising switching your attention from the 'horror video' to the 'reality video'?

Reminders of your trauma can mean that you do not simply remember what happened to you, but you re-experience it again, almost as if you are back at the scene of the accident. When this happens the difference between 'then' and 'now' becomes blurred. Common reminders are smells, sounds or seeing your trauma on TV. These reminders have become 'transporters', taking you back in time. Unfortunately, reminders are always about, but you can learn how not to board the 'transporter' by letting yourself experience what that the particular smell, sound or sight means today. For example, if the smell of petrol takes you back to re-experiencing your accident, you might deliberately let yourself smell petrol, all the while reminding yourself that you are safe as you do so – you are just smelling it in the garage. Possibly it is the sight of a particular car, a knife or a loud bang that acts as a reminder. Simply looking and listening to these now, either in real life or on the internet, can teach you that they do not always have awful consequences. In this way you recognise some similarity between the reminder and your trauma but at the same time you can see very important differences. When you come across any reminder, play 'spot the differences', like the childhood game – the more differences you come up with, the better you have done.

Guilt is often associated with PTSD. For example, you might be a bus driver who knocked down and killed an elderly person who, without warning, stepped from the pavement into your path. In such circumstances it is easy to feel very guilty. Perhaps you are haunted by the expression of the person as the bus went towards them. But you can take a different angle using the responsibility pie shown in Figure G.7.

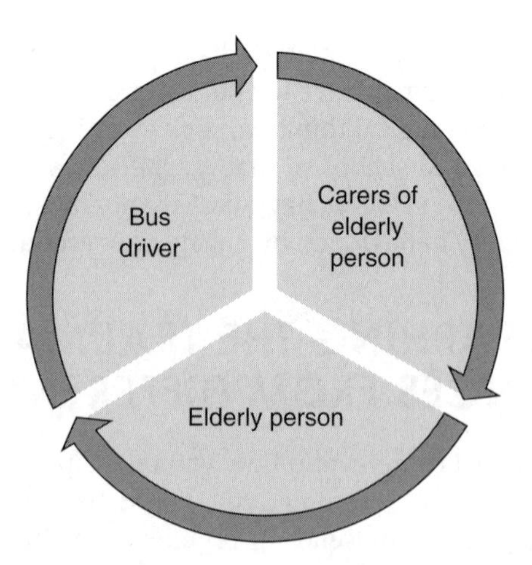


**Figure G.7** Responsibility Pie

Going clockwise around the pie, you might decide that the carers of the elderly person bear some responsibility for letting them out unsupervised, and it may be that the elderly person deserves a slice of the pie because of their carelessness. That would leave only a small slice of pie for the driver. Indeed, the driver's slice may be even smaller if the bus was poorly maintained. Using the pie, people often conclude that they are much less blameworthy than they first thought.

# 6. PTSD AND NEGATIVITY

PTSD sufferers have problems not only with the past but also with the future: when they think of the past they cannot get beyond the trauma and when they imagine what is likely to happen in the coming days they use a trauma-based construction kit (Figure G.8).

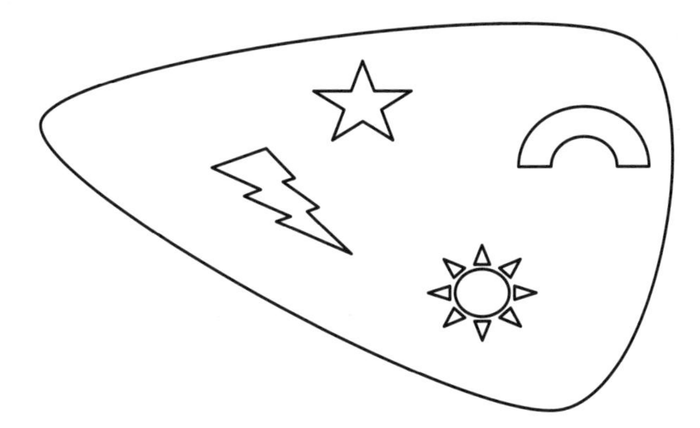

**Figure G.8** Trauma-based Construction Kit for Future Events

The sufferer uses different parts of the traumatic memory, thoughts, feelings, bodily reactions and behaviours to predict, say, what is going to happen as they go through a set of traffic lights when the lights are on green (even though their trauma might be unrelated to an accident at lights), and a typical 'picture' they might assemble is shown in Figure G.9.

Thus, though nothing might actually happen, when the person goes through the lights on green, they are nevertheless upset by their imaginings and may continue to be upset even when they find that they have safely gone through the lights. The 'picture' they have created of going through the lights on green is disturbing and unstable (unstable in the sense that it inaccurately predicts what happens). By contrast, most people use a quite different construction kit when building a 'picture' of a forthcoming event. Their kit is based on, say, their lifetime history of driving through lights that are on green (see Figure G.10).

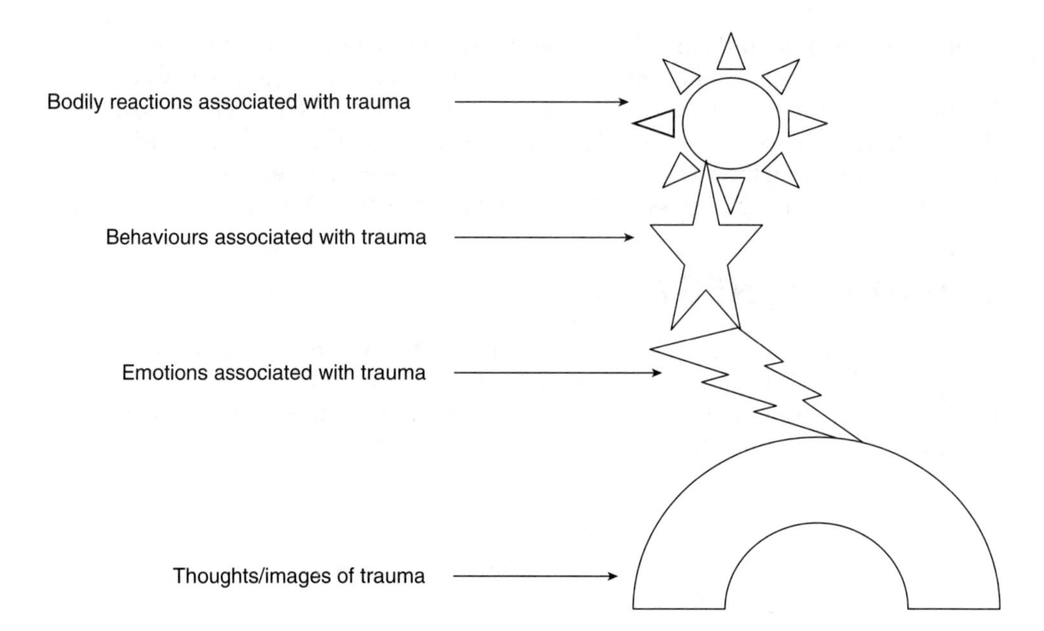


**Figure G.9** Assembled Likely Event

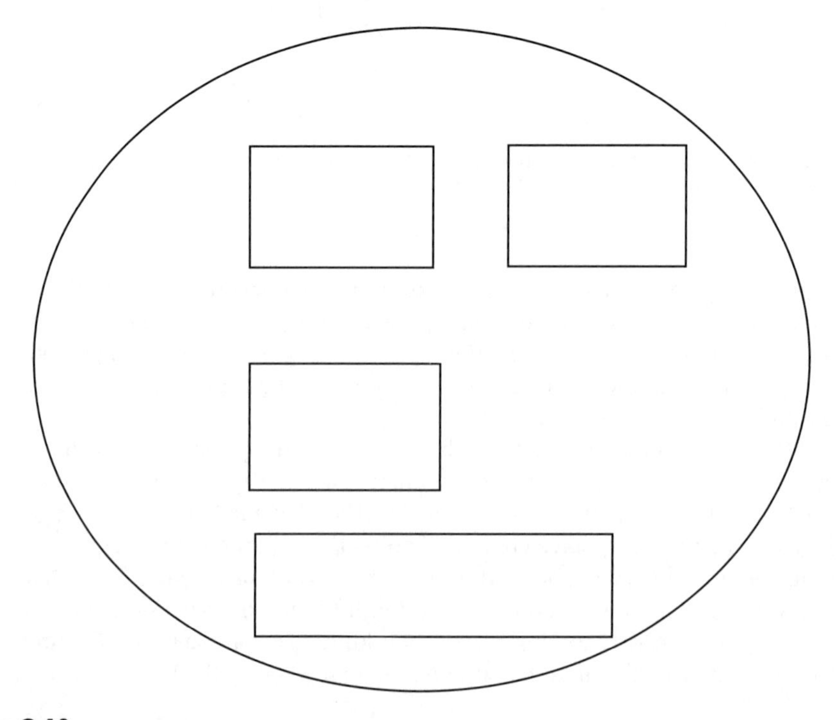


**Figure G.10**

And the 'picture' they assemble of a likely event, as if going through traffic lights on green just before reaching work, is shown in Figure G.11.

| Thoughts/images associated with similar events | | |
|---|---|---|
| Emotions associated with similar events | Behaviours associated with similar events | Bodily reactions associated with similar events |

**Figure G.11** Assembled Construction of Likely Event

Figure G.10 is a stable prediction in that it accurately predicts what happens. Negativity about forthcoming events can be reduced by recognising that the disturbing 'picture' is a 'mosaic' from the trauma and then switching attention to a 'realistic picture' by recalling, say, all the occasions you had passed through a set of traffic lights on green just before reaching your place of work. The realistic picture should be as specific and detailed as possible and relate exactly to the forthcoming event. For example, it is too vague to say 'I'm sure I will be OK going through this set of lights on green' to offset the traumatic memory that comes on-stream. Rather, it is necessary to place another more realistic, detailed image alongside it. With practice, you will gradually find that you access the realistic image much more frequently, but on occasion the traumatic image may come to mind, for example if you had a near miss going through the lights on green.

Negativity may relate not only to the past and the future but also to the self and can be fuelled by guilt. The guilt may relate to the incident or to the consequences of the incident. For example, you might think 'I should have warned the driver when I saw the oncoming car', or 'I should be over this by now', or 'I should be working/providing'. Alternatively, the negativity can be focused on blaming others (e.g. 'The emergency service vehicle should have been better maintained and shouldn't have been speeding'). Such negative automatic first thoughts can have the sting taken out of them by coming up with more realistic second thoughts. One way of doing this is to use the MOOD chart (Table G.3). The 'M' of MOOD stands for 'Monitor your mood', the first 'O' stands for 'Observe your thinking', i.e. what it sounds as if you have said to yourself, the second 'O' is for 'Objective thinking', i.e. your more realistic second thoughts, and 'D' is for 'Deciding what to do and Doing it'.

Whenever your mood dips you will have greater access to the memory of the incident – it will seem more vivid and real. It is therefore important to take the sting out your reflex negative thought as quickly as possible. The longer you pick at or ruminate about the automatic thought, the more difficult it is to take a photograph from a different angle. In theory, you can come up with better second thoughts without writing things down using the MOOD Chart, but it is a bit like learning maths for the first time and trying to do the sums in your head.

It is as if the negative view of self, others and the world (the fourth ripple in Figure G.1) gets washed up on the 'shore line', solidifies and becomes a

**Table G.3** MOOD Chart

| **Monitor Mood** | **Observe Thinking** | **Objective Thinking** | **Decide What to Do and Do It** |
|---|---|---|---|
| 1. Mood dipped standing drinking coffee looking out of the window | I should be over this by now | Who said I should? It is not my fault if I have not had the right tools to get over PTSD | I could dare myself to go swimming |
| 2. Mood dipped when I saw my neighbour going to work | I am weak. I can't face going back to where it happened | I can't be that weak. I have started some dares, I'll get back to work gradually, I just have to pace it | I will ring some colleagues and meet up with them socially first |
| | | | |
| | | | |
| | | | |
| | | | |
| | | | |
| | | | |
| | | | |
| | | | |

magnifying glass, through which anything negative is 'read'. For example, the unexpected visit of a relative is viewed not as a slight hassle, but as a catastrophe. Operating with the 'magnifying glass' becomes so familiar to PTSD sufferers that they often do not realise they are using it. But the habitual use of the magnifying glass results in feelings of detachment and estrangement from others. The first step in weaning yourself off using the magnifying glass is to become aware of the differences in your 'reading' with and without this apparent 'aid'.

Spend a few minutes completing Table G.4 and the questions that follow.

**Table G.4** My Views Before and Now

| | Myself | Others | The World | The Future |
|---|---|---|---|---|
| View Now | | | | |
| View Before | | | | |

What do you think others close to you think of you now? ............................................
.......................................................................................................................
.......................................................................................................................

Do they agree with you about the amount of danger you are in?.....................................

.......................................................................................................................
.......................................................................................................................

If they don't agree about the level of danger, why might that be?...................................
.......................................................................................................................
.......................................................................................................................

Do they agree with how you look at what happened in the incident?..............................
.......................................................................................................................
.......................................................................................................................

Looking back at your answers, they are probably very different depending on when you took the photograph (before or now) and whether it is your view or that of others. The social support provided by others, or indeed the lack of it, can also influence your observed thinking. If your observed thinking is exaggeratedly negative, this will influence your behaviour, which is likely to be avoidant.

# 7. RESTORING RELATIONSHIPS

PTSD puts a great strain on relationships. Often the sufferer is irritable over the most minor of events, no longer shows affection and cuts themselves off from relatives and friends. Many sufferers feel guilty that they no longer have feelings of warmth towards their partner. The apparent demands of others exceed their resources and they feel as though they are 'on a short fuse' (see Figure G.12).

High levels of stress are experienced when the felt demands exceed the resources and the see-saw tips up. The imbalance is expressed through irritability, and this puts a strain on relationships. Yet those who view themselves as supported are more likely to recover.

One way of helping to restore relationships is to question what you take to be the demands of others. For example, how true is it that your partner and children insist you provide financially in the way you did before the incident? How true is it that friends see you as a lesser person for not being able to do what you did before? Who is setting unrealistic standards – yourself or those around you?

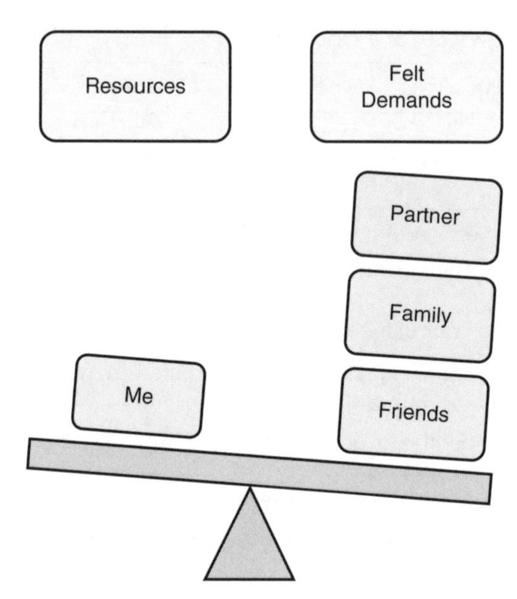


**Figure G.12** Disturbed relationships

Sufferers from PTSD tend to go into their own world, the 'Bubble' in Figure G.3, and stop investing in relations and friends. But because there is no investment there can be no return. Recovery from PTSD depends on gradually beginning to invest in those close to you again. You might start off with going for a walk with your partner, asking them about their day, giving them a hug, or perhaps telephoning a friend for a few minutes. To begin with you may well feel that you are going through the motions but eventually some enthusiasm will come back.

In order to moderate your outbursts you might imagine a set of traffic lights on red as soon as you notice the first signs of irritability. Then when the lights go to amber ask yourself whether what has just happened really is the end of the world? Did they really do it deliberately to wind you up? Then when the lights go to green, go into another room to calm down. To begin with many people go through the lights on red and it may take a few weeks' practice to learn to obey them. It may be that if you trust your partner or family member enough, you can ask them to remind you to use the traffic lights when you are getting irate.

Many PTSD sufferers stop communicating with family members after their trauma and the latter are left bewildered as to how to cope. Initially, rather than try to explain yourself, ask those around you to read this Manual. This may act as a stepping stone to their understanding the trauma self-help book, *Moving on after Trauma* (Scott 2008).

## 8. WRITING THE GAMEPLAN FOR THE NEXT CHAPTER OF YOUR AUTOBIOGRAPHY

Because the trauma has had such a big influence on your life, it can become the only lens through which you look at the world. Though you might recall pleasures and achievements from before the incident, you will probably only do so briefly and just long enough to dwell on what you have lost as a consequence of the trauma.

The first step forward is to recognise that you are using a trauma lens, then to stand back and instead see the bigger picture. To do this, spend some time collecting photographs, memorabilia and writing in graphic detail about your pleasures and achievements before the trauma. You could regard this as a first chapter of your autobiography. The second chapter you have already written or dictated is about the trauma. The following chapters are all about the life you are going to construct and your gameplan for dealing with likely difficulties. In writing Chapter Three onwards you could summarise in your own words those strategies you have found most useful in stopping domination by the trauma. In this way Chapter Three onwards becomes your own personalised Survival Manual that you can make ready reference to at the first sign of difficulties.

# Appendix H

**Table H.1** Severity of Psychosocial Stressors (based on *DSM IV TR* Axis IV)

| | No problem 0 | Mild problem 1 | Moderate problem 2 | Severe problem 3 |
|---|---|---|---|---|
| 1. How have things been with those closest to you? | | | | |
| 2. How have you felt you are fitting in with people in general? | | | | |
| 3. Do you have any problems with regard to studying, reading or writing? | | | | |
| 4. Do you have any problems with working or not working? | | | | |
| 5. Do you have any problems with housing? | | | | |
| 6. Do you have any financial problems? | | | | |
| 7. Do you have any problems with the health services? | | | | |
| 8. Do you have any problems with the police or legal services? | | | | |
| 9. Are there any other problems you are having? If 'yes', ask which ones bother you the most? | | | | |

# Appendix I

**Table I.1** Proposed *DSM V* Criteria for PTSD in Preschool Children

| **Subtype: Posttraumatic Stress Disorder in Preschool Children** | |
|---|---|
| A. | In children (less than age 6 years), exposure to one or more of the following events: death or threatened death, actual or threatened serious injury, or actual or threatened sexual violation, in one or more of the following ways:<br>1. directly experiencing the event(s)<br>2. witnessing, in person, the event(s) as they occurred to others, especially primary caregivers (Note: Witnessing does not include events that are witnessed only in electronic media, television, movies or pictures.)<br>3. learning that the traumatic event(s) occurred to a parent or caregiving figure; |
| B. | Presence of one or more intrusion symptoms associated with the traumatic event(s) , beginning after the traumatic event(s) occurred:<br>1. spontaneous or cued recurrent, involuntary, and intrusive distressing memories of the traumatic event(s) (Note: spontaneous and intrusive memories may not necessarily appear distressing and may be expressed as play re-enactment.)<br>2. recurrent distressing dreams in which the content and/or affect of the dream is related to the traumatic event(s) (Note: it may not be possible to ascertain that the frightening content is related to the traumatic event.)<br>3. dissociative reactions in which the child feels or acts as if the traumatic event(s) were recurring, (such reactions may occur on a continuum with the most extreme expression being a complete loss of awareness of present surroundings). Such trauma-specific re-enactment may occur in play.<br>4. intense or prolonged psychological distress at exposure to internal or external cues that symbolize or resemble an aspect of the traumatic event(s)<br>5. marked physiological reactions to reminders of the traumatic event(s)<br>One item from criterion C or D below: |
| C. | Persistent avoidance of stimuli associated with the traumatic event, beginning after the traumatic event occurred, as evidenced by avoidance or efforts to avoid:<br>1. activities, places, or physical reminders that arouse recollections of the traumatic event<br>2. people, conversations, or interpersonal situations that arouse recollections of the traumatic event. |

*(Continued)*

| | |
|---|---|
| D. | Negative alterations in cognitions and mood associated with the traumatic event, beginning or worsening after the traumatic event occurred, as evidenced by one or more of the following:<br>1. markedly diminished interest or participation in significant activities, including constriction of play<br>2. socially withdrawn behavior<br>3. persistent reduction in expression of positive emotions |
| E. | Alterations in arousal and reactivity associated with the traumatic event, beginning or worsening after the traumatic event occurred, as evidenced by two or more of the following:<br>1. irritable, angry, or aggressive behavior, including extreme temper tantrums<br>2. hypervigilance<br>3. exaggerated startle response<br>4. problems with concentration<br>5. sleep disturbance (e.g., difficulty falling or staying asleep or restless sleep) |
| F. | Duration of the disturbance (Criteria B, C, D and E) is more than 1 month. |
| G. | The disturbance causes clinically significant distress or impairment in relationships with parents, siblings, peers, or other caregivers or with school behavior. |
| H. | The disturbance is not attributable to another medical condition. |

**Table I.2** Proposed *DSM V* Criteria for PTSD in Adults, Adolescents, and Children Older than Six

The following criteria apply to adults, adolescents, and children older than six.

| | |
|---|---|
| A. | Exposure to actual or threatened a) death, b) serious injury, or c) sexual violation, in one or more of the following ways:<br>1. directly experiencing the traumatic event(s)<br>2. witnessing, in person, the traumatic event(s) as they occurred to others<br>3. learning that the traumatic event(s) occurred to a close family member or close friend; cases of actual or threatened death must have been violent or accidental<br>4. experiencing repeated or extreme exposure to aversive details of the traumatic event(s) (e.g., first responders collecting human remains; police officers repeatedly exposed to details of child abuse); this does not apply to exposure through electronic media, television, movies, or pictures, unless this exposure is work-related. |

| | |
|---|---|
| B. | Presence of one or more of the following intrusion symptoms associated with the traumatic event(s), beginning after the traumatic event(s) occurred:<br>1. spontaneous or cued recurrent, involuntary, and intrusive distressing memories of the traumatic event(s) (Note: In children, repetitive play may occur in which themes or aspects of the traumatic event(s) are expressed.)<br>2. recurrent distressing dreams in which the content or affect of the dream is related to the event(s) (Note: In children, there may be frightening dreams without recognizable content. )<br>3. dissociative reactions (e.g., flashbacks) in which the individual feels or acts as if the traumatic event(s) are recurring (such reactions may occur on a continuum, with the most extreme expression being a complete loss of awareness of present surroundings. (Note: In children, trauma-specific reenactment may occur in play.)<br>4. intense or prolonged psychological distress at exposure to internal or external cues that symbolize or resemble an aspect of the traumatic event(s)<br>5. marked physiological reactions to reminders of the traumatic event(s) |
| C. | Persistent avoidance of stimuli associated with the traumatic event(s), beginning after the traumatic event(s) occurred, as evidenced by avoidance or efforts to avoid one or more of the following:<br>1. distressing memories, thoughts, or feelings about or closely associated with the traumatic event(s)<br>2. external reminders (i.e., people, places, conversations, activities, objects, situations) that arouse distressing memories, thoughts, or feelings about, or that are closely associated with, the traumatic event(s) |
| D. | Negative alterations in cognitions and mood associated with the traumatic event(s), beginning or worsening after the traumatic event(s) occurred), as evidenced by two or more of the following:<br>1. inability to remember an important aspect of the traumatic event(s) (typically due to dissociative amnesia that is not due to head injury, alcohol, or drugs)<br>2. persistent and exaggerated negative beliefs or expectations about oneself, others, or the world (e.g., "I am bad," "No one can be trusted," "The world is completely dangerous"). (Alternatively, this might be expressed as, e.g., "I've lost my soul forever," or "My whole nervous system is permanently ruined").<br>3. persistent, distorted blame of self or others about the cause or consequences of the traumatic event(s)<br>4. persistent negative emotional state (e.g., fear, horror, anger, guilt, or shame)<br>5. markedly diminished interest or participation in significant activities<br>6. feelings of detachment or estrangement from others<br>7. persistent inability to experience positive emotions (e.g., unable to have loving feelings, psychic numbing) |

| | |
|---|---|
| E. | Marked alterations in arousal and reactivity associated with the traumatic event(s), beginning or worsening after the traumatic event(s) occurred, as evidenced by two or more of the following:<br>1. irritable or aggressive behavior<br>2. reckless or self-destructive behavior<br>3. hypervigilance<br>4. exaggerated startle response<br>5. problems with concentration<br>6. sleep disturbance (e.g., difficulty falling or staying asleep or restless sleep) |
| F. | Duration of the disturbance (Criteria B, C, D, and E) is more than 1 month. |
| G. | The disturbance causes clinically significant distress or impairment in social, occupational, or other important areas of functioning. |
| H. | The disturbance is not attributed to the direct physiological effects of a substance (e.g., medication, drugs, or alcohol) or another medical condition (e.g. traumatic brain injury). |
| | Specify if:<br>With Delayed Expression: if the diagnostic threshold is not exceeded until at least 6 months after the event (although the onset and expression of some symptoms may be immediate). |

# REFERENCES


Alford, B.A. and Beck A.T. (1997) *The Integrative Power of Cognitive Therapy*. New York: Guilford Press.

American Congress of Rehabilitation Medicine (ACoRM) (1993) Definition of mild brain injury. *Journal of Head Trauma Rehabilitation*, 8, 86–87.

American Psychiatric Association (2000) *DSM IV TR*. Washington, DC: American Psychiatric Press.

American Psychiatric Association (in press) *DSM V*. Washington, DC: American Psychiatric Press.

Arroll, B., Goodyear-Smith, F., Kerse, N., Fishman, T. and Gunn, J. (2005) Effect of the addition of a 'help' question to two screening questions on specificity for diagnosis of depression in general practice: diagnostic validity study. *British Medical Journal*, 331, 884–886.

Barlow, D.H., Craske, M.G., Cerny, J.A. and Klosko, J.S. (1989) Behavioral treatment of panic disorder. *Behavior Therapy*, 20, 261–282.

Beck, A.T. (1983) Cognitive therapy of depression: new perspectives. In P.J. Clayton and J.E. Barrett (Eds.), *Treatment of Depression: Old Controversies and New Approaches*. New York: Raven Press, pp. 265–290.

Beck, J.G., Grant, D.M. and Read, J.P. (2008) The Impact of Event Scale-Revised: psychometric properties in a sample of motor vehicle accident survivors. *Journal of Anxiety Disorders*, 22, 187–198.

Bisson, J. and Andrew, M. (2009) Psychological treatment of post-traumatic stress disorder. *The Cochrane Collaboration*. Chichester: John Wiley & Son Ltd.

Bisson, J.I., Tavakily, B. and Witteveen, A.B. (2010) TENTS guidelines: development of post-disaster psychosocial care guidelines through a Delphi process. *British Journal of Psychiatry*, 196, 69–74.

Blanchard, E.B. and Hickling, E.J. (1997) *After the Crash: Assessment and Treatment of Motor Vehicle Accident Survivors*. Washington, DC: American Psychological Association.

Blanchard, E.B., Hickling, E.J. and Devenini, T. (2003) A controlled evaluation of cognitive behavioural therapy for posttraumatic stress in motor vehicle accident survivors. *Behaviour Research and Therapy*, 41, 79–96.

Bomyea, J., Amir, N. and Lang, A.J. (2012) The relationship between cognitive control and posttraumatic stress symptoms. *Journal of Behavior Therapy and Experimental Psychiatry*, 43, 844–848.

Bradley, R., Greene, J., Russ, E., Dutra, L. and Westen, D. (2005) A multi-dimensional meta-analysis of psychotherapy for PTSD. *American Journal of Psychiatry*, 162, 214–227.

Brewin, C.R. (2008) What is it that a neurobiological model of PTSD must explain? *Progress in Brain Research*, 167, 217–228.

Brewin, C.R. and Holmes, E.A. (2003) Psychological theories of posttraumatic stress disorder. *Clinical Psychology Review*, 23, 339–376.

Bryant, R.A. (2008) Disentangling mild traumatic brain injury and stress reactions. *New England Journal of Medicine*, 358, 525–527.

Bryant, R.A., Friedman, M.J., Spiegel, D., Ursano, R. and Strain, J. (2011) A review of acute stress disorder in DSM-5. *Depression and Anxiety*, 28, 802–817.

Buckley, T.C., Blanchard, E.B. and Hickling, E.J. (1996) A prospective examination of delayed onset PTSD secondary to motor vehicle accidents. *Journal of Abnormal Psychology*, 105, 617–625.

Buhlmann, U., Marques, L.K. and Wilhelm, S. (2012) Traumatic experiences in individuals with body dysmorphic disorder. *Journal of Nervous and Mental Disease*, 200, 91–94.

Butler, A.C., Brown, G.K., Beck, A.T. and Grisham, J.R. (2002) Assessment of dysfunctional beliefs in borderline personality disorder. *Behaviour Research and Therapy*, 40, 1231–1240.

Butler, A.C., Chapman, J.E., Forman, E.M. and Beck A.T. (2006) The empirical status of cognitive-behavioral therapy: a review of meta-analyses. *Clinical Psychology Review*, 26, 17–31.

Callcott, P., Standart, S. and Turkington, D. (2004) Trauma within psychosis: using a CBT model for PTSD in psychosis. *Behavioural and Cognitive Psychotherapy*, 32, 239–244.

Cameron, L.D. and Moss-Morris, R. (2010) Illness-related cognitions and behaviour. In D. French (Ed.), *Health Psychology* (2nd edition). Oxford: Blackwell.

Champion, L.A. and Power, M.J. (1995) Social and cognitive approaches to depression: towards a new synthesis. *British Journal of Clinical Psychology*, 34, 485–503.

Chard, K.M. (2005) An evaluation of cognitive processing therapy for the treatment of posttraumatic stress disorder related to childhood sexual abuse. *Journal of Consulting and Clinical Psychology*, 73, 965–971.

Chard, K.M., Schumm, J.A. and McIlvain, S.M. (2011) Exploring the efficacy of a residential treatment program incorporating cognitive processing therapy for veterans with PTSD and traumatic brain injury. *Journal of Traumatic Stress*, 24, 347–351.

Choy, Y., Fryer, A.J. and Lipsitz, J.D. (2007) Treatment of specific phobia in adults. *Clinical Psychology Review*, 27, 266–286.

Clark, D.M. (1986) A cognitive model of panic. *Behavior Research and Therapy*, 24, 461–470.

Cloitre, M., Stovall-McClough, K.C., Zorbas, P., Cherry, S., Jackson, C.L., Gan, W. and Petkova, E. (2010) Treatment for PTSD related to childhood abuse: a randomized controlled trial. *American Journal of Psychiatry*, 167: 915–924.

Craske, M.G. and Barlow, D.H. (2008) Panic disorder and agoraphobia. In D.H. Barlow (Ed.), *Clinical Handbook of Psychological Disorders* (4th edition). New York: Guilford Press.

Creamer, M., Bell, R. and Failla, S. (2003) Psychometric properties of the Impact of Events Scale–Revised. *Behaviour Research and Therapy*, 41, 1489–1496.

Cukor, J., Wyka, K., Jayasinghe, N. and Difede, J. (2010) The nature and course of subthreshold PTSD. *Journal of Anxiety Disorders*, 24, 918–923.

Diekelmann, S., Büchel, C., Born, J. and Rasch, B. (2011) Labile or stable: opposing consequences for memory when reactivated during waking and sleep. *Nature Neurosciences*, 14, 381–387.

D'Zurilla, T.J. and Nezu, A.M. (2007) *Problem-solving Therapy: A Positive Approach to Clinical Intervention* (3rd edition). New York: Springer.

Echiverri, A.E., Jaeger, J.J., Chen, J.A., Moore, S.A. and Zoellner, L.A. (2011) 'Dwelling in the past': the role of rumination in the treatment of posttraumatic stress disorder. *Cognitive and Behavioral Practice*, 18, 338–349.

Ehlers, A., Bisson, J., Clark, D.M., Creamer, M., Pilling, S. and Richards, A. (2010) Do all psychological treatments really work the same in posttraumatic stress disorder? *Clinical Psychology Review*, 30, 269–276.

Ehlers, A. and Clark, D.M. (2000) A cognitive model of posttraumatic stress disorder. *Behaviour Research and Therapy*, 38, 319–345.

Epictetus (2011) *The Golden Sayings of Epictetus*. BiblioBazaar.

Ewing, J.A. (1984) Detecting alcoholism: the CAGE Questionnaire. *JAMA*, 252, 1905–1907.

Eyberg, S.M. and Ross, A.W. (1978) Assessment of child behavior problems: the validation of a new inventory. *Journal of Clinical Child Psychology*, 7, 113–116.

Fezner, M.G., McMillan, K.A. and Sareen, J. (2011) What is the association between traumatic life events and alcohol abuse/dependence in people with and without PTSD? Findings from a nationally representative sample. *Depression and Anxiety*, 28, 632–638.

Fineberg, N.A., O'Doherty, C. and Rajagopal, S. (2003) How common is obsessive compulsive disorder in a dermatology outpatient clinic. *Journal of Clinical Psychiatry*, 64, 152–155.

First, M.B., Gibbon, M., Spitzer, R.L., Williams, J.B.W. and Benjamin, L.S. (1997b) *Structured Clinical Interview for DSM-IV Axis II Personality Disorders (SCID-II)*. Washington, DC: American Psychiatric Press

First, M.B., Spitzer, R.L., Gibbon, M. and Williams, J.B.W. (1997a) *Structured Clinical Interview for DSM-IV Axis I Disorders – Clinician Version (SCID-CV)*. Washington, DC: American Psychiatric Press..

Foa, E.B., Dancu, C.V., Hembree, E.A., Jaycox, L.H., Meadows, E.A. and Atreet, G.P. (1999a) A comparison of exposure therapy, stress inoculation training and their combination for reducing posttraumatic stress disorder in female assault victims. *Journal of Consulting and Clinical Psychology*, 67, 194–200.

Foa, E.B., Ehlers, A., Clark, D.M., Tolin, D.F. and Orsillo, S.M. (1999b) The Posttraumatic Cognitions Inventory (PTCI): development and validation. *Psychological Assessment*, 11, 303–314.

Foa, E.B., Rothbaum, B.O., Riggs, D.S. and Murdock, T.B. (1991) Treatment of post-traumatic stress disorder in rape victims: a comparison between cognitive-behavioural procedures and counselling. *Journal of Consulting and Clinical Psychology*, 59, 715–723.

Galovski, T.E. and Resick, P.A. (2008) Cognitive processing therapy for posttraumatic stress disorder secondary to a motor vehicle accident: a single-subject report. *Cognitive and Behavioral Practice*, 15, 287–295.

Gottlieb, J.D., Muser, K.T., Rosenberg, S.D., Xie, H. and Wolfe, R.S. (2011) Psychotic depression, posttraumatic stress disorder, and engagement in cognitive behavioural therapy within an outpatient sample of adults with serious mental illness. *Comprehensive Psychiatry*, 52, 41–49.

Graham, D.P. and Cardon, A.L. (2008) An update on substance use and treatment following traumatic brain injury. *Annals of New York Academy of Science*, 1141, 148–162.

Handley, R.V., Salkovskis, P.M. and Ehlers, A. (2009) Treating clinically significant avoidance of public transport following the London bombings *Behavioural and Cognitive Psychotherapy*, 37, 87–93.

Harris, D. (1997) Types, causes and physical treatment of visible differences. In R. Lansdown, N. Rumsey, E. Bradbury, T. Carr and J. Partridge (Eds.), *Visibly Different: Coping with Disfigurement*. Oxford: Butterworth-Heinemann, pp. 79–90.

Hien, D.A., Jiang, H., Campbell, A.N., Hu, M.C., Miele, G.M., Cohen, L.R., Brigham, G.S., Capstick, C., Kulaga, A., Robinson, J., Suarez-Morales, L. and Nunes, E.V. (2010) Do treatment improvements in PTSD severity affect substance use outcomes? A secondary analysis from a randomized clinical trial in NIDA's clinical trials network. *American Journal of Psychiatry*, 167, 95–101.

Hooley, J.M., Orley, J. and Teasdale, J.D. (1986) Levels of expressed emotion and relapse in depressed patients. *British Journal of Psychiatry*, 148, 642–647.

Hou, R., Moss-Morris, R. and Peveler, R. (2012) When a minor head injury results in enduring symptoms: a prospective investigation of risk factors for postconcussional syndrome after mild traumatic brain injury. *Journal of Neurology, Neurosurgery and Psychiatry*, 83, 217–223.

Huband, N., Duggan, C. and Evans, C. (2007) Social problem-solving plus psychoeducation for adults with personality disorder: pragmatic randomised controlled trial. *British Journal of Psychiatry*, 190, 307–313.

IAPT (2011) *The IAPT Data Handbook v.2.0.1. Appendices*. Improving Access to Psychological Therapies.

Iverson, G.I. (2006) Misdiagnosis of the persistent postconcussion syndrome in patients with depression. *Archives of Clinical Neuropsychology*, 21, 303–310.

Jensen, M.P., Romano, J.M. and Turner, J.A. (1999) Patient beliefs predict patient functioning: further support for a cognitive-behavioral model of chronic pain. *Pain*, 81, 95–104.

Kahneman, D. (2011) *Thinking, Fast and Slow*. London: Allen Lane.

Kay, A. and Teasdale, G. (2001) Head injury in the United Kingdom. *World Journal of Surgery*, 25, 1210e20.

Kessler, R.C., Chiu, W.T., Demler, O. and Walters, E.E. (2005) Prevalence, severity and comorbidity of twelve-month DSM IV disorders in the National Comorbidity Survey Replication (NCS-R). *Archives of General Psychiatry*, 62, 617–627.

Kessler, R.C., Sonnega, A., Bromet, E., Hughes, M. and Nelson, C.B. (1995) Posttraumatic stress disorder in the National Comorbidity Survey. *Archives of General Psychiatry*, 52, 1048–1060.

Kroenke, K., Spitzer, R.L. and Williams, J.B. (2001) The PHQ-9: validity of a brief depression measure. *Journal of General Internal Medicine*, 16, 606–613.

Kroenke, K., Spitzer, R.L. and Williams, J.B. (2007) Anxiety disorders in primary care: prevalence, impairment, comorbidity and detection. *Annals of Internal Medicine*, 146, 317–325.

Lancaster, S.L., Rodriguez, B.F. and Watson, R. (2011) Path analytic examination of a cognitive model of PTSD. *Behaviour Research and Therapy*, 49, 194–201.

Lazarus, R.S. (2006) *Stress and Emotion: A New Synthesis*. New York: Springer.

LeDoux, J.E. (1998) *The Emotional Brain: The Mysterious Underpinnings of Emotional Life*. London: Weidenfeld and Nicolson.

Lee, B.H., Scharff, L. and Sethna, N.F. (2002) Physical therapy and cognitive-behavioral treatment for complex regional pain syndromes. *Journal of Paediatrics*, 141, 135–140.

Lee, J.L.C. (2009) Reconsolidation: maintaining memory relevance. *Trends in Neurosciences*, 32, 413–420.

Linehan, M.M. (1993) *Cognitive-Behavioral Treatment of Borderline Personality Disorder*. New York: Guilford Press.

Lu, W., Fite, R. and Kim, E. (2009) Cognitive-behavioral treatment of PTSD in severe mental illness: pilot study replication in an ethnically diverse population. *American Journal of Psychiatric Rehabilitation*, 12, 73–91.

MacIver, K., Lloyd, D.M. and Kelly, S.C. (2008) Phantom limb pain, cortical reorganisation and the therapeutic effect of mental imagery. *Brain*, 131, 2181–2191.

MacIver, K. and Lloyd, D. (2010) Management of phantom limb pain in amputation, prostheses use and phantom limb pain: an interdisciplinary perspective. In C. Murray (Ed.), *Amputation,Prosthesis Use and Phantom Limb Pain: An Interdisciplinary Perspective*. New York: Springer.

McCrea, M.A. (2008) *Mild Traumatic Brain Injury and Postconcussion Syndrome*. Oxford: Oxford University Press.

McGovern, M.P., Lambert-Harris, C. and Acquilano, S. (2009) A cognitive behavioural therapy for co-occurring substance use and posttraumatic stress disorder. *Addiction Behaviour*, 34, 892–897.

McMurran, M., Huband, N. and Duggan, C. (2008) The role of social problem solving in improving social functioning in therapy for adults with personality disorder. *Personality and Mental Health*, 2, 1–6.

Maercker, A., Zollner, T., Menning, H., Rabe, S. and Karl, A. (2006) Dresden PTSD treatment study: randomised control trial of motor vehicle accident survivors. *BMC Psychiatry*, 6, 6–29.

Marinus, M., Moseley, G.L. and Birklein, F. (2011) Clinical features and pathophysiology of complex regional pain syndrome. *The Lancet*, 10, 637–645.

Marsh, C. (2003) A psycho-physiological comparison of post-traumatic and prolonged duress stress disorders. *Behavioural and Cognitive Psychotherapy*, 31, 109–112.

Meares, S., Shores, E.A. and Taylor, A.J. (2008) Mild traumatic brain injury does not predict acute posttconcussion syndrome. *Journal of Neurology Neurosurgery and Psychiatry*, 79, 300–306.

Meichenbaum, D. (1985) *Stress Inoculation Training*. New York: Pergamon Press.

Meiser-Stedman, R.A., Dalgleish, T., Glucksman, E., Yule, W. and Smith, P. (2009a) Maladaptive cognitive appraisals mediate the evolution of posttraumatic stress reactions: a 6-month follow-up of child and adolescent assault and motor vehicle accident survivors. *Journal of Abnormal Psychology*, 118, 778–787.

Meiser-Stedman, R.A., Smith, P., Bryant, R., Salmon, K., Yule, W., Dalgleish, T. and Nixon, R.D.V. (2009b) Development and validation of the Child Post-Traumatic Cognitions Inventory (CPTCI). *Journal of Child Psychology and Psychiatry*, 50, 432–440.

Meiser-Stedman, R.A., Yule, W., Dalgleish, T., Smith, P. and Glucksman, E. (2006) The role of the family in child and adolescent posttraumatic stress following attendance at an emergency department. *Journal of Pediatric Psychology*, 31, 397–402.

Mueser, K.T., Goodman, L.A. and Trumbetta, S.L. (1998) Trauma and posttraumatic stress disorder in severe mental illness. *Journal of Consulting and Clinical Psychology*, 66, 493–499.

Mueser, K.T., Rosenberg, S.D., Xie, H. and Jankowski, M.K. (2008) A randomized controlled trial of cognitive-behavioral treatment for posttraumatic stress disorder in severe mental illness. *Journal of Consulting and Clinical Psychology*, 76, 259–271.

Neuner, F., Schaver, M., Klaschik, C., Karunakera, U. and Elbert, T. (2004) A comparison of narrative exposure therapy, support counselling and psycho education for treating post-traumatic stress disorder in an African refugee settlement. *Journal of Consulting and Clinical Psychology*, 72, 579–587.

Newell, R. and Marks, I. (2000) Phobic nature of social difficulty in facially disfigured people. *British Journal of Psychiatry*, 176, 177–181.

Nezu, A.M., Nezu, C.M. and Perri, M.G. (1989) *Problem-solving Therapy for Depression: Theory Research and Clinical Guidelines*. New York: John Wiley & Son.

NICE (2004) *Depression: Management of Depression in Primary and Secondary Care* (Clinical Guideline 23). London: National Institute for Clinical Excellence (www.nice.org).

NICE (2005a) *Post-Traumatic Stress Disorder (PTSD): The Management of PTSD in Adults and Children in Primary and Secondary Care* (Clinical Guideline 26). London: National Institute for Clinical Excellence (www.nice.org).

Pagura, J., Stein, M.B. and Bolton, J.M. (2010) Comorbidity of borderline personality disorder and posttraumatic stress disorder in the US population. *Journal of Psychiatry Research*, 44, 1190–1198.

Palyo, S.A. and Beck J.G. (2005) Post-traumatic stress disorder symptoms, pain, and perceived life control: associations with psychosocial and physical functioning. *Pain*, 117, 121–127.

Pennebaker, J.W. and Chung, C.K. (2011) Expressive writing, emotional upheavals and health. In H.S. Friedman (Ed.), *The Oxford Handbook of Health Psychology*. New York: Oxford University Press.

Pepys, S. (2003) *The Diaries of Samuel Pepys – a Selection*. Harmondsworth: Penguin Books.

Petty, R.E. and Cacioppo, J.T. (1986) The elaboration likelihood model of persuasion. *Advances in Experimental Social Psychology*, 19, 124–181.

Phillips, K.A., Menard, W., Fay, C. and Weisberg, R. (2005) Demographic characteristics, phenomenology, comorbidity and family history in 200 individuals with body dysmorphic disorder. *Psychosomatics*, 46, 317–325.

Phillips, K.A., Didie, E.R., Feusner, J and Wilhelm, S (2008) Body dysmorphic disorder: treating an unrecognized disorder. *American Journal of Psychiatry*, 165, 111–1116.

Pincus, D. and Sheikh, A.A. (2009) *Imagery for Pain Relief*. New York: Routledge.

Pine, D.C. and Cohen, J.A. (2002) Trauma in children and adolescents: risk and treatment of psychiatric sequelae. *Biological Psychiatry*, 51, 519–531.

Potter, C.M., Vujanovic, A.A. and Marshall-Berenz, E.C. (2011) Posttraumatic stress and marijuana use coping motives: the mediating role of distress tolerance. *Journal of Anxiety Disorders*, 25, 437–443.

Prigatano, G.P. and Gale, S.D. (2011) The current status of postconcussion syndrome. *Current Opinion in Psychiatry*, 24, 243–250.

Prins, A., Ouimette, P. and Kimerling, R. (2004) The primary care PTSD screen (PC-PTSD): development and operating characteristics. *Primary Care Psychiatry*, 9, 9–14.

Resick, P.A., Galovski, T.A., O'Brien Uhlmansiek, M., Scher, C.D., Clum, G.A. and Young-Xu, Y. (2008) A randomized clinical trial to dismantle components of cognitive processing therapy for posttraumatic stress disorder in female victims of interpersonal violence. *Journal of Consulting and Clinical Psychology*, 76, 243–258.

Resick, P.A. and Schnicke, M.K. (1992) Cognitive processing therapy for sexual assault victims. *Journal of Consulting and Clinical Psychology*, 60, 748–756.

Resick, P.A. and Schnicke, M.K. (1993) *Cognitive Processing Therapy for Rape Victims: A Treatment Manual*. Newbury Park, CA: Sage.

Resnick, S.C., Bond, G.R. and Mueser, K.T. (2003) Trauma and posttraumatic stress disorder in people with schizophrenia. *Journal of Abnormal Psychology*, 112, 415–423.

Roberts, N.P., Kitchiner, N.J., Kenardy, J. and Bisson, J.I. (2009) Systematic review and meta-analysis of multiple session early interventions following traumatic events. *American Journal of Psychiatry*, 166, 293–301.

Rosen, J.C. and Reiter, J. (1996) Development of the body disorder examination. *Behaviour Research and Therapy*, 34, 77–84.

Rosen, J.C., Reiter, J. and Orosan, P. (1995) Cognitive behavioral body image therapy for body dysmorphic disorder. *Journal of Consulting and Clinical Psychology*, 63, 263–269.

Roskes, E. (1999) Body dysmorphic disorder and a prosthesis. *Psychosomatics*, 40, 436–437.

Schacter, D.L., Addis, D.R. and Buckner, R.L. (2007) Remembering the past to imagine the future: the prospective brain. *Nature*, 8, 657–661.

Scocco, P., Barbieri, I. and Frank, E. (2007) Interpersonal problem areas and onset of panic disorder. *Psychopathology*, 40, 8–13.

Scott, M.J. (1989) *A Cognitive-Behavioral Approach to Clients' Problems*. New York. Routledge

Scott, M.J. (2008) *Moving on after Trauma: A Guide for Survivors, Family and Friends*. London: Routledge.

Scott, M.J. (2009) *Simply Effective Cognitive Behaviour Therapy: A Guide for Practitioners*. London: Routledge.

Scott, M.J. (2010) *Moving on after Trauma: A Guide for Survivors, Family and Friends*). Jordan: Hanan Zenin Edin.

Scott, M.J. (2011) *Simply Effective Group Cognitive Behaviour Therapy: A Guide for Practitioners*. London: Routledge.

Scott, M.J. (In Press) *Simply Effective CBT Supervision. A Guide for Practitioners.* London: Routledge.

Scott, M.J. and Stradling, S.G. (1990) The evaluation of a group parent training programme. *Behavioural Psychotherapy*, 18, 1–19.

Scott, M.J. and Stradling, S.G. (1994) Post-traumatic stress disorder without the trauma. *British Journal of Clinical Psychology*, 33, 71–74.

Scott, M.J. and Stradling, S.G. (1997) Client compliance with exposure treatments for posttraumatic stress disorder. *Journal of Traumatic Stress*, 10, 523–526.

Scott, M.J. and Stradling, S.G. (2006) *Counselling for Post-Traumatic Stress Disorder* (3rd edition). London: Sage.

Shear, M.K., Greeno, C. and Kang, J. (2000) Diagnosis of nonpsychotic patients in community clinics. *American Journal of Psychiatry*, 157, 581–587.

Shemesh, E., Newcor, J.H. and Rockmore, L. (2005) Comparison of parent and child reports of emotional trauma symptoms in paediatric outpatient settings. *Pediatrics*, 115, e582–e589.

Smucker, M.R. and Niederee, J.L. (1995) Treating incest-related PTSD and pathogenic schemas through imaginal exposure and rescripting. *Cognitive and Behavioral Practice*, 2, 63–93.

Stein, M.B. and McAllister, T.W. (2009) Exploring the convergence of posttraumatic stress disorder and mild traumatic brain injury. *American Journal of Psychiatry*, 166, 768–776.

Strain, J.J. and Friedman, M.J. (2011) Considering adjustment disorders as stress response syndromes for DSM-5. *Depression and Anxiety*, 28, 818–823.

Subica, A.M., Claypoole, K.H. and Wylie A.M. (2012) PTSD's mediation of the relationships between trauma, depression, substance abuse, mental health and physical health in individuals with severe mental illness: evaluating a comprehensive model. *Schizophrenia Research*, 136, 104–109.

Sullivan, M.J.L., Bishop, S.R. and Pivik, J. (1995) The Pain Catastrophizing Scale: development and validation. *Psychological Assessment*, 7, 524–532.

Teasdale, G. and Jennett, B. (1974) Assessment of coma and impaired consciousness: a practical scale. *The Lancet*, 13, 81–84.

Thorn, B.E. (2004) *Cognitive Therapy for Chronic Pain: A Step by Step Guide*. New York: Guilford Press.

Tull, M.T., Barrett, H.M. and McMillan, F.S. (2007) A preliminary investigation of the relationship between emotion regulation difficulties and posttraumatic stress symptoms. *Behavior Therapy*, 38, 303–313.

van Bilsen, H. and Thomson, B. (2011) *CBT for Personality Disorders*. London: Sage.

Veale, D., Gournay, K. and Dryden, W. (1996) Body dysmorphic disorder: a cognitive behavioural model and pilot randomised controlled trial. *Behaviour Research and Therapy*, 34, 717–729.

Vlaeyen, J.W.S., de Jong, J., Sieben, J. and Crombez, G. (2002) Graded exposure in vivo for pain-related fear. In R.J. Gatchel and D.C. Turk (Eds.), *Psychological Approaches to Pain Management*. New York: Guilford Press. pp. 210–233.

Vujanovic, A.A., Marshall-Berenz, E.C. and Zvolensky, M.J. (2011) Posttraumatic stress and alcohol use motives: a test of the incremental and mediating role of distress tolerance. *Journal of Cognitive Psychotherapy*, 25, 130–141.

Vythilingham, M., Blair, S. and McCaffrey, D. (2007) Biased emotional attention in posttraumatic stress disorder: a help as well as a hindrance? *Psychological Medicine*, 37, 1445–1455.

Weaver, T.I., Resnick, H.S., Kokosa, M.S. and Etzel, J.C. (2007) Appearance-related residual injury, posttraumatic stress and body image: associations within a sample of female victims of intimate partner violence. *Journal of Traumatic Stress*, 20, 999–1008.

Weerasekera, P. (1996) *Multiperspective Case Formulation: A Step Towards Treatment Integration*. Malabar, FL: Krieger Publishing.

Wells, A. (1997) *Cognitive Therapy of Anxiety Disorders: A Practice Manual and Conceptual Guide*. Chichester: John Wiley & Sons.

Wells, A. and Sembi, S. (2004) Metacognitive therapy for PTSD: a core treatment manual. *Cognitive and Behavioral Practice*, 11, 365–377.

Wenzlaff, E.M. and Wegner, D.M. (2000) Thought suppression. *Annual Review of Psychology*, 51, 59–91.

Weston, S. (1989) *Walking Tall*. London: Bloomsbury.

Wicksell, R.K., Olsson, G.L. and Hayes, S.C. (2010) Psychological flexibility as a mediator of improvement in acceptance and commitment therapy for patients with chronic pain following whiplash. *European Journal of Pain*, 14, 1059.e1–1059.e.11.

Wilhelm, S., Buhlman, U., Hayward, L.C., Greenberg, J.L. and Dimaite, R. (2010) A cognitive-behavioral treatment approach for body dysmorphic disorder. *Cognitive and Behavioral Practice*, 17, 241–247.

World Health Organisation (1992) *International Classification of Disorders* (10th edition). Geneva: WHO.

Zayfert, C., DeViva, J.C., Becker, C.B., Pike, J.L., Gillock, K.L. and Hayes, S.A. (2005) Exposure utilization and completion of cognitive behavioural therapy for PTSD in a 'Real World' clinical practice. *Journal of Traumatic Stress*, 18, 637–645.

Zimmerman, M. and Mattia, J.I. (1999) Axis I diagnostic comorbidity and borderline personality disorder. *Comprehensive Psychiatry*, 40, 245–252.

Zimmerman, M. and Mattia, J.I. (2000) Principal and additional DSM IV disorders for which outpatients seek treatment. *Psychiatric Services*, 51, 1299–1304.

Zimmerman, M., McGlinchey, J.B., Chelminski, I. and Young, D. (2008) Diagnostic comorbidity in 2300 psychiatric out-patients presenting for treatment evaluated with a semi-structured diagnostic interview. *Psychological Medicine*, 38, 199–210.

# INDEX

Note: Page numbers in *italic* refer to figures and tables.